THE

DRAVIDIAN NIGHTS

ENTERTAINMENTS

THE

DRAVIDIAN NIGHTS

ENTERTAINMENTS:

BEING A TRANSLATION OF

MADANAKAMARAJANKADAI.

BY

PANDIT S. M. NATESA SASTRI

GYAN

Published by

Gyan Publishing House
5, Ansari Road
Daryaganj, New Delhi-110002
Phone: 011-47034999, 9811692060
E-mail: books@gyanbooks.com

Distribution Network
gyanbooks.com
India, USA, Canada, UK, Australia

ISBN: 978-93-6208-058-5 (PB)
First Published, 1886

2nd Impression 2024

Printed at: Gyan Press, Delhi.

THE DRAVIDIAN NIGHTS ENTERTAINMENTS:
Author: PANDIT S. M. NATESA SASTRI

THE

DRAVIDIAN NIGHTS

ENTERTAINMENTS:

BEING A TRANSLATION OF

MADANAKAMARAJANKADAI.

BY

PANDIT S. M. NATESA SASTRI,

Government Archæological Survey

MADRAS:

PRINTED AT THE EXCELSIOR PRESS, BROADWAY.

1886.

TO BE HAD FROM MR. V. SAMBAMURTI AYYAR, NUNGUMBAKAM, MADRAS. PRICE WITH POSTAGE RS. 1-12-0 OR 3s. 6d.

CONTENTS.

PREFACE.

I BEG to offer for the perusal of the public my translation of the Tamil stories of the *Madanakâmarâjankadai* under the head of "*The Dravidian Nights.*" The English title to these tales is in imitation of the *Arabian Nights*. There a minister's daughter beguiles away the hours of the night by Arabian tales before her lord the Pâdushâh. Here, in the *Dravidian Nights*, a minister's son does in the same manner relate stories to two princesses.

Madanakâmarâja, the prince of Mahêndrapurî, falls in love with two female figures represented in a picture. His minister goes in search of them, finds them out after a great deal of difficulty and succeeds in getting them apparently wedded to himself. The ladies approach each in her turn, the side of their lord, to give him, their company. But as he has meant one of them to be the wife of his master the prince, and as he himself must choose his wife only after the prince has chosen his,—he keeps them off by relating fine stories in which the adventures, half probable, half improbable, but always very beautiful and pleasing, of some great prince or other hero, are enumerated.

In the *Arabian Nights* a lady who fears the safety of her own head each day, relates stories to her husband with her eyes swimming in tears. But here we find the minister's son going on pleasantly with his stories, after having successfully accomplished his mission and secured in his possession the two objects of his master's affection. By giving the conclusion of " And must not such a youth marry you my gem of womankind," to every story, he prepares them to accept their lord for the future.

The idea of a wife relating stories, and the husband listening to them, is not quite in keeping with the traditions of the Hindûs. So here, in the *Dravidian Nights*, we find the relater a male, the husband or apparent husband and the listeners his seeming wives.

Every original story must be read and appreciated in its original language. And Tamil stories have so many peculiarities and beauties that it is almost impossible to produce a translation which, while retaining the many idioms peculiar to the Tamil, shall, nevertheless, be in strict grammatical accord with the language in which I have written it. Fortunately for me, these stories are devoid of the several indecencies, we so often meet with in the *Arabian Nights*, which always produce a sort of disgust to the readers of both sexes, but especially to those of the softer sex. Bearing in mind that many of these expressions which now shock persons in this more refined age were not by any means considered indelicate in the time at which they were written, I have tried to avoid these as much as possible, but in the translation generally I have made it as literal as I can. I trust therefore that, on this ground, any expression which are not strictly in keeping with English idioms, may be overlooked. I have tried my best to stick to the original where-ever possible. But translators are always said to be traitors. They are compelled, much against their conscience, to put in or leave out some portion or other of the original stories. My principal object in publishing these translations is not to show that I am any bit of an author or translator, but that stories in Tamil are in no way inferior in their richness of thought, soundness of morality and luxuriance of imagination, to the other stories of Oriental romance. This is the great object which has principally influenced me in placing this translation, before English readers. Till now there has been a great negligence towards our national stories among, I am almost ashamed to say, our own Tamil public. Very few Tamil scholars, who are *Agastyas* in the other departments of Tamil literature, have ever given even a mite of their learned attention to the folk-lore and mediæval tales of their country. While European scholars like Messrs. Temple, Clouston, Knowles, Madame Steele and others, are devoting a great portion of their time and labour towards Oriental tales in some part of India or other, we have been leaving our rich store of mediæval literature to be eaten away by moth in some palm-leaf book tightly tied up and opened once a year, and that out of pure formality only, during the day of worship of our goddess of learning—I mean the *Sarasvatî pûjâ.* After I began collecting the Folk-lore in Southern India, I am happy to see it announced in the *Indian Antiquary* that a countryman of ours has taken up that interesting subject in

Western India; and I sincerely hope that my *Dravidian Nights* may soon bring to the platform of the Hindû public several interesting stories hitherto unnoticed, may bring us *Andhra Nights*, *Mâharatta Nights*, &c., and even *Days*, and thus supply, a sad want in our story-telling publications.

As to the author of the original tales, everything, as far as my present inquiries have gone, leave his name a mystery. He, most probably, was more an intelligent compiler of the stories he found round about him than an author. Though we cannot with great certainty speak on the native place of the author or compiler of these stories, there are internal evidences to show that he must have belonged to the Tirunelvêli District—internal evidences of words and phrases peculiar to that district, more than to others in Southern India.*

The compiler seems to have made a most successful attempt at stringing together twelve different

---

* வேங்கியம், *vêngiyam* : for shame; குடுமி, *kudumi* : for serpent charmer; பண்டிதன், *pandita* : for doctor; வலிக்கிறது, *valikkiradu* : for drawing up; புறம்பு, *purambu* : for forest; துகில்வெளுக்கிறது, *tukilvelukkiradu*, for washing dirty clothes; தப்புகிறது, *tappukiradu*, for washing cloth; களைந்துவைக்கிறது, *kalaiduvaikkiradu* : for removing and keeping (cloths)—unrobing, and several others peculiar to the Tirunelvêli District are met with throughout the book. Of course one or two may belong also to some other of the Tamil Districts, but the major portion belongs as is now proved by the prevailing language in that part of the country, to the Tirunelvêli District.

stories, each of which supplies an example. Almost any long story related by a story-teller in Southern India and even the other parts of the country, may be put under the head of one of these tales in its outline, development and conclusion. There are several tales which may here and there differ in shadings and colourings, but the skeleton will be the same almost throughout. And perceiving this, the learned compiler of the original of the *Dravidian Nights* has limited the number to twelve.

To the main aim of my translation of these tales, already stated, it may not be out of place if I were also to add that, I greatly wish to show these twelve examples of the Dravidian stories to the learned European Orientalists labouring in this direction and to profit by their generalisations. Each of these tales goes to illustrate a moral which I have attached at the end. These stories resemble in their general features the *Mediæval tales*, *Monks Tales*, &c., of Europe. The probable date of these stories may be laid in the 17th century, as now and then a name or two of the Vijayanagar sovereigns of that period occurs, though these are placed by the compiler as ruling over some imaginary towns.

Before closing this preface I would request my readers to be lenient towards the style which I have adopted in writing these stories if it is not everywhere in keeping with strict idiom; but bearing in mind my former remarks on this subject, I trust that the fact also of my being a Hindû writing in a foreign language, whose depth is unfathomable even to its own intellectual sons, may be accepted as an excuse for any shortcomings.

In conclusion, I beg to offer my humble regards to Mr. A. Rea. First Assistant, Archæological Survey, for his having kindly looked over my manuscripts.

MADRAS, *Novr.* 1885. S. M. N.

INTRODUCTION.

On the face of the large world surrounded by seas, there was a city named Mahêndrapurî—famous for the fertility of the soil and inhabited by rich landlords. Over that city ruled a king named Mahêndra, learned in the four *Vêdas*,[1]

(1)The four *Vêdas*—(1) *Rig Vêda*,(2) *Yajur Vêda*,(3) *Sâma Vêda*, (4) *Atharva Vêda*—are the celebrated holy writings on the religion of the Hindûs. The first three only are the regular *Vêdas* and the last was afterwards added.

(2) *Aru Sâstram.* The six sciences. These are :

1. வேதாந்தம். (*Vêdânta.*)—Theology, as the highest knowledge. The theological portion of the *Vêdas* as contained in the *Upanishads.* The founder of this last school was Vyâsa, and its most celebrated supporter was *Sankarâchârya.*

2. வைசேஷிகம். (*Vaisêshika.*)—The *Vaisêshika* doctrine, morality, or ethics, a branch of the *Nyâya* or logical school instituted by *Kânâda.*

3. பாட்டா. (*Bhâttâ.*)—The system of *Bhâttâchârya*, in an epic poem containing narrations.

4. பிரபாகரம். (*Pirapâkara.*) Ceremonial law.

5. பூர்வமீமாஞ்சை. (*Pûrva-mîmâmsâ.*)—" *Pûrva-mîmâmsâ* an enquiry into the first or ritual portion of the *Vêda* (hence sometimes also called *Karma-mîmâmsâ*, as opposed to *Uttara-mîmâmsâ* or *Brahma-mîmâmsâ*, which is rather an exposition of the later portion of the *Vêda* or *Upanishads* ; the *Pûrva-mîmâmsâ* forms one of the six systems of philosophy and is attributed to

six *Sâstras*,[2] the sixty-four varieties of philoso-

Jaimini ; it is really an interpretation of the text of the *Vêda*, and is generally called the *Mîmâmâ*, the term *Vêdânta* being applied to the *Uttara-mîmâmsâ* ; though scarcely a system of philosophy, yet in the course of its critical explanation of the Vedic text, the *Pûrvamîmâmsâ* discusses various philosophical questions, one of its speculations being the doctrine of the eternity of sound or of an eternal sound underlying all temporary sound and by some identifical with Brahma."

6. உத்திர மீமாஞ்சை. (*Uttaramîmâmsâ.*)—" *Uttaramîmâmsâ*, examination of the later portion or *Jñanakânda* of the *Vêda, i. e.*, of that portion contained in the *Aranyakas* and *Upanishads* (which teach the knowledge of Brahma or the Universal spirit) stands out prominently by itself as representing the popular pantheistic creed of the Hindûs of the present day, which is really based on the *Upanishads* and constitutes the true *Vêda* of the modern cultivated Brâhman underlying also all the polytheism and multiform mythology of the people; it explains the universe synthetically as a development from one principle, and so differs from the analytical *Nyâya* which treats of the various objects constituting the material world as it finds them, without investigating their mutual relation of effect and cause, and from the *Sànkhya* which, although also synthetic, propounds a duality of principles to account for the visible universe; according to the *Vêdànta* doctrine, Brahma, or the supreme soul also called *Paramâtman*, is both the efficient and material cause of the world ; the *âtman* or individual human soul, as well as all the phenomena of nature, being really identical with the *Paramâtman*, and their existence being only the result of *Ajñâna* or an assumed ignorance on the part of this supreme soul, who is described as both Creator and Creation, Actor and Act,

phy,[3] the Codes of Manu, &c. He had a minister

Existence, knowledge, joy, and as devoid of the three qualities, or *guna* the liberation of the human soul, its deliverance from transmigrations, and re-union with the *Paramâtman*, with which it is really identified, is only to be effected by a removal of that ignorance which prevents the consciousness of this identity and by a proper understanding of the truth of the *Vêdânta*; this system is also sometimes called *Brahma-mîmâmsâ* and *Sarîraka-mîmâmsâ*, investigation of the embodied soul. The founder of the school is said to have been Vyâsa also called Bâdarâyana, and its most eminent teacher was Sankarâchârya."

(3) *Kalaijñânam, Arupattunâlu.*—The knowledge of the 64 Sciences. They are as follows:—

"1. அக்கர விலக்கணம். (*Akkaravilakkanam.*)—The knowledge of spelling and reading, orthography, the science of reading. 2. இலிகிதம். (*Likhita.*)—Caligraphy, penmanship. 3. கணிதம். (*Ganita.*)—The art of computation, arithmetic, the science of numbers. 4. வேதம். (*Vêda.*)—The Hindû *Vêda*. 5. புராணம். (*Purâna.*)—A class of sacred books comprising the whole body of Hindû theology. 6. வியாகரணம். (*Vyâkarnam.*)—Grammar. 7. நீதி சாத்திரம். (*Nîtisâstra.*)—Jurisprudence. 8. சோதிட சாத்திரம். (*Sôtidasâttira.*)—Astronomy including astrology. 9. தரும சாத்திரம். (*Dharmasâstra*)—Ethics, moral philosophy, code of laws. 10. யோக சாத்திரம். (*Yôgasâstra*).—The knowledge of abstract or silent devotion, rules for religious and abstract meditations. 11. மந்திர சாத்திரம். (*Mantrasâstra.*)—A division of the *Vêdas* in the first or practical part; it includes prayers and hymns addressed to particular dieties and used at particular sacrifices, and it also comprehends incantation in religion, magic, medicine and every other

named Manâiyâlan, eight times more dear to him

art or practice in which enchantments are used. 12. சகுனசாத்திரம். (*Sakunasâstra.*)—The science of prognosticating by omens and augury. 13. சிற்பசாத்திரம். (*Sirpasâstra.*)--Architecture and mechanics, symmetry, shapes in general, including sculpture, painting features, lines, hairs, &c., of the human system, and their various effects on life. 14. வைத்தியசாஸ்திரம். (*Vaidyasâstra.*)—Science of healing, physic, pharmacy and surgery which may include restoration to life of the dead, the reunion of several limbs, &c. 15. உருவசாத்திரம், (*Uruvasâstra.*)—Physiognomy the art of discovering the temper and foreknowing the fortune by the features of the face, netoposcopy, chiromancy, the art of foretelling the events of life by inspecting the hand. சாமுத்திரிகம். (*Sâmudrika.*) 16. இதிகாசம். (*Itihâsa.*)—History, traditional accounts of former events, heroic history—as found in the *Bhârata* and *Râmâyana.* 17. காவியம். (*Kâvya.*)—Epic poetry—as சிந்தாமணி, நைடதம் &c. 18. அலங்காரம். (*Alankâra.*) —Science of rhetoric. 19. மதுரபாடணம். (*Madura-bhâshana.*)—Eloquence. 20. நாடகம். (*Nâtaka.*)—Dramatic science. 21. நிருத்தம். (*Nritta.*) The art of dancing. 22. சத்தப்பிரமம். (*Sabdabhrama.*) Directions for the modulation of sounds. 23. வீணை. (*Vînâ.*) —The art of playing on the lute or stringed instruments. 24. வேணு. (*Vênû.*)—The art of playing on the lute or stringed instruments. 25. மிருதங்கம். (*Mridanga.*)—The art of beating the tambourine. 26. தாளம். (*Tâla.*) — The art of beating the cymbals. 27. அத்திரபரிட்சை. (*Astraparîkshâ.*)—Archery, the art of throwing darts. 28. கனகபரிட்சை. (*Kanakaparîkshâ.*)—The art of an assayer in gold, &c. 29. இரதபரிட்சை. (*Rathaparîkshâ.*)—The art of

than his own life. The king ruled conferring peace

driving chariots, charioteering. 30. கசபரிட்சை. (*Gaja-parîkshâ.*)—The knowledge of the marks of an elephant. 31. அசுவபரிட்சை. (*Asvaparîkshâ.*)—The knowledge of the marks of a horse. 32. இரத்தினபரிட்சை. (*Ratnaparîkshâ.*)—The art of examining and choosing gems, knowledge of precious stones. 33. பூமி பரிட்சை. (*Bhûmiparîkshâ.*)—The knowledge of the different kinds of soil, rules for determining by the surface, the nature and depth of soils underneath which water is to be found, &c. 34. சங்கிராமவிலக்கணம். (*Sangrâma Lakshana.*)—Military art, tactics. 35. மல் லயுத்தம். (*Mallayuddha.*)—Wrestling, gymnastics, athletic art, boxing. 36. ஆகருடணம். (*Akarudana.*)—The art of calling and summoning by enchantment. 37. உச்சாடணம். (*Uchchatana.*) — Exorcism, dislodging devils or exciting them to injure others. 38. வித் துவேடணம். (*Vidveshana.*)—Exciting hatred between parties by magical spells.—One of the eight performances of enchantment. 39. மதனசாத்திரம். (*Madana sâstra.*)—Erotics, modus cocundi. 40. மோகனம். (*Mohana.*) — Libidinous fascinations occasioned by enchantment. 41. வசீகரணம். (*Vasîkarana.*)—The art of subduction by magic, the art of bringing one over to another's side or interest by enchantment. 42. இரசவாதம். (*Rasavâda..*)—Alchymy and chemistry. 43. காந்தருவவாதம். (*Gandharvavâda.*)—The knowledge of the condition of the celestial choristers. 44. பைபீலவாதம். (*Paippilavâda.*) — The language of brute creatures from emminets upwards. 45. கவுத்துகவாதம், (*Kavuttukavâda.*)—The art of restoring pleasure to a sorrowful mind. 46. தாது வாதம். (*Dhâtuvâdam*).—The knowledge of the pulse. 47. காருடம். (*Gârudam.*)—Charms, incan-

and prosperity over his kingdom. He was such a

---

tations against poison. 48. நட்டம். (*Nashtam*)—Information respecting a thing lost obtained by astronomical calculations. 49. முட்டி. (*Mushthi.*)—Information respecting any thing concealed in the palms of the hand, in the fist. 50. ஆகாய பிரவேசம். (*Akâsapravêsa.*)—The art of entering into the air and becoming invisible 51. ஆகாயகமனம். (*Akâsagamana.*)—The art ofwalking-in the air. 52. பரகாயபிரவேசம். (*Parakâyapravêsa.*)—The power of leaving ones own body and entering another lifeless body or substance at pleasure. 53. அதிரிசயம். (*Adarsya*)—The power of making ones self invisible. 54. இந்திரசாலம். (*Indrajâla.*)—The art of conjuring, juggling, &c. 55. மகேந்திரசாலம். (*Mahêndrajâla*)—The art of performing wonders in heaven and earth. 56. அக்கினித்தம்பம்; (*Agnisthambha*)—Restraining the action of fire. 57. சலத்தம்பம். (*Jalastambha*) —The art of counteracting the yielding quality of water so as to be able to walk on its surface. 58. வாயுத்தம்பம். (*Vâyustambha*)—The art of restraining the power of the wind. 59. திட்டித்தம்பம். (*Drishtistambha.*)—The art of fascinating the eyes. 60. வாக்குத்தம்பம். (*Vâkkustambha.*)—The art of fascinating the mouth. 61. சுக்கிலத்தம்பம். (*Suklastambha*)—The art of restoring the semen virile. 62. கன்னத்தம்பம். (*Kannastambha*)—The art of preventing the discovery of things concealed. 63. கட்கத்தம்பம். (*Khadgastambha.*)—The art by which the power of the sword or any other weapon is nullified. 64. அவத்திபிரயோகம். (*Avasthaiprayôga.*)—The power of stationing the soul at pleasure in any of the five stages by virtue of abstract devotion."

good man that he regarded the life of every one of his subjects as his own. Though the king and the minister had all the happiness to their allotment, there was still one great want. They had no children; and being much afflicted at heart on that account, consecrated several shrines to *Siva*, Vishnu, Brahmâ and other gods, had their festivals celebrated, distributed food and money to the poor and performed all the sixteen kinds of donations[4] and thirty-two of sub-donations,[5] as prescribed by rules, till, after all, God, in

---

4. Sixteen donations. Generally ten donations only are enumerated. They are (1) *Gôdâna*, gift of cow; (2) *Bhûmi-dâna*, gift of lands; (3) *Tiladâna*, gift of sesamum; (4) *Svarnadâna*, gift of gold; (5) *Ghritadâna* gift of *ghî*; (6) *Vastradâna*, gift of cloth; (7) *Guladâna* gift of molasses; (8) *Dhânyadâna*, gift of paddy; (9) *Rajatadâna*, gift of silver and (10) *Lavanadâna*, gift of salt, to Brâhmans in each case. The other six may be *Sayyâdâna*, the gift of a cushion; *Pâtradâna*, gift of a vessel; *Chhatradâna*, gift of an umbrella; *Pâdukâdâna*, gift of sandals for the feet; *Dandadâna*, gift of a walking stick to the weak and *Châmaradâna*—gift of a fan for the tired.

5. *Arams* are thirtytwo in number; they are "1. ஆதுலர்க்குச்சாலை. (*âtularkkuchchâlai*) Building houses for the poor. 2. ஓதுவார்க்குணவு. (*Oduvârkkunavu.*) Giving maintenance and education. 3. அறுசமயத்தார்க்குண்டி. (*Arusamayattârkkundi.*) Feeding persons of either of the six religious sects. 4. பசுவுக்கு வாயுறை. (*Pasuvukkuvâyurai.*) Feeding cows. 5. சிறைச்சோறு.

(*Siraichchôru.*) Feeding prisoners. 6. ஐயம். (*Aiyam*) Giving alms. 7. இன்பண்டநல்கல். (*Tinpandanalkal.*) Providing for travellers. 8. அறவைச்சோறு. *Ara-vaichchôru.*) Feeding the destitute. 9. மகப்பெறுவித்தல். (*Makapperuvittal.*) Rendering assistance in childbirth. 10. மகவுவளர்த்தல். (*Makavuvalarttal.*) Nourishing children. 11. மகப்பால்வார்த்தல். (*Ma-kappâlvârttal.*) Giving milk to infants. 12. அறவைப்பிணஞ்சுடுதல். (*Aravaippinansududal.*) Burning or burying the poor. 13. அறவைத்தூரியம். (*Aravaittûriyam.*) Furnishing clothes to the destitute. 14. சுண்ணம். (*Sunnam.*) Giving chunam to use with betel. 15. நோய்மருந்து. (*Nôymarundu.*) Giving medicine to the sick. 16. வண்ணார். (*Vannâr.*) Paying for washing the clothes of the poor. 17. நாவிதர். (*Nâvidar.*) *Paying* for shaving. 18. கண்ணாடி. (*Kannâdi.*) Giving the looking glass. 19. காதோலை. (*Kâdôlai.*) Giving palm leaf rolls to women for their ears. 20. கண்மருந்து (*Kanmarundu.*) Giving black paint to women for the eyes, 21. தலைக்கெண்ணெய். (*Talaikkennai.*) Giving oil for the head. 22. பெண்போகம். (*Penbhôgam.*) Pecuniary aid to the poor to celebrate their wedding. 23. பிறர்துயர்காத்தல். (*Pirartuyarkâttal.*) Redressing injuries. 24. தண்ணீர்ப்பந்தல். (*Tannirppandal.*) Keeping water pandals, to give drink to the thirsty. 25. மடம். (*Matham*) Erecting inns or buildings for the reception of Brâhman pilgrims, ascetics &c. 26. தடாகம். (*Tatâkam.*) Making tanks. 27. சோலை. (*Sôlai*) Planting topes groves, &c. 28. ஆவுரிஞ்சுதறி. (*âvuriñjutari.*) Erect-

each a son. The king named his son Madanakâmarâja and brought him up very tenderly. The minister gave the name of Buddhichâturya to his boy and took all requisite care of him. Soon as the boys reached their fifth year, their parents gave them over to a teacher, on an auspicious day, for their education. The teacher regarded these two boys as his two eyes, and being amply rewarded by the king and the minister and expecting more, left no stone unturned for their education. As the boys were naturally intelligent, they very easily learnt at the very first teaching what their master taught them, and soon became proficients in the four *Vêdas*, six *Sâstras,* sixty-four varieties of philosophy, the Codes of Manu, &c. Rewarding the pains of their master as became their positions and more, they left their books for their weapons, and entering the arsenal underwent regular tuition in the usage of arms. They soon became experts in the aiming of the arrows, in the wielding of their bows, the handling of all the weapons and the management of horses and elephants. They were also deeply educated in the politics of the

---

ing stakes at which cows may rub themselves. 29. விலங்கிற்குணவு. (*Vilangirkunavu*) Feeding all kinds of animals. 30. எறுவிடுதல். (*Eruvidudal.*) Giving a bull for covering a cow. 31. விலைகொடுத்துயிர்காத்தல் (*Vilaikoduttuyirkâttal.*) Giving money to save life. 32. கன்னிகாதானம். (*Kannikâdânam.*) Giving assistance towards marriage, of the twice born sect, especially Brâhmans.

country, and thus were made eligible to succeed their parents in the government of the realm. The king and the minister finding out suitable wives for their sons, had their marriages celebrated and left the pairs to the free enjoyment of their youth. These two boys regarded themselves as king and minister from their very young age and were in close friendship.

The following was their daily routine:—Soon as they left their beds in the morning, they were used to go direct to the tank of their city and there clean their teeth. After washing their face and sending up their prayers, they delighted themselves in a sport which was rather a mischievous one. The prince Madanakâmarâja was used to aim one dry mud bullet from his bow and break the pots which the females carried filled with water over their heads; and Buddhichâturya, the minister's son, before the water escaped out of the pot, was used to shut the gap up with a wet mud bullet, which he instantaly aimed at all the pots which the prince broke mischievously. In this kind of sport they were engaged till the tenth *ghatikâ*[6] in the morning, and returning home had their breakfast which was prepared with the six.

---

(6) *Ghatikâ* is equal to 24 minutes. The story being Hindû, the Hindû mode of reckoning time is kept up in those tales.

delicacies : after their meals they chewed some betel-leaves and went separately for their own duties. This was their daily routine.

One early morning while thus they were engaged in breaking and gapping up the pots of the females that left the tank after taking water, the minister's son felt extremely hungry and said, "O, my king! I am very hungry to-day. Let us return home a little early and have our breakfast." The prince laughed at his companion being hungry so early as that, and when Buddhichâturya again and again pressed him, he exclaimed, "Well, if you are hungry, then you may go before me this day." The minister's son was extremely grieved to leave the prince alone there, and extracted an oath from him not to touch his bow till his return, to which the prince consented.

Thus Madanakâmarâja was left alone on the tank-bank and the minister's son was hastening home to have his breakfast. The king of the town, Madanakâma's father, had an household priest whose daughter was a great admirer of the prince's beauty, so much so, that she entertained unlawful love towards him. She was only wait-

---

(7) அறுசுவை. (*Arusuvai.*) The six delicacies or flavours. They are 1, கைப்பு. (*Kaippu.*) Bitterness. 2. இனிப்பு. (*Inippu.*) Sweetness. 3. புளிப்பு. (*Pulippu.*) Sourness. 4. உவர்ப்பு. (*Uvarppu.*) Saltness. 5. துவர்ப்பு. (*Tuvarppu.*) Astringency. 6. கார்ப்பு. (*Kârppu.*) Pungency.

ing for an opportunity to see the prince separate; so, on the day the minister's son returned home a little early, she set before her father, the priest, all his necessaries for the performance of his worship, and taking a vessel on her hip came to the tank with the apparent object of storing up water. Leaving the pot by the water-side she approached the prince and enquired the cause of his being alone. Madana, soon as he saw the daughter of the priest of his father approaching him, welcomed her with all respect due to her position and explained the cause of the absence of the minister's son. The priest's daughter with a lascivious smile on her face, replied as follows :—

"O prince! Your having allowed the minister's son to satisfy his hunger is not a great thing. A greater thing I beg of you, and that is, that you must satisfy my appetite of long-cherished love towards you." Thus spoke the preceptor's daughter, banishing fear, shame and delicacy from her heart, and pointed to a grove as if inviting the prince to that place. He was greatly alarmed, and with great uneasiness of mind replied as follows : "O maid ! That you being the daughter of a preceptor should talk like a ruthless female in a shameless way seems most strange to me. He that gives us birth, he that helps us in difficulty, he that gives us meals, he that gives us refuge and he that instructs us—

these five persons we must regard as our fathers. So says Manu. So, instead of your keeping sisterly affection on me, that you should have led astray your mind for evil passions is most painful. Therefore I beg of you never to mistake me." The pure prince thus spoke and refused her shameless call. She, blinded by headstrong passion, pointed out several rules by which men ought not to refuse the involuntary request of females and began to kiss him forcibly. The prince escaping from her sinful embraces called out help in the name of God, pronouncing, "O, Thou the most merciful! Thou the lord of Kailâsa! Thou the lord of Pârvatî! Thou the lord of the three worlds,[8] come and protect me in this delicate moment." Like a mad man he again and again begged of her to banish from her mind all evil thoughts and that he shall never heed to her as he regarded her as his sister.

The preceptor's daughter was now burning with anger on account of her rejected love. Shame at the refusal and the unfulfilment of her intentions, provoked her so much, that she wanted to bring him to trouble at once, and vowed before him that she would cause his murder in one *muhûrta*. No sooner she uttered the threat than she loosened her locks and made

8. Several epithets applied to Siva.

9. A *muhûrta* is an hour and half or three and thee-quarters *ghatikas*.

them hang in all sorts of disorderly ways, broke her glass bracelets, wounded her body by the sharp edges of those broken pieces, and assumed the character of a chaste female that had been dishonoured by a bad person and that had, notwithstanding all his personal compulsion, refused his temptations. Raising up a great alarm by her loud cries she ran to her house and fell down before her father who had just then sat down for his worship. The father was thunderstruck, and taking the girl in his lap enquired out the cause of her distress and the name of the offender.

"My dear father! After setting before you all the requisites for the *pūjā,* I just went to the tank to supply the house with water. The son of the king who rules over this city seems to have been there, on the tank bank. He barred my way and forced me to accept his embraces. And when I refused, he dishonoured me in this way." Thus ended the daughter and the father's rage knew no bounds. Fierce like Rudra[10] in his anger he walked in haste to the palace. Soon as he approached the gates, the guards who had been watching from a distance his angry countenance, reported his sudden arrival to the king, as also the symptoms of plain anger on his face.

The king ran out to welcome him, and falling down with the eight members of his body

10 *Rudra*—Śiva in his anger.

touching the ground,[11] humbly addressed him thus:—

"My preceptor, my god! May I know the reason of your reverence's sudden appearance in a time when your reverence should have been sitting for worship?" The preceptor, with his countenance burning in anger, related how the prince had spoiled the honour of his daughter, and wished to know how his subjects would manage to live in a country where such daring crimes were rife. The king was much ashamed at what he heard and pacified the preceptor by promising to take away the life of that abominable criminal for whom he had no longer any affection though he was his son. Then he invited the preceptor to the *sabhâmandapam* or council hall and there paid him all the sixteen kinds of respects.[12] He

---

11. *Sâshtânga namaskâra.* A kind of salutation among Brâhmans and other high caste Hindûs in which the younger falls down before the elder with the eight members of his body touching the ground. The eight members are the two hands, breast, forehead, two eyes, throat and the middle of the back.

(12) *Upachâra* or *Shôdasôpachâra* or the 16 kinds of external honours done to God or to any holy person. They are,—1. தூபம். (*Dhûpa.*) Burning incense. 2. தீபம். (*Dîpa.*) Placing lamps before an idol. 3. நைவேத்தியம். (*Naivêdya.*) Offering etables or sacred rice. 4. தாம்பூலம். (*Tâmbûla.*) Betel

sent for the minister Manaiyâlan, told him the prince's crime and the punishment he deserved for it, and pulling out his signet ring ordered it to be given to the executioners as the permission to murder Madanakâma. The minister had a great regard for the royal preceptor and took the prince for a real offender. He had every reason to think so, taking into consideration Madanakâma's prime youth; so, he gave the ring and ordered the executioners to do their duty.

They accordingly went to the tank and showing the ring asked him to prepare himself for death. The prince was greatly startled at first and by degrees became bold. "If the will of God be so, then what could I, a mortal, do in this affair.

---

and nut offering. 5. சந்தனம். (*Chandana.*) Sandal wood, &c., for anointing. 6. புட்பம். (*Pushpa.*) Offering of flowers in the act of worship. 7. கர்ப்பூரம் (*Karpûra.*) Presentation of camphor. 8. சலம். (*Jala*) Pouring of water in the feet, &c. 9. எண்ணெய் (*Enney* Sans. *Taila*) anointing. 10. கண்ணாடி. (*Kannâdi.* Sans: *Darpana.*) Presentation of mirrors 11. சாமரை. (*Châmara.*) Presentation of chauries. 12. குடை. (*Kudai*: Sans: *Chhatra.*) Presentation of umbrella. 13. கொடி. (*Kodi*: Sans: *Ketu* or *Dhvaja.*) Flags. 14. விசிறி. (*Visiri.* Sans: *Tâla-vrinta.*) Offering of fans. 15. ஆலவட்டம். (*Alavatta.*) Offering of large circular fans. 16. வஸ்திரம். (*Vastra.*) Offering of cloths.

I was put to all these calamities by the absence of my minister for a short time, though it may be. Let me now see him before I die." So thinking, Madanakâma intimated the executioners that he was ready for death and that he had an only request to be gratified. When they, pitying a prince in peril, asked him to communicate that request, he said: "Kindly bring me my minister before I die. I must see his face and give him a few instructions. He just left me for his breakfast and has not yet come back. Kindly inform him that I am in trouble and that I want to see him."

One of the executioners watched the prince and the other went to bring the minister's son who had then sat before his leaf for his meals after his bath and ablutions. He took in the first morsel and was raising his hand for a second one, when a servant of his stood before him with a dismal face and informed him of the executioner that had come from the prince. The minister's son left his leaf suddenly, and going to the executioner asked him the reason for his sudden appearance. "My lord, I know only this much. The king is enraged at a report from his preceptor that the prince attempted the spoliation of the latter's daughter; your honour's father gave me his signet ring of the king as an order to murder the prince. When I went to do my duty, his honour the prince wanted me to inform your honour of this order," was all the executioner's reply.

Buddhichâturya was extremely vexed, at what he heard and did not know what to do. He had very great respect for the moral character of the prince. But then was his youth to be blamed? No, (he thought), let me arrive at no conclusions now, till I see him. So thinking, he went to the stalls, saddled two *Pañchakalyânî*[13] fleeters, and prepared for the worst, went to Madanakâma and asked him to tell him the truth. Soon as he heard the real facts, Buddhichâturya fell into the following contemplations. "If we are out with the secret, people may not believe us now. They may not think us to be on the right side. The poor king would then be blamed for his partiality to his son. The world may talk of an unjust king who let away unpunished a criminal that was his son." All these thoughts passed over his mind in the twinkling of an eye, and he addressed the executioners as follows:—"Well, my friends, what say you now to this case. The crime is with one party, and another who is innocent has the punishment." The executioners were watching all the marks in the prince's face, and were fully convinced of his innocence and hence replied as follows:—

---

13. A horse whose four feet and forehead are white.

"Your Highness! This king has an only son who is in every way qualified to reign. We see plainly who the offender is. The king will excuse us in future, if we tell his majesty the truth. We shall murder some beast or bird and produce that blood as the life-blood of the prince. And we request your majesties not to remain in this town but to run away to some place or other till the truth is out."

Buddhichâturya was extremely delighted at the words of the executioners who were so merciful on the occasion. He made the prince mount one of the horses, and himself getting up on the other rode fast, leaving the direction to the choice of the fleeters themselves.

Galloping without food and drink all the forests, mountains, thickets and jungles and much overcome by fatigue and hunger, they reached a town which on enquiry they found out to be Indrapuram. The first thing they did was to enquire out any hotel or feeding house for themselves and their horses. They, not wishing to expose themselves to the public, chose the house of an old woman, who promised to give meals to them and grass and gram to their horses for a pagoda per day. Agreeing to her conditions they boarded there, and under the kind protection of that old woman forgot their homes. Thus passed several days.

One day Buddhichâturya and Madanakâma set out to see the sceneries of the town, and, admiring all they saw on their way, reached the *Siva* temple of that place. It was unfortunately shut. When they enquired the reason for it, they found that the high officer of that town had shut the gates of the temple as the subjects did not pay their tax. They went to that officer and convinced him, how unjust it was to direct the temple gates to be shut for an offence which the subjects had committed. The taxes ought to be collected by force from the inhabitants, and not the temple gates shut, spoke they to the officer who, being ashamed of his unlawful course, at once opened the gates of the temple and gave due orders for the resuming of the *pûjâ*, which was accordingly done. Madanakâma and Buddhichâturya went on circumambulating the God, admiring several paintings on the *prâkâra* (circuit) walls of the temple. They discovered in a part of the wall a drawing hung up. There were two charming beauties in it. Madanakâma went very near the drawing, eyed it closely, and fell down in a swoon enchanted by the beauty of those figures. The minister's son who was engaged in admiring the beauties of another portion of the *prâkâra* was aroused by the staggering down of the prince. Flying at once to his rescue and taking him on his lap, he tried all his best to bring him back to his senses. Wishing to know the cause of Madanakâma's swoon, he eyed round about him and discovered the life-like paintings. Judging that the beauties on the drawing must have been the cause of Madanakâma's loss of senses, the prince proceeded in the requisite treatment and succeeded in restoring him to his senses. Madanakâma, no sooner had he returned to his senses than he turned his eyes towards the pictures and again fell down in a swoon. Again the prince was brought back to his senses. Buddhichâturya was now more than certain that the prince's love was towards the objects in the drawings and removed him to a place where he could no more see them. The only way of giving perfect restoration to the failing understanding of the prince was, thought Buddhichâturya, the bringing of the damsels drawn in the picture; so he called the *Dharmakartâs* or the temple authorities to his side and enquired of them all about the drawings. Who drew it? Who the objects were that it represented? How it came to be hung up in that temple? And the *Dharmakartâ* gave the following reply: "Gentleman! There is a town named Dêvakîpuram near this place. In it lives a painter named Vengaiyan. He now and then comes to this temple on pilgrimage, and on one occasion he brought with him this piece of workmanship and had it suspended here. That is all we know about it." Thus ended the *Dharmakartâ* and the minister's son replied as follows: "I have not a greater friend here than yourself. The prince, my master, is now almost enslaved by the beauties of the paintings. I am determined to bring him those objects though I shall have to undergo twelve years labour for it. Till I return successfully, the prince must remain here under your kind protection. I shall render you all help in money." Thus arranging with the *Dharmakartâ* and the old woman as regards the care-taking of Madanakâmaâ, Buddhichâturya mounted his horse to go in search of Vengaiyan in Dêvakîpuram, and after much travelling reached him in three days. Making his acquaintance, he moved with him closely for ten days till their acquaintance turned into friendship. On the eleventh day, just when there was no third party, Buddhichâ-âturya spoke as it came of by itself about the abovesaid painting and who, the objects represented in it, were. The painter replied that he never saw those objects himself, that in the town of Vîmâ (Bhîmâ) purî, fifty *kôs* from that place, he had a friend—an oil-rubber, employed under the king of that place, and that that friend gave him a hair from which he had, by the rules of his art, worked up the objects in the picture. Buddhichâturya now cunningly questioned everything about that oil-rubber, the names of his relations, their places of residence, his wealth, position, &c., &c. The painter replied as follows :

"Well, my friend, the name of that oil-rubber is Mutyâlunâyakkan. His wife's name is Ilakshumakkâ*l*. Her mother country is Vidarbhadêsa. She has, since she came away there, never gone back to her mother's house, and none of her mother's people visited her there." The minister's son heard all the story, as if he was quite unconcerned, remained three days more with the painter to arouse no suspicion and went away as if going to some other place after the formal leave-taking. He reached Vîmâpurî, and going into the bâzâr street, bought clothes for all the members, big and small—of the family, and with turmeric, nuts and betel-leaves reached the neighbouring house of the oil-rubber. When the inmates of the house enquired as to who he was, the minister's son said, "I have my brother-in-law here in this town employed as the chief oil-rubber in the palace. My sister's name is Ilakshumakkâ*l*. We gave her away in marriage when she was very young. Through several inconveniences we were not able to see her. I have now come in search of her; is this her house?" The next house people at once sent word to Ilakshumakkâ*l* that her brother had come and as soon as she came to meet him, the minister's son sobbed out, "Oh, my sister! We gave you away in marriage when you were only five years old. Several family circumstances, when our father was alive, prevented me from seeing you, and after our father's death the family concerns devolved on me, which gave me so much work that I was not able to see you ere now." He then followed her to her house and there distributed his presents and fruits to the children. And, by that time Mutyâlunâyakkan, the oil-rubber, returned from the palace to whom the minister's son,—the brother-in-law gave all the presents. Feasts for the brother-in-law followed. Mutyâlunâyakkan gave special attention to his brother-in-law's horse. And Buddhichâturya passed twenty days in (the supposed brother-in-law) the oil-rubber's house.

Medicine and feast for three days says the (Tamil) proverb. Mutyâlunâyakkan exhausted the savings of pagodas he had in hand for the feast of twenty days' duration that he was giving his brother-in-law. On the twenty-first night he spoke to his wife of the prolonged stay of her brother. The minister's son, her supposed brother, overheard it from the veranda outside, and soon as morning dawned, requested permission to return to Vidarbhadêsa. Ilakkshumakkâ*l* gave him some breakfast, which when he was eating, Mutyâlunayâkkan came home. He inquired the cause of his brother-in-law's breakfasting rather early, and when he replied that he intended going to his country, Mutyâlunâyakkan requested him to stay three days more.

It was only at this time that Buddhichâturya enquired of his brother-in-law or supposed brother-in-law whether the king of that country had any children. Mutyâlunâyakkan said that the king had no sons but had two daughters yet unmarried. " Have you ever seen them," asked Buddhichâturya. " No. It is impossible to see them" replied Mutyâlunâyakkan, and added as follows :—

" If any one demands the princesses in marriage, he is at once murdered by the king. So, no one dares ask them in marriage. They are strongly guarded and it is impossible to see them."

Buddhichâturya, whose sole object was to take a sight of them, to know whether they were the same represented in the picture, suggested the following plan to Mutyâlunâyakkan, which would enable him to see them. "My dear brother-in-law ! Kindly take a vessel full of oil to the palace, to the spot next the window of the princesses' rooms. And I shall follow you and sit down there for an oil-rubbing, you shall go on rubbing the oil with the thirty-two strokes. They would open their windows and ask you the reason of your making a noise there. Then you shall tell them that the king detained you there that day, and, as your brother-in-law wanted

---

* Which thinly two, to the best of my enquiring, I am not a'le to ascertain.

to go away to his country, you apply the oil there to his head. I shall somehow manage to see them."

So spoke the supposed brother-in-law, and Mutyâlunayâkkan promising to gratify his wishes, took him to the palace to apply the oil. When the strokes were falling with all sorts of symmetry, the princesses opened the windows and wanted to know the reason for the disturbance, and Mutyâlunâyakkan, who was instructed by his brother-in-law already, gave out what was said before. Their features were seen reflected on the surface of the oil, and Buddhichâturya was fully satisfied within himself that they were the same persons he saw in the painting. The princesses closed their windows and Mutyâlu's brother-in-law too finished his bath. After the three days were over he took leave of Ilakshumakkâ*l* and her husband, and much vexed at heart at the oath of the king to murder the demander of his daughters' hands in marriage, and knowing no other way of returning to Madanakâma without taking with him those princesses, wished to put an end to his life. So, he turned the horse towards the sea coast and leaving him free there to himself addressed him thus: "O my jewel of a horse! You were under my kind patronage so long. Now I enter this sea to get myself drowned and thus give up my life, as I no longer like to live in this world without fulfilling the prince's wishes. You may go now and roam at large wherever you like." Thus addressing the horse, the minister's son entered the sea. The noble animal, as if pitying his master and not caring a bit more for his own life, followed him close behind in the waters. To his great wonder Buddhichâturya found the waters only neck deep wherever he went. Go wherever he may, there was no water to drown him. His grief knew no bounds. He called up help in the name of God. "O, the ever Merciful! The Lord of Pârvati! The Destroyer of the three cities! The Protector of the world, why dost Thou not take me under Thy protection in the Heavens? Thus the minister's son called out, and it was to his own fortune that he did so. For these calls for help fell on the ears of Pârvatî, who, with Paramasiva, was passing very near that place. She insisted upon her husband's helping the man in distress, and accordingly *S*iva stood before him. As Buddhichâturya was naturally intelligent, he at once concluded that the person who stood before him must be no one except Isvara, and so began his loud and respectful extollations of *S*iva, Sankara, *S*ambho, &c. Isvara wanted o know his distress, and Buddhichâturya addressed him as follows: "My god, I came in search of two princesses with whom my master the prince has fallen in love. I left no stone unturned in my efforts to search them. Just when I found them out I had to give up the idea of ever securing them at all, as their father had proclaimed to put to death him who requests their hand in marriage. Instead of returning to him with empty hands, I just resolved to throw myself into this ocean, which again disappoints me by being only neck-deep wherever I go." Isvara pitied the prince and promised to assist him. The god assured him of success and gave him the following directions. "Well, my boy, come to the shore from the water; go to that town and be living there for a few days. On a certain day you shall hear the sound of a bell. It shall fall on your ears only. Soon as you hear it, adorn yourself with all princely ornaments and be walking the streets. The ministers shall come and invite you for a wedding. You had better say that you are a sojourner and that you would not like the idea of becoming a son-in-law. Then the king shall come and invite you in person. You shall then proceed to the palace and have the marriage badges tied round the neck of the princesses by a Brâhmanî's hand, and taking them to your own country marry the younger yourself and give the other in marriage to the prince." Thus pointing him out the course, Isvara disappeared. Buddhichâturya much pleased at his success returned to Vîmâpurî and there sojourned in expectation of the time. Siva hid his goddess Pârvatî and his vehicle the bull in the hollow of a fig tree, and assuming the character of a *Sanyâsi* or an ascetic robed in dyed clothes, and holding a *Kamandalu,*[14] came to the palace of the king. When the god Isvara himself assumed the shape of a *Sanyâsi,* who can describe the majesty of it. The king was highly pleased at the approach of a sage towards his mansion and running headlong welcomed him for his meals at his house that day. The *Sanyâsi* apparently accepted the invitation. The king seated him in a gold plank, and spreading a leaf before him requested him to partake of his dinner. The ascetic Isvara cunningly asked the king before his partaking of the meals whether he had any sons. The king said that he had no sons and that he had two daughters. The *Sanyâsi* wanted to see them and distribute the *prasâdam*[15] of sacred water to them. By the king's order the princesses came nad stood before the sage, who distributed water to them and asked them to drink it and sprinkle it on their heads ; and they did accordingly. The sage now inquired of the king whether his daughters were married, and the king replied in the negative. "Then have I come to a wretch's house for my meals. A man who has two grown up daughters unmarried. I shall never taste a grain of food here. Thus crying out in anger the *Sanyâsi* disappeared in the place

14. An earthen or wooden water pot.

15. Remnants of the holy water and *Tulasi* or *Bilva* leaf after worshipping an idol.

where he was seated. The king was greatly affected by the event. "Pity on me that I should have become such a sinner. The *Sanyâsi* must have been the God himself for who could thus have suddenly disappeared. As I never gave out my daughters in marriage, and as I proclaimed that I would kill him who would demand their hands, the great God was highly displeased and subjected me to this everlasting remorse. I must give them in marriage in a *muhûrta* to any prince and then only taste my food to day." Thus maddened by grief and tearing his hair at the loss of Isvara, whom he had a moment ago for his guest, the king sent his ministers in search of a fitting match, and sending for the priests fixed an auspicious hour for the wedding.

Isvara, after his disappearance, went to the fig tree, and taking possession of his goddess Pârvatî and his vehicle Rishabha, rung as promised his victorious bell, which the minister's son only heard. Dancing and capering with joy, praising every moment the great god *Siva*, he adorned his body with all sorts of costly ornaments and loitered in the bâzâr street, where the ministers of that city discovered him, and invited him extolling his fortune to accept the princesses' hands. Buddhichâturya refused; the ministers again and again told him how he cast away the fortune that wishes to cling to his feet. Even then he refused, and cuttingly pointed out to the king's order of murdering the persons who demanded the princesses in marriage. The ministers could not convince Buddhichâturya, rather the latter in obeying the order of Mahêsvara pretended that he had no confidence. They now returned to the king and informed him of their success in having found out one, and at the same time in not having convinced him of the change of the king's resolution. Now the king flew to the spot with all the parahphernalia for the invitation of a bridegroom, and requested him to accept his daughter's hands in marriage.

The minister's son replied to him thus: "O, king! You once had a rule of murdering him who came to demand your daughter in marriage; and now you yourself come of your own accord to request me. I have no confidence in you." The king begged his pardon, and told him of the change that he had lately to make in his own resolution. Then the minister's son wanted to have his own system of marriage, and the king agreeing to it brought him to the palace. The wedding hall was hastily decorated. The news that the king had suddenly resolved to give away his daughters in marriage spread throughout the town. The *purôhita* or the officiating priest or the marriage ceremony was asked to conduct all the preliminaries, the *hôma* or sacred fire, donation, &c., of the marriage. The brides were hastily decorated and brought to the hall. The Brâhman g ving the marriage badges to the minister's son, wanted him to tie them round the brides' necks, and as the minister's son had quite a different plan in his mind, as we all know about the marriage affair, he directed saying that that was the custom of his country, to have the marriage badge tied, as ordered by Paramêsvara, by the hands of Bhâmanî's. With this single exception, all the ceremonies pertaining to the marriage were regularly conducted.

The busy day was drawing to its close. The minister's son as soon as the sun set in the western mountains had his supper, and entering the bed room pretended to be sound asleep. The eldest of the princesses bathed in the evening and adorning herself with all ornaments, and repleting with all sorts of sweet odours and taking in her hand, a platter containing sweet fruits and betel-leaves and nuts as well as a lovely violin entered the bed chamber. Seeing her lord asleep, instead of awakening him herself, she played for some time on her violin. Finding that her music was not able to do its intended work, and much enraged at finding so retired a husband who would go to sleep on the very first day instead of waiting for an affectionate wife, determined to do away with him by one stroke of her sword, if he did not rise at the tap of her fingers on his back. Buddhichâturya who was only pretending sleep slyly watched all the movements of her face, and concluding with himself that he would highly provoke her if he remained in that state for a longer time, awoke as if from deep slumber.

"How is it my lord that you went away to sleep so early as that?" were the words which the princess spoke to her drowsy or apparently drowsy husband. The minister's son begged pardon for his neglect, and pointed out the bustle of the day as the reason for his weariness.

The princess was satisfied by the reason and requested him to accept the fruits, sweetmeats, &c., that she had brought and also herself. Buddhichâturya did full justice to what she brought in the platter, and after washing his hands began to chew betel-leaves and nuts. The princess not much pleased with the retired spirit of her husband, and wishing to arouse his love by artificial means played some lovely songs on her guitar. The minister's son never returned her loves and kept on closely to his *tâmbûla*-chewing.

Let us not think for one moment even Buddhichâturya to be unfit to return her loves. He, as the *Sanyâsi* robed Sankara had ordered, had meant the elder of the princesses for his king Madanakâma and so kept aloof from her regardless of her love evincements towards him. But when she came very near him with a smiling countenance, he devised a plan of wiling away the night time by a pleasant story and addressed her as follows :—

"My dearest love! Permit me first to relate you a pleasant story. We shall sleep after that." The princess agreeing to it, kept to her own seat. The minister's son Buddhichâturya, sat up on his bed and possessing all the natural advantages of an impressive story teller—silvery tone, fine gestures as befitting the occasion, apt allusions to serve as illustrations, &c., began as follows :—

FIRST STORY.

LISTEN, Oh you best of womankind! There was a town named Dharmâpurî. Over it ruled a king Dharmananda. He regarding the lives of his subjects as his own life, ruled them very justly with his fellow officers—the minister, councillors, commanders, captains and lieutenants. During the fifty years of his prosperous reign there was not even a single day on which he swerved from the Codes of Manu. But for all his charitable disposition he had not the happiness of a son to his allotment. Of course, this defect worked much in his mind. He consecrated several shrines to *Brahmâ*, *Rudra*, *Vishnu* and other Gods, had their festivals regularly conducted, distributed food to the poor, made the sixteen kinds of donations [1] to deserving men, and sent up prayers to God on the three occasions of morning, noon and evening with the intention of securing a son. After all his devotions seemed to have effect, and God gave him a son. The king distributed sugar on account of that happy news, and brought him up very tenderly. In the third year after this event, the king had another son, who was also being carefully brought up.

A few days after, all on a sudden, an enemy invaded the town of Dharmâpurî, and totally

1 See Note 4, Introduction.

defeating him, drove him outside the town with his wife and children. The king was much vexed at the calamity that came over him, and cursing his own evil-star, went to another town and was earning his livelihood by begging there in the streets till his elder son was seven years of age and his younger five. Thinking that it was a sin to ruin the boys without giving them their education, he took them to a distant village, where an old learned Brâhma*n* was keeping a school. He gave the sons over to the charge of that village schoolmaster, and addressed him as follows :—

"These two are my sons ; I am extremely poor and so quite unable to pay anything for their education. But if you would kindly educate them, I mean rewarding your pains by presenting you with one of these boys." The schoolmaster agreed to the conditions, and so the king and his queen, after leaving their children there, went away to some other town to pass their days like the lowest of men in begging.

The Brâhma*n* teacher appointed the eldest son to the domestic task of grazing the cows and buffalos, and educated with all possible means the second son, who duly learnt the four *Vêdas*, [2] six *Sâstras*, sixty-four varieties of philosophy, the Codes of Manu, and even the objectionable science of jugglery, the magic art of infusing ones own soul into different bodies and other tricks in which his master the old Brâhma*n* was a great

---

2 See Notes 1, 2 & 3, Introduction.

expert. He also acquired from him the faculty of *Jñânadrishti.** Thus he passed several years in study and acquired perfection in one and all the departments of knowledge.

One day, just when he had attained mastery of the science of *Jñânadrishti,* he experimented it to see where his parents were dwelling then, and when he found out by his newly acquired power their whereabouts, he wanted to go and see them secretly. They have forgot us so long and are now mere beggars in the streets. I shall now go and see them and make arrangements to relieve them from their calamity. They may then ask me about my brother ; why should my master not educate him but appoint him to only low works. Let me now dive at his motives by my *Jñânadrishti.* Thus pondering over in his mind, he thought for a time and exclaimed, "Vile wretch! For henceforth I must only regard you so, as you want to deceive my parents when they come to demand one of us. You also mean to make me sit in the sun as a student that is very careless and never pays any attention whatever to his books ; of course, they will choose my elder brother, being deceived by his position of a monitor in the class, though he knows nothing. Thus you mean to deceive my poor parents. Oh! I know how to deceive you." These

---

* The knowing eye, a faculty of diving into others inward feelings and motives.

were the thoughts of the prince—the second son —and they were quite natural. He saw only then the evil intentions of his teacher. He wanted to inform his parents of them and was waiting for the night to proceed to them.

The night came on. After his duties of the evening as a student were over, he retired for rest or rather pretended to retire for rest. For no sleep could now close down his eye-lids since the evil intentions of his master became plain to him. He therefore left his bed and walked out to the public road. To his joy he found there the dead body of a kite. He transferred himself into its corpse, flew at once to his parents and reached them in the dead of night. Then resuming his own shape he awakened them from their slumber. They were surprised at first, and when they were certain that it was one of their sons who stood before them, kissed their boy and inquired into the welfare of his brother and the way by which he managed to come such a long distance. Their second son related to them in haste everything; how he acquired all the rare arts, how his elder brother had been ruined, how the master's intention stood, and how they must act themselves. He also requested them to come soon and reclaim him and not to take the elder brother who would be quite useless, then, for them. He assured them that he would afterwards himself manage for his rescue. Thus advising them, the second son flew back, assuming the shape of a kite, in the same night to his master's house, and resuming his former shape fell in sound slumber.

Soon as the morning dawned, the father-king and the mother-queen set out to the Brâhman teacher's village, which they reached after several days' journey. They entered his house. The teacher welcomed them with a cheerful countenance and made arrangements for giving them a grand dinner. Secretly he called a student to his side and sent him to fetch the eldest son who was grazing the cattle. As soon as the boy arrived, he dressed him up with all pomp and sent him to the school as the monitor of the highest class. And he made the second son to sit in the scorching sun, as a fit punishment, as he said, for his not studying his lesssons well. The parents saw what was before them, and concluded with themselves of the extreme truthfulness in the second son's statement.

The feasts were over. The master was over-hospitable to his poor but royal guests. He extolled the high proficiencies of the eldest son, and of his having raised himself by his own exertions to a monitor's position in the highest class of the school ; and he also spoke very poorly of the attainments of the second son, who spent the greater portion of the day in sitting in the sun for his carelessness and stupidity.

The king saw too well the tricks of the master; therefore he spoke to the Brâhman thus: "Sir, many thanks for your having devoted so much of attention to my first son. Him I give to you only, as I think, he may not in the pride of his overlearning obey me. Stupid as he is, I prefer the second son, as I can make him obey me." Thus taking the second son, the king returned with him to his place. The master was sorely disappointed at his own ruin, and sent the eldest son as usual to look after his cattle.

The old king and queen retired to a certain town with their second son, who now asked for some food. They said that he must fast that night with them, and as soon as morning dawned they shall beg in the streets and give him his breakfast. The son was extremely vexed at the imprudence of his parents, who had never saved anything during all their past period of begging. So he spoke to them thus: "My dear father, I am very sorry to see that you have been begging so long without having saved even a single pie for the future. Let what is past be past and let us no more think of it. For the present kindly do as I request you. The king of this town has a big cock for which all along his life he had been searching a hen. He has not even now succeeded in procuring one for it. I shall transform myself, by the power of the magic art that I have recently learnt, into a hen. When I begin to crow in the morning the people would be attracted towards me by my voice, and report to the king of the existence of a suitable match for his cock. He shall then demand me of you in sale. If you ask one hundred pagodas he shall offer them and take me disguised as a hen from you. I shall then rejoin you." So advising his father, he assumed the shape of a hen and began to crow. Early morning crowds began to collect before the abode of the beggar king. The news reached the ears of the king of that town, who at once came to the spot to see, in person, the hen reported to be a fair match to his cock ; for his mania for these fowls had always been very great. The father and now the owner of the hen demanded one hundred pagodas for it, which the king of the town offered without grudging, and walked home fully rejoiced to have secured such a good fowl. He gave her over to the fowlers, who preserved her in an iron basket which they set over her and placed a weight over the basket. No sooner these persons left the hen to herself, then she—rather the prince in disguise—assumed the shape of a bandicoote, and boring a hole underground escaped from his confinement, and, crossing all the palace mansions, reached the outside of the town and went to the place where his father was staying. The parents had kept meals ready and were waiting for their son. So they were highly pleased to see him return safe, and first serving him meals, sat down themselves for their dinner after him.

The ki ng of that country who was always thinking of his highly bought hen, soon as he had some leisure, ordered the fowlers to bring her to him ; and when they went for her they found in that place a hole. Their confusion may be more imagined than described. So flying back in anguish they reported the strange phenomena of a hole in the place of a hen that they safely secured in an iron basket over which they had put a heavy weight.

The king was extremely vexed at the mystery of the disappearance of his hen. "Can a bandicoote ever kill a hen and eat her up. May kill perhaps ! Let us now examine the hole and its winding, and dragging it out kill it." So thinking he ordered his men to bring him at least the murderer of his hen—the bandicoote. Pickaxes, spades, hoes and crowbars were freely administered to all the windings of the hole of the bandicoote till more than half the palace was ploughed down. All the search, of course, proved vain, and the king doubly mortified, sanctioned at once new estimates for the repair of his mansion.

Let us turn to the prince. He lived in peace outside the town with his parents, who took great care of him till every pie of the hundred pagodas was spent. When that sum was exhausted they informed their son of it, who now devising within himself of another scheme, spoke thus to his father:—"There lives a rich merchant named Dhanapâla *Setti* in this town. He has an only son who prefers walking only instead of riding, which his father daily compels him to do. I shall assume the shape of a *Pañchakalyâni*[3] horse. You shall walk with me to the tank side where the merchant's son will come in the morning for his bath. He shall have a liking for the horse and ask of you the price. You had better demand one thousand pagodas. He will conduct you to his father, count you out the money, and take me to the stables. I shall somehow manage to come away from my confinement." Thus instructing, the son assumed the shape of a horse and stood before his father neighing most melodiously. The father was extremely delighted at the beauty of the horse, which was no other except his own son, and as instructed took him to the tank side. The merchant's son came, and as prophesied already, promised to offer pagodas one thousand for it. So he took the seller with his horse to Dhanapâla *Setti* his father.

Now, it unfortunately happened, that the Brâhman master who instructed the transferred prince, was sitting by the side of the merchant. He, as soon as he saw the horse, fully concluded within himself that it was no other than the trickish disciple of his who had overpowered him by his own art. And he now devised plans to kill him by some tricks, and with this evil desire spoke to

---

3 See Note 13, Introduction,

the merchant : "My dear merchant, you have an only son. And this horse is a very rough and mischievous animal, not fit to be used by such untrained riders like him. So it is not fit for him. And if you or he persist in buying the horse, you shall never see the face of him getting down from it. Therefore, as I know riding better, I wish to have it ; give me please a loan of one thousand pagodas. I shall return you the money as soon as I go home. You shall now see yourself the tricks of this animal." So saying the Brâhma*n* master procured one thousand pagodas from the merchant, and counting them out to the seller, secured the horse, nay, his student whom he had all along, ever since his father walked away with him, been hating.

The master got upon the horse and began to whip it right and left. It took him to all the places he drove till it was entirely exhausted. Now the rider took it to a dirty pool to water it and thus to kill it. The transformed prince saw the evil intentions of his master-enemy, and so entered the body of a dead fish inside the water leaving that of a horse. The life now left the horse and hence it fell down. The Brâhma*n* now saw by his *Jñânadrishti* that his student had transformed himself into a fish, and so calling all his school-boys ordered them to pour out the water in the tank and kill all the fish in it. And they were executing their master's order. The prince in the shape of the fish was greatly confused. He saw on that tank bank the dead body of a buffalo which the cobblers had left there and went to fetch their weapons to dissect it. The prince entered its body and began to run away. The master was watching all the prince's movements, and so following the buffalo ordered the cobbler to torture it. The prince in confusion assumed the shape of a parrot, the carcass of which he discovered in a tree. And the master taking the shape of a kite (*garuda*) followed him furiously through mountains, forests, thickets and jungles, till at last both of them reached a town. The prince finding it impossible to escape the beaks of a kite flew in the direction of the palace. To his joy the windows of the room of the princess of that town were open, and she herself was sitting in her cushion undoing the knots of the hair over her head. The parrot-prince flew through the windows and fell on her lap. She was extremely delighted at the sight of the parrot, and taking it up on her hands kissed it close to her breast. She immediately sent for a goldsmith, and measuring out rubies from her treasury asked him to make a suitable cage for her parrot. And the goldsmith did accordingly. The kite waited for some time outside the window, and vowing by signs to take away the parrot's life in a week flew away. The prince-parrot poo-phooed the idea by signs and felt himself perfectly secure in the cage. The princess dandled her pet during the whole day, and at night fed it with milk, fruits and condiments and retired for her usual sleep.

At about midnight the parrot left its cage, and assuming its own form of a prince sat beside the sleeping princess, smeared sandal over her body, ate all the sweetmeats that she had left on her table, and converting himself again into a parrot, was quietly dozing away the night in its cage. At about the tenth *ghatikâ* [4] in the night, the princess arose from her deep slumber. It was then that she came to know of something that had been put upon her while in sleep without her knowledge. The sandal cup was empty; the scent boxes had exhausted their contents; all her body was rubbed over with sweet scent. "Who could have done it in this strictly guarded place? The *Zanâna* is most jealously watched by soldiers and eunuchs. Who could have managed to throw dust into the eyes of one and all the watches? Why should that expert man who had managed to cross all the so many barriers not awake me; let me watch next night." So thought the princess, and with that thought the morning dawned. During the day she nursed the parrot as usual; when it became dark she retired for rest and kept herself awake till about midnight, and afterwards unconsciously fell in deep slumber. The prince-parrot watching the

4 See Note 6, Introduction.

carefulness of the princess never left its cage till she was snoring. Then it came out, and resuming it original shape applied sandal to the sleeping princess's body and went into the cage. She, on leaving her bed next morning, saw in her body the signs of the shameful act repeated, and much astonished at her own carelessness and at the dexterity of the secret frequenter of her room, and fully determining within herself to catch out the thief the next night, took little breakfast and slept the whole day to be cautious during the night. For all that, the parrot did not lose its care ; for before going to bed, she fed him well, and on rising from her sleep in the evening, she nourished him with milk and fruits. After a light supper, to keep herself awake, she retired to her bed and, covering her body with a blanket from head to foot, pretended to sleep. The parrot-prince watched all her movements. He knew quite well that she was wide awake. But he thought it best, to come out of the cage and disclose his history to her. He was also eager to instruct her as to her future course. So, he came out of the cage resuming his original form, and chewing betel sat beside the princess in her couch. She now caught hold of his arm and sitting up in her bed spoke thus: "I have watched you, leaving your parrot's body and resuming this princely shape. Tell me now who you are, why you have assumed this shape, and what made you come to me." The prince then related his parentage, education and adventures, how his elder brother had been ruined, how he first transformed himself into a hen, then a horse, then a fish, then a buffalo, and at last into a parrot, and how his bitter enemy the teacher pursued him throughout his transformations and teased him. He then addressed the princess as follows : " I prophesied with myself that you must become my wife, and hence resulted my secret visits to your bed. Even now, knowing that you were wide awake, I came to you as I wished to instruct you previously about the course of action you ought to follow. My master who hates me from the very bottom of his heart, has vowed to kill me in eight days. Three days are already over. In five days more he will come to your father—the king of this country, with a band of rope-dancers. He will perform before him so excellently that your father shall make up his mind to give him whatever he demands. The master, as he comes with the sole view of killing me, will demand the parrot. The maid servants will come to you from your father and request you to give them the bird. You had better first refuse. Then they will again come for it. You shall then break the neck of the parrot and give it into their hands. Be not afraid of having killed me, for I shall then run over to your pearl necklace. The servants shall again come to you saying that your father wanted the necklace Then, you had better break the necklace in pieces and cast away the pearls in the courtyard. Then, there shall take place a wonder which you can very well see from this topmost mansion." Thus ended the prince. The princess was extremely delighted at the harangue of her lover. For henceforth, so he must be called. The princess was enslaved by all his qualities, personal as well as mental, and sent up prayers to God for his having given her such a noble and clever husband. All the prince was relating seemed more a fairy tale to her. She was greatly amazed at all his wonderful attainments, and was glad after all that the intruder was none but himself. With an elated mind she slept soundly by the side of the prince that night, and soon as it was morning requested him to assume the shape of a parrot. Thus passed five days. The prince continued as a parrot during all the day time and resumed his own shape during the nights.

Just as the prince prophesied, a band of rope dancers arrived at the palace portals on the morning of the sixth day. The king himself was given up for such sports. He therefore invited them and ordered them to give a performance in the palace. The master and his band of dancers did their tricks so very well, that the king was highly delighted at their execution. He told them to demand what presents they wanted after first rewarding them with clothes and money. The chief dancer—the

Brâhman master in disguise — demanded the princess's parrot; unless it came to his hands, he said, he will not get down from the rope-swing. The king sent certain maid-servants to bring the parrot. They returned with a negative reply. But the rope-dancer persisting in the request, the king ordered his daughter to give up the parrot; and when the servants went in with the order, she writhed her parrot's neck and threw the pieces into their hands. They placed the bits before the king, who, though vexed at his daughter's disobedience, did not carry the matter further.

But the rope-dancer would not come down. He now asked the king to give his daughter's necklace. The king sent for it, and the princess enraged at the pliancy of her father to the words of a rope-dancer, tore her necklace and threw the pearls into the courtyard. She was unusually astonished at the events which literally followed the prince's narrations and was watching what more would take place. As soon as the pearls fell down on the courtyard, they were all converted into worms. The master saw by his *Jñânadrishti* that the prince was in one of the worms. So he remained in the rope as a man and assumed a second shape as a cock. He, now in his latter shape, began to peck at every worm. The prince, who was better up in these tricks than the master who taught him, now assumed the shape of a cat and pouncing upon the cock caught it by its neck.

The spectators were startled at what they saw before them. The cock in human voice demanded help. The cat in still younger human voice cried out that he *must* kill his enemy. The king and the other spectators interfered and wanted to know who they were, why they fought so in beastly shape and what was the cause of their enmity. The prince now related everything of his master and himself. The master acknowledged before the assembly his evil intentions. He also swore before them all, that he gave up all such intentions from that day as he found his student a better expert than himself. They both resumed their original shapes.

The king was highly pleased at the beauty of the prince. He also respected the teacher. Calling the prince to his side he spoke to him thus: "You have remained with my daughter, though it be in the shape of a parrot for one week. So, you must ever remain with her, that is, marry her." True to the sayings that the happy events must be instantly celebrated, the king celebrated the marriage that very day. The master too, overcome by the superiority of the prince, was perfectly reconciled to him. He gave a grand feast to the royal pair and gave the prince his brother also, whom he ever sent after his cows. The prince reclaiming his elder brother and also receiving all sorts of presents from his father-in-law went to his original country prepared for a battle in the act of conquering it; his parents also followed him.

The usurper of Dharmâpurî was taken unawares. He thought it best to surrender his kingdom without a battle and did accordingly. Thus the second son, without a blow, got back his lost country Dharmâpurî. He then educated his elder brother also and had him married to a princess. He ruled over that country for several years, conferring peace and prosperity over the inhabitants.

Thus Buddhichâturya finished his story. Before concluding, he added one sentence. "Must it not be such a prince that ought to become your husband? Oh my love!" By that time the day dawned and the minister's son and the princess left their bed chamber.

[The moral of the story is, that the deceiver shall be deceived. We here find that the Brâhman teacher, who troubled and harassed his student—the second prince—was in the end overpowered by his own intended victim.]

SECOND STORY.

THE minister's son Buddhichâturya left his bed in the morning and attended to his daily duties, baths, meals, &c. When it grew dark, he had his supper and returned to his bed-room. The second princess having already bathed in the evening and ornamented herself, entered the bed chamber with sweet scents smeared over her body, taking in her hand a platter bearing all kinds of sweet fruits and confections for her lord. She had also the violin on the other hand, on which she played for a time, thinking that that would awaken her husband instead of herself rising him up unmannerly. The minister's son never opened his eyes, for he would have done so, had he been sleeping. He only pretended sleep, and so secretly admired all the pleasant tunes of his future wife. But the princess mistook him for a spiritless man and shook the couch. Then also Buddhichâturya kept to his slumber. She was now highly enraged. She then determined within herself to pat him on his back lightly, and that if he did not open his eyes she would call him an ass. Thus thinking she slightly touched him with her fingers. Buddhichâturya, who had watched her emotions, now opened his eyes. She, in humble words, asked him the reason of his sound sleep; and he replied; — "My dear love! Have you not heard of the proverb of the nuptial barriers, several stupid circumstances—sleep, sickness and other such mishaps? This dirty sleep is one of the number and hence I was not my master. Kindly excuse me for what is past. So saying he, with a smiling face, took some of the fruits and sweetmeats that she brought in the platter and asked the princess also to taste what she liked best. They then chewed betel-leaves after which the princess pleased the ears of Buddhichâturya with some love songs. The latter wishing to subside her passions by a fine story thus addressed her: "My dear love! I have a very fine story to relate. You had better listen to it first. Then we shall go to rest. She agreeing to it, he began as follows:—

"Listen, Oh my love! There was during the good old days a famous town A*l*akâpurî, ruled over by a king named A*l*akêsa. He regarded the life of each of his subjects as his own life, and was very popular among one and all of them. He had a very good wife for his partner in the pleasures of the world. They had a son, and most unfortunately when the boy was only three years of age, the king was carried away by an untimely death. He left behind him a younger brother also who, in the name of his brother's son, managed the state and protected the prince and his widowed mother. But this continued only for a time. Before long ambition, to get the throne for himself, and envy that, if the prince continued powerful, he may not have the chance of becoming a king, began to cloud his mind, and these worked in him so much that he, little by little, gave up the protection of the prince and his widowed mother. They had therefore to shift for themselves. They left the palace and came to the streets as common beggars. The mother, some time after the event, left the son alone and went to her father's house. Sometime after, her heart again fondly turned, as of course it ought to, to her son. So with great difficulty she procured one hundred pagodas returned to her son and spoke thus ; "My son, your father was in his days the ruler of this city, and if we should beg here, will not people laugh at us? So I have brought you here one hundred pagodas. You must try to get some income by it, by investing it in some trade or other." These words seemed very reasonable to him and he agreed to do so. The mother gave the hundred pagodas she had with her, and with that sum he started to bring some wares to trade with.

He was walking through a thicket when he met a man coming opposite with a heavy gunny bag on his head. He was a farmer in whose house an old cat brought to bed several kittens which had become a great nuisance to him. To get rid of them he had put them all in a gunny bag and brought them to that copse to let them out and get himself rid of their nuisance. Now the prince demanded the farmer the price of each of the kittens inside the bag. The farmer by his words well understood him to be a crack and so wanted five hundred pagodas on each of his valuable kittens as he represented them to be. Then the prince showed him his one hundred pagodas and begged of him to accept that sum and sell him one of the kittens. The farmer, though glad at heart, reluctantly parted with one of the kittens to the prince, who, greatly elated at his valuable purchase, returned to his mother. She was extremely vexed at the stupidity, which she thought must be invincible, of her own son. The former too praising all his Gods for their having given him one hundred pagodas for a worthless kitten returned to his cottage.

The widowed mother again left her son to himself and returned to her parent's house. The boy-prince with the kitten went abegging house by house. The people pitied the prince and his cat, and so, gave him always something more to feed his kitten also. Thus he passed some days. The mother, after a few days stay in her parent's house, returned for a second time with a hundred pagodas, thinking that her son must have improved by that time. She gave him the money and advised him to get better wares for trading,.

than a cat; that time. And he accordingly left that city in search of better wares.

The prince in passing outside the town saw a snake-charmer approaching him. He carried in two baskets, suspended in the ends of a large bamboo supported on his neck, several serpents and other snakes. Among them was the son of A'disêsha(1) too. That serpent left his palace in the infernal regions and came to take a view of the world. The snake-charmer perceiving him took hold of him unawares by the superiority of the incantations that he used over serpents, and hence that son of A'disêsha was among the enslaved snakes. When the prince saw the snake-charmer he asked him what goods his baskets contained and what they were worth: The man said, "Gentleman, this contains the finest serpents ever caught in the world, and I shall get for each of them five hundred pagodas if I just made them play their tricks before my king." Now, the prince in earnest words requested him to sell one of the serpents to him for a hundred pagodas which, by the bye, was the only sum he had with him. The snake-charmer, though glad at heart, reluctantly parted or rather seemed reluctantly to part with one of his serpents—the very son of A'disêsha—to the prince, and thanking all his Gods for the hundred pagodas they gave him went his way. The prince too went to his mother a

(1) Adisêsha—the first serpent—the king of serpents.

second time with a serpent—the bitterest enemy to mankind. She was extremely vexed at his stupidity, and accusing all her stars for her having given birth to such a stupid son, went away disgusted with his conduct a third time to her parents' house.

The prince had now to his cat a serpent also and with these he begged from door to door. Giving a portion of what he collected to his animal friends and pets he tasted the remainder. So passed full twelve years. After such a long separation the mother's heart again longed to see her son. She went to him this time with no money and requested him in kind words to abandon the serpent. "As long as you have this enemy of mankind, my son, no one will approach you. So kindly leave him in the place where you made his purchase." The son, who was very regular in obeying his mother, took the serpent in his hand and proceeding to the wood where he first met the serpent-charmer, left him there and said, "My dear serpent, we were bosom friends for the last twelve years. Now by my mother's order I abandon you. Hence go your own way now, without being displeased at my conduct." Thus addressing the serpent and leaving him to himself, the prince began to retract his way home. Already the serpent had watched, for the last twelve years, the prince's character. He was extremely delighted at all his kindness to him and wanted to do something in return to his benefactor. So, when he was tracing his way back, the serpent called him out by his name. The prince was astonished to hear a human voice in the midst of a forest. He had never heard his serpent speak out, during the twelve years of his stay under him. So he never expected him to call out. He again and again heard the call, and finding it proceed from the serpent's place, went near him. What was his astonishment when he heard him speak out in the following human voice: "My prince! My protector! My father! For, henceforth I must regard you as such. For, he that gives birth to us, he that delivers us from difficulty, he that heartily gives us meals, he that instructs us and he that gives us moral teaching—all these we should regard as our fathers. And, as you protected me for twelve years, I regard you as my father. For you renounce me in this wood in obedience to your mother's order, and I call you now to do you some good in return for all your kindness. I am the son of the serpent-king, Ádisêsha, who now pines away in sorrow for my separation. You had better be here for some time till I go to him. He would be highly pleased to see me, and after kissing me with affection will ask me to sit by his side. I shall then refuse saying that I must have the consent of my father to do so. Ádisêsha will be astonished to hear of my terming another person as my father and will ask me the reason of it. I shall then praise all your kinduess to me. He will be highly pleased at it and send for you several serpent-servants with palanquin on their heads; you had better come down in it and see my father. He will respect you highly for all your cares over me and give you a grand feast. Then he will request you to speak to me and make me stay in the nether world (*Pâtâlalôka.*) You shall then do so and make me consent. For I will make up my mind to stop with my father only. But A'dsêsha thinking that by your recommendation I was made to stay there, will be highly pleased with you and ask you to demand any presents from him. You had better then request him to give you his ring which he will do full willingly. By that ring you will accomplish wonders in the world to you and to others. If you only put it on your finger and, extolling Paramêsvara, think of what you want, that will be instansly before you." Thus advising the prince, the son of the serpent-king, himself anxious to see his father, went to the nether world. Every thing occurred there as was already prophesied by the serpent. The prince who protected him for twelve years was invited to that world, was feasted grandly, was requested to use his influence to make the son serpent to stay there and was presented with the ring on his having successfully accomplished his act. Giving out the ring, the king of the nether world, the great A'di*s*êsha Bhagavân, spoke thus to the prince. My dear brother ! This ring I would not have given even to Indra if he had requested this of me. But since you, who protected my son for the past twelve years, want this, I give this to you. You must take special care of this and not allow it to be taken away from you by any one. For if you once leave it off, your fortune shall abandon you." Thus extolling the ring and presenting the prince with it, *S*êsharâja conducted him to the upper world, and taking leave of him returned to his own place.

Highly delighted at all adventures and at the way in which a serpent, bought for a hundred pagodas, repaid his kindness in an indescribable manner, the prince now went inside a thick jungle, and taking his stand in the midst of it, thought of the god Paramê*s*vara—the supreme lord of all in the world, and spoke to the ring thus: "May this wood to a distance of five hundred *kôs* round about me, with all the objects in it except myself, be burnt to ashes! May those people that protected me during my calamity come here to be my subjects! May here rise mansions fit to accommodate them with their families! May they have fields, gardens, pleasure-villas and everything that they had in their towns! May broad rivers run throughout the year, in this country! May my mother and cat join me here!

May I have a palace to live in, persons for a minister, commander and every officer that constitute a government! And may this kingdom be known in the world as Nishadadêsa"! No sooner he uttered these words, than the whole wood was burnt down except himself. The people who protected him, his mother and cat made their appearance before him. Palaces, mansions, pleasure villas, temples, tanks and all other requirements of a Hindû dominion sprung up. Rivers began to flow through that land. And thus by the power of the ring which he obtained from Ádisêsha, in a moment a thick wood was converted into a busy country. The persons who, taking pity on a prince, supplied him once with meals were now very glad to be his subjects. The prince was also equally glad to be their master. The mother who once cursed her boy for his stupidity, which she then thought invincible, for having bought a serpent for a hundred pagodas, now thanked all her household gods for having sent the fortune, through that enemy of mankind. Thus by that son of Ádisêsha the prince had again a kingdom to govern, ministers, subjects, commanders, and other constituents of a state. Thus passed a few years.

One moonlight night, while the prince who had now reached his prime youth found it difficult to catch sleep, he just thought by the power of his ring as to whom Paramêsvara had meant to be his future queen. He just closed his eyes for one moment in deep contemplation, and found out that at a distance of five hundred *kôs* from his town there was another town named Svar*n*apurî ruled over by a king named Svar*nêsa*, and that Svar*nêsa*'s daughter was meant to be his future wife and queen. "May that princess be lifted up with her couch without the slightest disturbance to her sleep and placed before me!" said the prince, and lo! the couch descended and was beside him. She was soundly sleeping without any consciousness of the change that had come over her. The prince now slightly touched her. She opened her eyes, and wonder of wonders, she found herself in a different room, and had every reason to think in a different country also. She also found a prince touching her by his hand. Being very intelligent, she spoke to him thus: "Prince, for, so you appear to be by your countenance! Prince, you must be one of the greatest men in the world. That you must be so, is plain by your power in having brought me here without my knowledge. I am also a princess destined by God to be the wife of some prince or other. Since you have displayed your extraordinary abilities to me, I have determined in my mind to be your wife. So instead of our secret loves here, before the lawful performance of our marriages, let us wait a few more days. By your power take me back now to my original place. Give me kindly the name of your country. Tomorrow morning I shall intimate to my father of the existence of your dominions and my determination to marry you. You shall also send ministers to settle about our marriage. My husband! Your leave for the present." Thus kissing her future lord, and admiring his beauty and ability, she stood before him most obediently as if waiting for his order. The prince was extremely delighted at the sweet and sound advice of his future wife, and agreeing to all her requests and promising to despatch ministers to her father, sent her back on her couch to her own room in her native country by the power of his ring.

At Svar*n*apurî, just when the morning dawned, the princess left her bed, and after her bath and meals stood before her father, and raising up her hands in worship of him, requested in the following manner: "My dear father! I have been, long putting off my marriage as I did not find a suitable match for me. Last night I dreamed that at a distance of five hundred *kôs* from this place is the country of Nishadadê*s*a ruled over by a fair and powerful king. I have determined to marry him. Kindly ascertain through our ministers of the existence of such a country and king.

Svar*n*ê*s*a was astonished at the words of his daughter, and despatched ministers to the Nishadadê*s*a, thinking that there may be some divine influence in the dream.

Here at Nishadadê*s*a the prince was only waiting for the dawn. Soon as the day broke, he despatched his own ministers to Suvar*n*apurî ordering them to request the king of that country to give his daughter in marriage to the Nishada king. He also ordered them not to return without fixing the auspicious day for the celebration of the marriage.

Just a few days after the princess had disclosed, in the form of a dream, her intentions to marry the Nishada king, ministers arrived from that country to request for their king, the hands of Svar*n*adêsa princess. Svar*n*ê*s*a was highly pleased, so much so that he thought there must be some divine influence in his daughter's dream. He without delay fixed the *muhûrta* or the auspicious day of the marriage, and sending invitation cards to all his royal friends and relatives, despatched his own ministers to the Nishada country to bring the bridegroom.

When the courtiers of Svar*n*apurî came to Nishada and informed the king of the settlement of the marriage and the appointment of the auspicious day, the Nishada king started with his elephants, horses, chariots, and all other paraphernalia and reached Svar*n*apurî. Svar*n*ê*s*a welcomed Nishadê*s*a with proper respects due to his position as a bridegroom, had the nuptials of his daughter, and Nishadê*s*a celebrated most splendidly, and rewarding the bridegroom and all his party with appropriate presents, gave leave to them to return to their kingdom. Nishadê*s*a rejoiced at his splendid acquisition of an intelligent and obedient wife, reached his kingdom with his mother and cat, and reigned over it for a long time.

The princess had a great pleasure for sea-bathing. She was a very religious lady. So she requested her lord to construct a subterranean passage from her bedroom to the sea. The prince thought that there shall be such a passage, and in an instant it came into existence, which the princess used as the way to reach the sea for her bath. Thus passed several months.

One morning after her bath, one of her hairs fell off her head, and collecting itself into a ball by the dashing and breaking of the waves, was lying on the shore. The king of Kochchi (Cochin) happened to ride by that shore and his eyes saw the hair ball. He took it up and examined it, and unrolling it found it to be a single hair ten *bhâgams* (3) long. By the *Sâmudrikâlakshana*—

(3) A *bhâga* is equal to two yards.

or the art of reading the beauty and nature of human beings by anything belonging to them —Kochchi king at once concluded the woman of that hair to be a paragon of beauty ; his mind was now bent upon how to get that woman as his wife. He promised ample rewards to any one who would accomplish that business. An old double-bent woman offered herself for it, and ascertaining the place where the hair was discovered, reached that spot. Collecting some rotten timbers and wood, she heaped them up in a pile, and setting fire to it was crying by its side.

The queen of Nishada, as was her custom, came to her morning bath. Hearing the voice of a female crying, she was greatly affected and cast her eyes all round her, when she found an old woman mourning over a funeral pile. She ran to her to enquire into her miseries. The old woman, soon as she saw the queen approaching, threw her arms over her neck and said, " My daughter ! You left me in this poor age just a few hours ago for the other world. I am astonished to see that you have returned so soon." These words, of course, infused pity into the Nishada queen's heart. Thinking that that poor woman had lost a daughter of her age, and pitying for her mistaking her to be that daughter, she consoled her by appropriate words. The queen then enquired into her history. The old woman said ; "I had an only daughter ; we were going to a village near. Just when we reached this place my daughter died all of a sudden, leaving me in this poor age a prey to sorrow." Nishada queen pitied the old woman, as was very natural, and promised to take her under her protection. She requested her to stay in that very place that day, and that she would take her to her place next morning with the consent of her mother-in-law and husband. The old woman pretended to be highly pleased with all her promises of help and agreed to stay there that day.

The queen returned to her palace, and, after her daily worship of her husband and mother-in-law, related the poor woman's history to them. They were much affected at her condition, more on the relation of her state by the queen, and gave permission for her being received into the palace. Accordingly the queen, when she went to the sea the next day, returned home with her.

The old hag pretended all sorts of affections towards the queen and other members of the palace. Even Nishadêsa liked her, and concluded her to be a woman of extraordinary good nature. One day, when it was not the season for mango fruits, the old woman requested the queen to satisfy her taste by procuring one of those fruits. On the queen's intimating the king with it, and on his pronouncing 'Let there be a fruit by the power of this ring,' the old woman had one to satisfy her taste. She now at once concluded that everything lay in that magic ring, and that if she succeeded in getting it, she almost succeeded in getting the Nishada queen for the king of Kochchi.

With this evil intention, she one day pretended severe head-ache. All medical skills were tried; but they were of no effect; for how could that be possible in a case of pretence. The old woman called at last the queen to her side and said; "My daughter, no use of suggesting several remedies which would have no effect. I know of one which, if tried, will have instantaneous result, and that is, the ring of your husband. Why not get that for me for only a couple of minutes? If I only wear it for a few seconds on my finger, this troublesome headache will abandon me." The queen replied that it would be difficult for her to get the said ring, and that on no occasions would her husband part whith it to any one. The old-woman now sobbingly said: "If I had my daughter now, would she have replied to me in this way? Is it impossible for a female to get anything from her husband? Only, when in amorous sports he comes to you in the night, you refuse to sleep with him unless he gives you the ring, he must part with it for a few moments to you. As soon as you get it, come out on thepretence of going to answer your call of nature. Give it to me for a couple of minutes, and you shall find your mother no longer suffering from head-ache." These words of the old woman uttered before the queen in a sweet and pathetic way stirred up her pity. Without knowing what dangers may await her if she gave the ring to the old woman, the queen consented; and on that very night she became disobedient to her husband for the first time in her life. Nishadêsa, though he was astonished at the slight change which he, for the first time, observed in his wife, gave her the ring, as he had never any occasion to suspect anything bad from her. The queen too never dreamt of anything evil and would have been the last lady to have procured the ring to the old woman, had she only known her bad intentions. Having great confidence in her, and viewing every one to be highly honest as herself she brought the ring and gave it to her.

The old hag, whose only object of affection was the ring, as soon as she had it in her fingers, thought of her country and that she must be there. And to the confusion of the queen that sat by her side, after putting the ring in her fingers, she, the wretched hag, ascended into the sky and vanished. The queen tore her hair and beat her breast; for now the evil intention of the disappearing hag became plain to her. "The wretch has disappeared, and I do not know what calamity may come over one, my lord, and my mother-in-law. Pity this nasty wretch of me who met this old woman in an evil hour." Thus was the queen pining away in sorrow.

The old hag reached Kochchi in the twinkling of an eye, and placing the ring before the king and duly receiving the presents and rewards promised, told him that if he thought on the lady he admired putting the ring on his finger, he would have her by his side. The Kochchi king who was dying of love for the lady of the hair ball, at once contemplated on her, and lo! the queen of Nishada that was pining away in sorrow for the loss of the ring was lifted into the sky and placed by an unknown power before the king of Kochchi. This king was delighted at the power of the ring, and desired that the former husband of that princess should run mad, his kingdom be burnt to ashes; and accordingly these curses had their effect in Nishada.

The king of Kochchi had now successfully accomplished his desires. He wanted to induce the Nishada queen to be henceforth his queen. She, seeing her plight and thinking that if she denied she would have her chastity ruined by force, apparently consented and gave out one condition for her becoming his wife. When the Kochchi king asked her what that was, she said, "My lord, I always hold eight days' fast whenever I come into the possession of a new husband ; so you must excuse me for a week. During the fasting season I distribute money and food to the poor, for which you must supply me with all that I ask : you may now consider that I am entirely in your possession, and the amorous sports that you have with me *to-day* is the same as those that you shall have with this same woman this eighth day. All, that I do now, is for yourself and your long life." These seemingly sweet words, made a thousand times more sweet by all the arts of the Nishada queen, produced a great effect in the mind of the Kochchi king. He allowed her request and made arrangements for the supply of all that she needed for the fasting season. The queen fed every day several poor people of all classes and made a proclamation that all the deaf, dumb, &c., would be freely fed there. Daily thousands flocked to the place.

Let us enquire about the Nishada king. His country was burnt to ashes and himself became mad. For all his change of mind, he never gave up his cat. Taking it in his hand and decorating it with all sorts of wild flowers which he found on the way, and which he converted into garlands, he was roaming from place to place. There was none to feed him. With a famished body he, after seven days of wandering here and there, at last reached the kingdom of Kochchi. It was the seventh day of the fasting season to the Nishada queen and feasting season to the poor. When the mad Nishadarâja saw several people going to the place to be fed, he with his queerly decorated cat joined the company and took his seat with those beggars. When the leaves were spread for the dinner, the mad king fought with the leaf-spreader to lay one before his cat also. The queen had only just then seen her mad lord and his cat. She remonstrated with the leaf-spreader for his refusal to give a leaf to a cat which had also life as men, and thus from a distance fulfilled the desire of her former lord. Her sorrow knew no bounds to see her Nishada sitting among the beggars, and his swallowing voraciously all the dishes placed in his leaf. For, be it remembered, that Nishada never had a morsel of food for the past week. "Will there be an end to my lord's miseries and my anxieties ? If there is no end of these calamities, I must give up my life tomorrow evening, instead of surrendering my honour to my enemy, the Kochchi king." Thus was the Nishada queen buried in the sea of sorrow. By that time the Nishada lord too finished his dinner, and without even washing his hands fell upon the pyal, overcome by pain and exhaustion, and snored. His ever faithful cat sat on his breast.

The refuse leaves of the poor that were fed were thrown outside the palace just opposite the pyal where Nishada slept. Some rats and mice were feeding upon bitten puddings and sweetmeats. Among them was a stout rat who, by his prominent appearance and the respect paid to him by the sorrounding rats, appeared to be the rat-*râja* or king. The cat, who was pitying his master all the while, and wanted to try its best to reinstate him in his dominions, sprang at once on the rat-*râja*, and catching him by the neck, without the slightest injury, spoke to him thus: "I have now caught you by the neck. You shall never escape my jaws to-day. If you are able to do me one kindness, which it is not at all difficult for you, I shall give you your liberty." The rat-king hearing the word liberty, said, "Let me hear what you want. If possible I will do it and rebuy my life." The cat now spoke: "My master Nishada, who is now sound asleep, had a ring which is now with the Kochchi king. I do not know how you will get it; only if you bring it, you will live again in this world. If not, you will furnish my supper." The rat requested him to wait till his army tried its best to bring back the ring, and issued the order with his neck still in the cat's mouth to bring that ornament from the Kochchi king. The faithful rats now ran to examine one and all the boxes of that monarch to get the ring. To their great joy they found it in a certain box near which he was himself sleeping. Taking it they flew to the cat, and placing it before him, bought back the life of their king. The cat now placed the ring on the breast of Nishada, who now awoke from his slumber. The cat related the way in which the ring was lost, how calamities came over his kingdom, and how he got it back ; he now put it on his finger and was again restored to his senses. He thought that he must be carried back to his kingdom and again see it in its former state. It was instantly so. He had his faithful queen back and advised her never more to believe in old hags. He wished insanity to the Kochchi king and destruction to his kingdom. These were accomplished. Thus reclaiming everything which he lost by means of his cat friend, he reigned for a long time over Nishada.

" And must not such a prince be your husband my love*!*" said Buddhichâturya and finished the story.

The sun began to rise in the East and the prince now left his chamber.

[The moral attached to this story is, that assistance rendered to any one, even though it be to a reptile, shall never go without being repaid. The serpent that was bought by the prince, notwithstanding the admonitions of his mother, returned his master's gratitude by procuring him the magic ring and the cat by bringing back the lost ring.]

THIRD STORY.

On the third night, the elder of the princess entered the bedchamber and approached her husband with amorous desires. The minister's son Buddhichâturya wanted to subdue her love by a story and said: "I have a short story today also, and soon as that is over we shall retire to rest." The princess agreeing to it, the minister's son began as follows: "Listen, O, thou the gem of womankind! There was a city named Mathurâpurî ruled over by a king named Madanagirirâja. He reigned so well and just that during his time three rains washed the earth every month, all sorts of corns flourished luxuriantly, all castes of people adhered to their prescribed rules and the temple charities were duly conducted. He had an excellent wife for his companion, and had been reigning for a long time in peace and prosperity. He had his full share of happiness except the gift of a son. He performed many austerities, till at last by divine favour he had a male child. On casting the horoscope of the prince, they found him to be a man of extraordinary powers in future life. He was very beautiful like Kumâra.[1] The king was highly pleased and when the prince was of proper age, appointed teachers for his education, who left no stones unturned in giving him proper tuition. After attaining due proficiency in learn-

1. *Siva's eldest son.*

ing, he was put to the military profession, and under proper training soon learned all, that he ought to, in that department. The father's wish was now to find out a suitable match for his son. So sketching his face in a picture, he gave the drawing to his courtiers and sent them to go and fetch a princess resembling in beauty the drawing, and accordingly they went, and after searching in all directions in vain turned at last to the west.

There was another town named Vijayanagaram. The king of that place long practised austerities for a child, and at last had a daughter, and when she reached her maturiry, he wishing to procure her a husband, drew her shape in a picture, and like the Mathurâpurî king, giving the picture to his courtiers, and sent them out to fetch a partner resembling her. Both these messengers met in the midst cf a river which they were crossing from opposite directions, and seeing each others pictures, were highly delighted. They then exchanged their drawings. The messengers of the picture of the princess brought to her father the prince's picture, and those of the picture of the prince brought to his father the princess's picture. The royal parents settled about the marriage by letters. The princess's father—the king of Vijayanagaram—fixed a *muhûrta* or appropriate day for the marriage. Madanagirirâja, king of Mathurâpurî, started with his son and the royal paraphernalia of horses, elephants, &c., and reached

Vijayanagaram. The bride's father welcomed the bridegroom with all appropriate honour due to his relationship, and had the wedding of the pair celebrated most splendidly. He gave due honour to the bridegroom and his party. Madanagirirâja stayed for some more days after the marriage in Vijayanagaram, and returned to Mathurâpurî with his son and daughter-in-law. Wishing to give the pair the free enjoyment of their youth, Madanagiri built a separate palace, and placed them there with all requisite servants. Thus passed a couple of years.

One moonlight night the prince and the princess were sleeping on the top of their palace. The seven divine maidens used to pass that way daily to the sea for their bath. That night they saw the prince, who resembled Cupid as it were, and one and all of them fell in love with that sleeping mortal. They passed away quietly to the sea without opening their lips, of course, making up their mind to walk away with him on their return. Accordingly, on their way back, they fell into a dispute as to who of them should have the prince. Then they came to the conclusion that each of them shall live with him for a day, and that in a week they shall all live with him. With this agreement the eldest of the *Saptakanyâs*, or seven maids, sprinkled water on the prince without awaking his wife. He was turned into a flower garland which the eldest maid fastened round her neck and reached her heavenly mansion; placing the garland before her, she sprinkled some more water which made it a prince again. She lived with him that whole day, and on the next gave him over to the second maid. Thus each, in her turn, had the prince for a day.

Let us see what happened to the sleeping princess after the disappearance of her husband. She awoke in the morning and did not find him by her side. Startled at it, she enquired of all the servants in her palace and had no satisfactory reply. She at once sent word to her father-in-law about the mysterious disappearance of his son. He was greatly vexed at what had happened, and sent his courtiers all over the country to search the prince, and they all after careful search, came and informed him that his son was to be found nowhere.

Madanapurirâja was buried in the ocean of sorrow and consoled by soothing words his daughter-in-law. The seven maids, after retaining the prince for seven days in the heavens, had some compassion for the princess also—his lawful wife. So, every eighth day they were used to bring him to the side of his wife, and sprinkling water on her and making her unconscious, used to leave him there. In the morning just before dawn they again visited him and took him back to the heavens, reviving the princess from her swoon. Thus passed some time, till at last she became pregnant. The maid servants of the palace were astonished to hear of her pregnancy, while there was no husband near her, and while the *Zanâna* was so jealously guarded, and so reported the matter to her father-in-law Madanapurirâja. He came, and after making due enquiries, was not pleased with his daughter-in-law's replies. He made arrangements to banish her in a wood, and calling some of all his servants ordered them to tie her eyes up and abandon her in the midst of a jungle infested by wild beasts; and they did accordingly.

The princess's state of mind may be more imagined than described. She knew no sins and was punished for all her purity like a bad woman. How she became pregnant remained a mystery to her. She with great difficulty removed her blindman's-buff, and keeping up her life by eating berries, wandered here and there, till at last she reached a foot-path. She walked along by it till night, and to her great disappointment found no signs of human habitation. At about the tenth *ghatikâ* of the night she discovered a blazing fire before her. She flew to it and found it to be a funeral pile with a woman mourning by its side. That woman, soon as she saw the princess, threw her arms over the new comer's neck and addressed thus: "My daughter! You left me a few minutes ago to the other world, and how is it that you have returned so soon." The princess pitied her and said, "Grand-dame! There are similarity of features in the world. I am not at all your daughter, but a poor helpless beggar." The old woman heard those words and her heart was moved. She was by profession a dancing-woman. She had the previous day lost her daughter just in the prime of youth, and thus in an age to begin her profession. When she lost her she became utterly hopeless; and when on the same night another female figure of still more charming beauty stood before her, claiming protection, she was delighted and forgot even her departed daughter. She took the new-comer—the princess-to her house in Mathurâpurî. Thus the princess again reached her own town and lodged with a professional harlot.

The old dancing-woman daily gave her lectures about her profession, but the princess was always deaf to her instructions.

Her time of confinement approached fast. The old woman appointed nurses to attend on her and spoke to them thus: "I shall reward you amply if you would execute my commands. If this woman gives birth to a daughter it is well and good for our profession; but if a son we do not want him. So, just at the time of her bringing the child to bed, close her eyes. If you have a male child remove it to a place where you can kill it, and throwing a piece of timber on the ground, tell her that she gave birth to it." So the old lady instructed, and the avaricious nurses who cared more for money than for anything human, agreed to act according to her words.

The time of the delivery approached, and unfortunately for the old hag the princess gave birth to a son. Before that took place the nurses managed to close her eyes. They now took the baby to the neighbouring wood, and instead of killing it, were overcome by its beautiful face. They wanted to take it home themselves, and so returned hastily to the confinement room and threw a piece of timber on the ground. Soon as the princess recovered from the exhaustion of confinement and asked for her baby, they put the timber piece in her hand. She was astonished and reckoned it as one of the mysteries similar to her unknown pregnancy.

Now let us see what happened to the baby in the wood. Just a few yards opposite to the place where the baby was crying there was a Kâlî temple. The goddess pitied the baby in distress, and by her powers made a copse to spring round about the child. Just above the mouth of the child the goddess located a honeycomb, which shed honey drops when the child began to cry by hunger. Neither the sun nor the rain gave any injury to it. Thus, under the kind patronage of the divine Kâlî, the prince was growing as tenderly as he would in his own palace. The nurses came to take home the child, and finding a thick copse in the place where they left the baby, went away disappointed.

Under Kâlî's kind care the child grew up for three years. The goddess now wished to give up her responsibility of the prince. Moreover Madanagiri, the old king, was pining away in distress, and daily praying to that goddess to give him another son, since his son had by some mysterious way disappeared. So Kâlî appeared to Madanagiri in a dream and said, "Your prayers till now have not been thrown away in vain. Come to my temple tomorrow, you shall have a son." The old king rose up, and finding the time of his dream to be day-dawning time, hoped success. As soon as the day broke, he bathed, finished his ablutions, and stood before the Kâlî's temple. Wonder of wonders, he saw a child of three years come crying before him. It was his own grandson, which, of course, he had no reason to know then. He took the boy home, and regarding him as his own son, brought him up tenderly. When he reached his eighth age he put him to school. Kâlî herself had taught him all the departments of knowledge, even the speech of animals, the deciphering of birds' sounds, &c. He was next put under the military profession. Thus, before his sixteenth year, he learned all that is required of a prince. The old king already disgusted of his long reign wished to give the burden over to the son that Kâ*l*î gave him ; and, accordingly, he had the boy inaugurated as the king of Mathurâpurî. The young king on the day of this ceremony was carried throughout the town on the back of an elephant. He was also in the prime of his youth. While passing the dancing-girls' streets he saw a certain woman of the most charming beauty, and not being able to curb his desires, sent 30,000 pagodas to her house, informing her that he would be there that night. The woman that he saw was no other than his mother, which, of course, he did not know. For the past sixteen years and more the old hag was compelling her to take to her profession. The princess had all along refused. Now, when the old woman saw the large sum of 30,000 pagodas, she began to trouble and worry the princess to be prepared for that night at least to receive the new king. She was greatly perplexed. Cursing the day on which she was born in the world, she entered a closet, and bolting the locks inside, was sobbing in a corner.

The new king was only waiting for the evening. Soon as it was dark he bathed, scented his body, and overcome by love to the object that he saw in the morning, approached her house. There was a calf half asleep on the way ; he by mistake crushed its tail by treading over it. At once it called out to its mother and exclaimed, "See how a prince dishonours me." The cow in reply said, "This is no dishonour to him who wishes to sleep with the very woman who gave birth to him—his own mother." To others these words of the beasts would be an enigma. Having been educated by Kâlî in the secret language of the beasts, the prince heard well what passed between the cow and its calf, and at once retraced his steps. He was startled at what fell into his ears, "Have I become such a sinner! I have regarded the old king as my father. In that case the old queen must be my mother and not the woman that I saw this morning. Let me wait till the morn." So thinking within himself the new king returned to his palace, and as several thoughts were passing and repassing his mind, he had no sleep. Soon as there were signs of light in the morning he unsheathed his sword, and holding it in his arm, stood like an enraged lion before Madanagiri and addressed him thus: "Now tell me the truth; who is my father, who is my mother, and who are you? If you do not do so I will kill you."

The old king was extremely vexed, and told him his true origin, and how the goddess Kâlî gave him while a child and that he knew no more of it. The young king now flew to the Kâlî temple with the old king and queen, and all the courtiers running after him. He stood before the goddess with sword in hand like a mad man and exclaimed,

"If, my goddess, you do not name my parents and reveal the secrecy of my birth, I *will* commit suicide." The Kâlî was greatly afraid of his determination, and speaking out told the public everything about the boy prince. How his father the son of Madanagiri disappeared, and how the seven maidens were having him in turn, how he was allowed every eighth day to sleep with his own wife, though she had no knowledge of it, how she became pregnant, how she was banished most cruelly, how she gave birth to the young boy, how she, the goddess, protected the child and gave it to its grand-father, and how the mother was being cruelly treated by the dancing-hag. The goddess also suggested a way to bring back the lost prince Madanagirî's son. "Ask your mother to fast on eight Fridays. On the ninth Friday the maids shall appear before her and demand what she required. Then let your mother request her husband back, which will be granted." Thus revealing the mystery the goddess disappeared. The son was much satisfied. The dancing-girl was tortured for all her inducements. The mother was brought back. The father too joined his wife and son on the ninth Friday. The old king just in his last stage of life saw again the face of his long lost son who now succeeded to the throne.

"And should not such a prince be thy husband, thou gem of womankind?" Thus Buddhichâturya concluded his third story. The sun was beginning his course in the heavens by the time that the story ended. The princess and the minister's son left their bed-room and were engaged in their different duties of the day.

[MORAL.—This story illustrates how the Supreme power restores to the right person his lost property. The grandson comes back to his grand-father, the lost husband returns to his pining wife, and the vicious dancing-woman is condemned to the gallows.]

FOURTH STORY.

On the fourth night the minister's son Buddhichâturya with his bridegroom's dress entered the bed chamber. As it was the turn of the second princess for that night, she adorned her body with all her choice ornaments, and with guitar on one hand and sweetmeat platter on the other, entered the sleeping apartment. After soothing her lord's ears with well-chosen love songs, she approached his bed with amorous desires. And the minister's son seeing this, addressed her: "My dearest love! I have a short story this night also. And soon as that is over, we shall go to rest. On the princess agreeing to it, he began :—

"Listen, thou gem of womankind! There was a city named Mallikârjunapurî. A certain king named Ve*n*ka*t*arâja ruled over it. Though he reigned most justly for a long time, he had no son. Much grieved at heart he divorced his first wife, gave a separate building for her, made her to live there, fixed a certain amount of rice to be measured out daily to her, and married a second wife. Unfortunately she too bore no children. Then it was that Ve*n*ka*t*arâja began to see that every thing depended on the supreme will of God and not on men. This thought kindled in his mind a desire to propitiate Paramêsvara[1] by austerities. He accordingly gave the reins of his kingdom to his ministers and ordered them to bring no discredit to his name. He told them that he was going to a secluded forest to practise austerities. And he did as he told them. For a couple of years he put himself in severe penance till Mahêsvara[2] appeared before him. He danced and capered with joy with uplifted hands and projecting and famished ribs on one foot and extolled his long-longed God. The *S*ûlapâ*n*in[3] I*s*a[4] ordered him to mention his longings. The king requested a son. The God presenting him with a mango fruit, and instructing him to give it to his queen, disappeared. With a glad heart he returned to his country and gave the mango fruit to his second wife, mentioning its extraordinary merit. She squeezed the juice of it in a silver cup and threw away the seed in the courtyard. The maid servant of the first queen came as usual to receive her dole, and hearing the story of the fruit which was in the mouth of every one, and finding its seed cast away carelessly, she took it and gave it to her mistress—the first

---

(1) Parame*s*vara. God the supreme, mainly applied to *S*iva.

(2) Mahe*s*vara. God the great, mainly applied to *S*iva.

(3) *S*ûlapâ*n*in. Bearing on hand a trident—an epithet of *S*iva, the destroyer of the Hindû trinity.

(4) *Isa*. Literally complete master, a name of *S*iva as regent of the north-east quarter.

queen. She related to her its history also. The first queen thanked her maid servant for her prudence, and breaking the seeds she ate it herself and gave a portion of it to her faithful maid-servant. The second queen drank off the juice. All became pregnant. The second queen gave birth to two twin-princes. The first queen brought to bed a tortoise; and not at all displeased at it, nursed it up with all maternal care. The maid servant had also a son.

The king Ve*n*ka*t*arâja was highly pleased at his second queen's having given him two princes. He never knew of the first queen or her tortoise-son, or of her having procured the mango seed for her part. The tortoise was no tortoise. He was also a prince and, unlike the other princes, was a most beautiful child. Moreover he was the son born by the special favour of Paramê*s*vara by his mother having taken the seed with full heart and faith. The second queen, by her pride in squeezing only the juice of the dearly obtained fruit, stood aloof from that God's favour.

The first queen was feeding her son as she would a tortoise, as she thought him to be no better than that. This meal was all sufficient when the prince was young; but when he grew up he found it quite insufficient for his hunger. So he rose up one night when his mother was sound asleep, and removing his tortoise shell, went to the rice pot where the remnant of the night meals was soaking in water to serve for the next breakfast, and ate all that remained there; then he washed his hands and came back to his mother, where, putting on the tortoise shell, he slept. Thus passed on a couple of days.

The mother on one or two mornings found her cold rice, left for the breakfast, missing; she suspected the maid servant. On enquiry the suspicion was removed. So she wanted to watch the thief herself the next night and kept herself awake with closed eyes; just about midnight she found her son the tortoise leaving her side and slowly moving towards the pot. "What could a tortoise do with a cold rice pot" thought she, when, to her greatest wonder, she found a male child issuing out of the tortoise shell. Her sight was dimmed at the lustre of his body. She sent up a thousand prayers to Paramêsvara for his having given her such a fair son. Going up slowly to the place where the tortoise shell was kept, she took it and cracked it to pieces and pretended to sleep. The prince, after eating his belly-full and washing his hands, came to the place where he kept his cover of the tortoise shell, and not finding it, was much vexed. He had no other person to suspect than his own mother, and so awaking her up, demanded the shell. The mother begged pardon from her son for her having broken it, and wanted to know the reason of his having been under that disguise. The son was very sorry and said, "I need that disguise for some more time, but since you have broken away the shell, no use of repenting of what is already past. Now I request you to do me one piece of kindness. I must, for some secret reasons, be in disguise for some more time and then appear in my true colour. I shall smear soot and charcoal all over my body. You will lock me up in a big box and never open it except in the meal time." The mother agreed to these conditions, for she was a most sensible woman, and foresaw something extraordinary in her son. She accordingly smeared him with charcoal and locked him up most carefully.

The God Paramêsvara, by whose special favour Ve*n*ka*t*arâja of Mallikârjuna had his son, now called upon Nârada (5) and ordered him to go to that city and give all instructions, religious and political, to the prince in the box. And accordingly that divine R*ishi* (sage) came to the tortoise prince, taught him first *Pañchâkshar* (6),

---

(5). Nârada. A divine sage often occurring in the Hindû mythology as a messenger from gods to men and *vice versâ*: he is always represented with the lute in his hand, which musical instrument he is supposed to have invented.

6) *Pañchâkshari*. The (holy) five letters—*Na, mah, Si, vâ, ya*. Let us meditate upon *S*iva—literally Salutation to *S*iva—an incantation which every religious Advaiti Brâhma*n* ought to pronounce every day to obtain eternal felicity after death.

and then gave him all the requisite education in politics, religion and weapons. Thus, though in the box, the son of the first queen received a very sound education.

The twin sons of the second queen had all sorts of requirements for their education, but not having the favour of Paramêsvara, did not advance much. But they seemed much ideal perfection in everything—beauty, bravery, education, weapons, &c., to a doting father, like the king of Mallikârjuna. One day the father called his two sons to his side and said, "My dear children, they only deserve the names of sons who fulfil the desires of their parents. I have long entertained a desire which I now request you to fulfil, and bear the name of sons deservingly. To the extreme north of this country is the mountain named Himayagiri (7). In it there lives a princess to whom I have long entertained a deep love. I look up to you to get me married to her." The sons agreed and started at once to Himayagiri, rash like young colts and without knowing how to accomplish their undertaking. They promised to return with the princess of the mountains within one month.

The prince in the box who had acquired the gift of the *Jñânadrishti* (8) or the power of see-

(7) Himayagiri. The frosty mountain. The Himâlayas.

(8) See note* p. 3

ing into what was passing in the outer world without being himself personally present, learnt at once that his step-brothers were travelling to the Himayagiri to bring a princess from that mountain for their father. He also concluded with himself that unless he accompanied them they would not succeed in their undertaking. So he called his mother the first queen, and relating to her what he ought to do to his father, took leave of her. Rubbing some more soot and charcoal over his body, he followed the princes and was walking in their company, relating pleasant stories to them now and then to break the tediousness of the road. They took him for a mountaineer, but found his company very useful, as he had a fund of tales to amuse them with. Journeying and journeying for three days and crossing several woods, forests, mountains and jungles, they three approached a large city. Near it they saw what appeared to be a big river. The twin brothers were very thirsty and drank full from that river to pacify their thirst. The tortoise prince found out by the red colour and sweet scent of the water that it was not a natural stream, but the refuse water which had once served for the bath of the princess of that town. She almost used a river full of water for her bath daily, and the washed water flew like a river. She had set men on the banks of that stream to bring to her news of any adventurous man who crosses it without walking through it. The tortoise prince, soon as he found out that what lay before him as a river was nothing else but the refuse water of a princess, crossed it by the superiority of his strength and reached the other bank without placing his feet in the stream. The peons were astonished at the adventure of the black passenger, and requesting him to wait for a few moments, they ran to the princess of that town. The black prince not to be idly waiting there, again jumped on the other side of the bank, and taking his two step-brothers on his two arm-pits, came back to where he left the peon.

Now the princess of that town had made up her mind to marry him who would cross the stream of her bath-water. She was with an elated heart viewing from the uppermost storey of her palace all the adventures of the black prince. She came down, related to her father what her determination was, how it remained unaccomplished till then, and how on that day she saw it accomplished. She, in humble words, requested her father to get her married to that adventurous man. By that time the peons set on the shore of the bath-stream arrived with the joyful news of having found that day a black passenger who successfully crossed it. The king went in person to welcome his son-in-law and have the marriage celebrated. The black prince requested his fellow-travellers, the two princes, to stay with him that day, and that he would accompany them in their expedition the next day. They were highly delighted at the extraordinary powers of their dirty passenger, whom, of course, they had no reason to know to be their brother. They agreed to his request, and were present at his wedding. The black prince agreed to the marriage on one condition, that is, that he should not remove his black dye. The bride's party consented and the wedding was celebrated.

The bridegroom in his bedroom related everything about himself to his new married wife—that he was the son of the first queen of Mallikârjunapurî, that the others were the twin sons of the second queen, that they started to Himayagiri to bring a princess from that mountain to their father, that he, thinking that that was not possible for them, had accompanied them, and in the way had the pleasure of being married to her. She was extremely delighted at the royal parentage of her husband, and still more at his abilities. He took leave of her that very night to start the next morning, and told her that if she did not see him return that twenty-eighth day she must come to the Himayagiri in search of him.

At day-dawn the black passenger joined his royal travellers and started for the snowy mountains. They all travelled a day till they reached another large city. A peon met them on the way and gave each of them a pie, asking them to get firewood, leaf and oil for it, and to return the pie. The twin brothers accused the peon for his having lost his senses and went their way. The black passenger received (his) pie, calmly thought over it for a couple of (*nimishas*) minutes, went to the neighbouring field where there was a good crop of sesamum, and rooting out one of that plant, gave it with the pie to the peon who gave him the pie. The peon asked him to wait for some time and ran to the palace: for he was the person set by the princess of that town to do this with every one who came to that city, and report to her any person who undertakes to do it. And she had made that as a test to choose for her husband who successfully buys up these three things for a pie, returning at the same time the money. When the peon placed in her hand the pie and the sesamum plant, her joy knew no bounds. She found fuel in the stem and body of the sesamum plant. Its leaves supplied the leaves she wanted, and the sesamum ears contained the oil in them. She ran to her father, reported her having found out a man fit to be her husband and requested him to make arrangements for he wedding that day. The king of that city sent for the black traveller, and respecting merit in him in preference to his awkward body, which he persisted in keeping dirty, had the marriage celebrated that day. While in his bedroom the bridegroom related everything about himself to his second wife, and took leave of her to start to the mountain the next day. He also appointed a certain time to her, after which if he did not return he asked her to come to that place. Joining the princes whom he had a second time requested to wait, he started for the mountain at daybreak.

They went on journeying and journeying for a long time till, at last, they reached a city. The princess of that city was a great *Panditâ*(9). She had written a book on philosophy and vowed within herself to marry him who would write a satisfactory comment on it. For testing passengers she had set men on the roadside to present every one with a book, requesting him to write commentaries. Accordingly one of the men gave three books for the twin brothers and the black prince. The twin brothers returned away their books as they were not able to understand the right meaning of even a single sentence of what was written on it. The black prince sat down beneath a tree, and requesting the princes to wait for a couple of *Ghatikâs*(10), wrote the commentaries required, and with them returned the book to the princess's man, who now flew to the palace. She was highly pleased at the annotations, resolved within herself to marry the

---

(9) Panditâ. A learned lady.

(10) See note No. 6, p. xvi., Introduction.

annotator, and obtained her father's consent to it. The father at once welcomed the sooty bridegroom, and had his marriage with the princess regularly celebrated. As on the two former occasions, the black prince asked his fellow-passengers and step brothers to stop for that day in that city. They said, "We have no time to wait now. You marry a princess at every town; we waited on two former occasions; we will not wait any longer." So saying they went away in advance of their black bridegroom passenger.

The third marriage of the tortoise prince was duly celebrated. When in company with his third wife in her bedroom, he related to her his whole history, and requested permission of her to start to the snowy mountains in search of a maid. He asked her to come to that spot in search of him if he failed to come to her on that sixth day, to which his wife replied, "My lord! Do you know the way to search for her and successfully take her with you to your country." By these very words he found out that she knew that subject better than himself. So he requested her to tell him everything on that head, and she began as follows: "My dearest husband, soon as you reach the Himyagiri mountains you should circumambulate it. A slender creeper running from the top to the bottom of the mountain shall meet your eyes. Touch it gently with your hand. It will take you to the topmost peak, where you will find a golden hall, in the midst of which there sits a beautiful lady. She will come in great love to take embraces of you. You should at once prostrate yourself before her, call her by the name of mother, and say that you intended her to become the wife of your father. She will agree to it and follow you." Thus ended the third wife. The husband was greatly pleased at her account, and started next morning to the mountains. His step brothers were there before him. They were merely blinking at the mountain without any method before them as to the successful accomplishment of the intended purpose of their journey. The tortoise prince went round the mountain. His step-brothers followed him. He discovered the creeper and ascended to the top of the mountain and stood in front of the golden hall over it. He looked around him and saw a charming beauty coming running towards him with clear evincement of amorous desires. He thought the best way of checking her desires was to fall before her and name her as his mother, and so placing down his scimitar, which he always carried hanging down his hip, he prostrated himself before her and spoke, "My dearest mother! For henceforth I must call you so, as I have meant you for the loves of my father. Follow me to the plains, become his wife and grace our palace." The mountain maid left off all her loves towards him as soon as she heard him calling her his mother, and said, "Oh, you most beautiful prince, you have disappointed me. I had vowed to marry him who, after all obstacles, reaches this place. But as you have termed me your mother, I have now no other course to follow than to marry your father. Before I come down give me an account of yourself." The tortoise prince related to her his whole story—his unworldly birth and education, his marriage with the three princesses on the way of his following the twin brothers to the mountain Himyagiri, &c. She was highly pleased at every part of his story and copied them all in a paper that she had with her. Then the prince requested her to descend, and they both by the way of the creeper came to the plains.

Down the mountains the twin brothers with an envious heart saw their black fellow passenger ascending up to the top of the mountain and descending with the maid in search of whom they had come all the way. When the maid and her conductor reached the ground, the latter found out that while prostrating before the maid he had left his scimitar in the golden hall over the mountain. He asked her and his twin brothers to wait for a few minutes, went up to the top a second time, and was returning with his weapon. The princes at the foot of the mountain finding out by that time that the route between the base and the top was the creeper, cut its root, when the tortoise prince was approaching the base. By this break the descending prince fell down from a great height and was powdered to death.

The mountain maid's terrors may be more imagined than described. Her conductor from the top to the base of the mountain was now no more· She was at the mercy of two of the vilest princes who had most cruelly murdered one of the ablest men of the world. When the creeper was once cut away she lost forever the power of ascending again to her mansion. Now the two princes approached her, spoke to her about the iron-hand of fate, and that she must follow them to their country and there become their father's wife. As she had already heard from the tortoise prince everything, she consented, and calmly followed them to Mallikârjunapurî. The old king of that place was greatly pleased at his sons' abilities, and asked the princess to allow him to marry her. She wishing to wait some time till she could see that whether the dead prince would ever revive, spoke to the old king as follows—" My respected lord. There is no doubt now that I should one day or other become your wife. Since your sons have by their ability brought me here, I have one request to make to you, that is, that you must wait for six months, during which time I have a penance to perform. Daily thousands of Brâhmans must be fed on account of it, and you must make all the arrangements for it." The old king was greatly delighted at the religious bent of his would-be wife, made all arrangements for the feeding of the Brâhmans, and gave her, her own time. Thus was the mountain maid in penance, with the sole object that these penances should be useful to the revival of the dead prince.

Let us see what became of that unfortunate adventurer after his death. His wives, after waiting till the time fixed by him for his return, came separately to the foot of the snowy mountain and knew each other. They mourned over the dead and shattered body of their husband like three sisters. The last of the three wives, who was very intelligent and who pointed out the way first to her lord to reach the mountain maid, broke the mourning and said, "Sisters,—No use of useless weeping now like ignorant women." Our husband has now met an unnatural death; perhaps his brothers killed him in treachery. You will now gather up his shattered body in one of your laps putting all the members in their right place. I shall bathe and, contemplating upon the God that created us, pour some water over him. If God has favour on us poor women, he will live." So saying she went to the nearest tank to bathe, and the first wife collected the shattered members of the tortoise prince. The second wife sat down and arranged on her lap the different limbs. The third wife returned with her body wet all over and with water in hand, over which her tear-drops were freely falling, contemplated upon Paramêsvara, "If you, my God, have meant me to live a wife, give me back my husband." So said she, and sprinkled the water in her hand over the dead body of her husband which, notwithstanding its corruption, lay with full majesty on the lap of the second wife. Soon as the drops fell over the corpse, the dead members began to move, and the tortoise prince sat up in the midst of his wives as one arising from his deep slumber. He related his adventures, and his accidental death while returning with his weapon to his wives. They also related their doings to him. With his three wives he returned to his third father-in-law's house. There they gave him all the dowries and other presents which the third wife's people had meant for her. He received them all and returned to the house of the second wife. That royal father-in-law too gave all the requisite dowry. Receiving them all, he reached the first father-in-law's house. The same respect was repeated here too. Thus with the three wives and with all their presents the tortoise prince returned to his country, and thinking that it would be unwise to take them all to his mother, halted in a village near his town. He enquired for a big and spacious house, placed his wives and the required servants there, left all the presents of money, jewels, clothes, vessels, &c., with them, and returned singly to his mother. The old queen was greatly delighted when she saw her son back, and with open arms welcomed him to her bosom. He related to her all his adventures without omitting a point and sent her to meet her daughters-in-law, duly informing the latter of the interview. They waited with *Malli*,(11) *Mullai*,(12) *Iruvâkshi*(13) and other flowers, worshipped the feet of their mother-in-law, and did due respects to her position as befitted their duty and affection towards her. She was extremely pleased at her daughters-in-law and took them secretly to her own palace. Thus passed on some days till the mountain queen's term of six months approached its completion.

The old king now again requested that maid about her sanctioning of the marriage with him. Her anxiety was for the life of the tortoise prince. So she said within herself, "How to know whether that prince lives now or not. I shall demand now the golden lotus that is on the other side of the seven oceans. That dead prince only, if he is alive now, has got the power to bring it to me. If I get that flower I shall at once conclude that he is alive. If not he is dead and gone." These thoughts passed over her mind in a couple of minutes, and she spoke to the old king; "My lord,

(11) Malli—the jasmine (*Jasminum sambac.*)
(12) Mullai—another kind of jasmine (*Jasminum Trichotomum.*)
(13) Iruvâkshi—another kind of jasmine.

I beg your excuse this occasion also for a short time. My penance was to see the golden lotus on the other side of the seven mighty oceans. I have not seen it by that means. Your able sons who brought me from the snowy mountains must surely have also the power of bringing this lotus. Kindly order them after it, and soon as I have it I am at your disposal." The old king, though sorry for the delay and postponement of the marriage, was sure of his sons' accomplishing this feat also, and so gave them the order which they received and started.

They journeyed and journeyed and reached the sea-shore. How to cross the seas and reach the flower? Now they thought of the black passenger and their treachery to him. "Brother, surely if that kind man was living now he should be a great help to us," said the elder to the younger, who now replied: "Yes, No doubt of it. That is a prodigy. See how he crossed the river of the bath-waters, how he bought fuel, leaf and oil for a pie, returning the latter, how he wrote the notes, how he reached and brought successfully the mountain princess! Pity that we killed him." He had scarcely finished his speech and turned his back when he saw the black passenger coming towards him. "What? Is it he? Is it the poor passenger that we killed by cutting the creeper that approaches us now." Thus, while they were wondering, the tortoise prince approached them, told them that they cannot cross the oceans, that he would do it for them, and get then the flower.

How did that prince come here? He by his knowing eye or *jñânadrishti*, saw what passed on in the palace. When he came to know that his step-brothers were being commissioned after the golden lotus, he went to his mother and wives and took leave of them to start on that expedition. His third wife asked him how he would get it. Her very words indicated that she knew the process. The cunning husband replied: "Don't you know, my dearest of wives, that I have an intelligent counsellor in you. Why don't you tell me then the way," and she began as follows, giving into his hands seven pebbles and a note: "My dearest husband, take these pebbles and the note with you to the sea-shore. Throw one of these pebbles into the first sea and say, "May the sea dry before and swell behind." It shall at once occur so, and you may go on walking in the dry road, thus cut in the midst of the waters. Soon as the first sea is thus crossed, throw the second stone in the second sea, pronouncing the same words. There the same phenomena shall occur. Thus you shall cross the seven seas by these seven stones. Beyond these seven seas there is a sacred water called *Akilâudakoti brahmânda* (14) water. There go

---

14-15. *Akhilândakôtibrahmândanâyaka*—is the lord of the complete mundane egg—an epithet applied to Siva. The water is the special locality in the ocean sacred to that God.

and bawl out, "Oh, thou the lord *Akilândakôti brahmândanâyaka* (15). A certain *Râkshasa* (16) will come running toward you waving his huge club and bent on putting you to death. Do not fear his anger, but give the note that I have given you and see what follows." The husband the tortoise prince, was greatly pleased at the instructions, and starting reached the shores where his step-brothers were waiting.

He told them to wait for a couple of days till he would bring them the flower. They were speechess to express their joy to his repeated kindness for all their cruelty to him. The tortoise prince, as instructed by his wife, threw one of the pebbles into the ocean and said. "May the sea dry before and swell behind?" and behold it was accordingly done. His joy knew no bounds. He walked through the seven seas as on dry-land, and called upon the *Râkshasa* or giant of the sacred water there, to whom he gave the note undaunted at his embrandishments of his club. Soon as the note fell into his hands the giant left off all his proud posture and humbled himself like a wagging dog before the prince. He applied the note several times to his eyes and called a crocodile by its name. It stood before him with its mouth wide open. He threw the note into its mouth and ordered to carry it to their king. When the king saw the note he pull-

---

Rakshasâ—a Titan, demon.

ed out a golden lotus from the divine pool, and giving it to the crocodile with several valuable ornaments ordered it thus: "Now, thou crocodile, thou shalt take on thy back the prince waiting on the bank of the sacred *tīrtha* (17), carry him safe over the seven seas and leave him in his own country, giving him this flower and these jewels for the princess who sent us this note, and who was our mother in her former life. Fly thou at once." The crocodile received the order, and in one dive stood before the prince and communicated to him the giant king's *âjñâ* or order. The prince jumped on its back, and after a safe ride reached the shore with the lotus, which he gave to the twin brothers that waited there. He took the jewels home and presented them to his third wife. She was delighted at them and her husband having successfully accomplished that adventure. These princes too went to their father with the golden lotus which they told him they had brought. He was greatly delighted at their extraordinary powers, and producing it before the mountain maid asked her for the marriage. She, concluding within herself that the tortoise prince must have got back his life, as it must be he only who was fit to have brought the flower also, gave orders for the marriage and said, "Send notice about our

(17) *Tīrtha*—Meritorious spots along the course of holy rivers.

marriage to the kings of the world and decorate the hall. And, soon as everything is ready please come to me." The old king accordingly did everything, and reported the arrangements to the mountain-maid. She said, " My dearest lord, kindly go to your first queen, invite her to the marriage with her three daughters-in-law and her son, who will give me in marriage to you" The old king was thunderstruck, and thought within himself; 'What a son and three daughters-in-law to my first queen. I divorced her for being childless, and it is a great wonder to see her a mother and mother-in-law. Let us calmly see everything before wondering at them.' Thus thinking the old king agreed to invite the first queen. The tortoise prince also by his knowing eye *Jñānadhrikhti* saw everything that passed in the palace and made requisite arrangements to receive h father. When the old king entered the first queen's quarters, the three daughters-in-law and the queen herself welcomed him. He was in amazement, but did not like to display his ignorance. So he mannerly invited them all. The son—the tortoise prince now arrived with all his royal paraphernalia which he had received from his three fathers-in-law which he had kept back in the adjacent village. The old king, the father, was struck at the beauty and majesty of his son, whom he never dreamed till then to exist. For all that he mannerly invited him to the marriage

The kings of the world had already met in the marriage-hall. All the guests had come. The mountain maid sat behind a screen; by the side of the old king sat his first queen's son with his mother and three wives; in front of their father sat the other two princes. There prevailed a solemn silence before the commencement of the ceremony. The mountain maid just broke the silence by her sweet address to the assembly: "Royal gentlemen assembled here from all parts of the world! Hear, please, this short story that I shall relate to you all, and then permit the priests to proceed with the wedding ceremonies." They all were spell-bound as it were by her sweet voice and sat dumb. She in a few words related how the old king divorced his first wife, how he married a second wife, practised penance, obtained a mango fruit, how the first queen had the seed of it, and by it the son who brought her from the snowy mountains, and who was put to death treacherously by the other two sons born by the juice of the said fruit. She then wishing to know whether that prince had his life or not asked, for the divine golden lotus, and soon as she had it, concluded within herself that that prince must be alive, and that the flower must have been brought by him. On that opinion, she said, she gave the permission for the marriage.

All the kings present, and the old king of Mallikârjunapurî were astonished at what they heard. They now requested the tortoise prince to complete the narration by his relating how he acquired the lotus. He satisfied them with the other portion, which was not known to the mountain lady. The old king melted into tears on account of joy. He kissed his son a thousand times, passed his hands over him, who, for his sake fell down and lost his life on the snowy mountains, admired his intelligent daughters-in-law and told the tortoise prince to deal with his treacherous step-brothers as he chose. He was of so good a nature that he excused all their faults and took them to his side. The marriage of their father and the mountain maid was duly celebrated with all pomp. The kings of the world honoured the pair with appropriate presents, and after a short stay returned to their country. The old king had also his three wives, the first queen, the second queen and the mountain maid. With these and his three sons and three daughters-in-law he lived for a long time.

"And must not such a brave prince like the tortoise prince marry thee? Oh thou gem of womankind!" Thus Buddhichâturya ended his fourth story. The sun began to rise in the east and the pair now left their bed chamber.

[Moral.—The moral that follows this story is, that faith is always rewarded. The first queen of the story by her faith in Paramêsvara gives birth to a dutiful son whom the Great God himself instucects, through Nârada the sage, in all branches of knowledge. This son, without revealing his relationship, follows his treacherous brothers and procures the lady desired by his father and is rewarded in the end by his father's affection.]

FIFTH STORY.

On the fifth night the minister's son Buddhichâturya retired to his bed chamber after his supper: and the first of the princesses whose turn it was for that night adorned her body with the costliest ornaments and entered the chamber chewing betel-leaf. She hastened to the side of her husband with great love. Buddhichâturya with his usual mode to allay those desires, spoke out, "My gem of womankind! I have to-day also a story to relate to you. Soon as that is over we shall retire to rest." The princess out of decency's sake was compelled to agree; and the minister's son began as follows:—

There was a town named Udayagiri ruled over by a king named Lôkâdhipa. He had seven sons whom he instructed in the four *Vêdas*, six *Sâtras*, sixty-four arts, the Codes of Manu and in the usage of different weapons, the management of horses and elephants. When they all attained their youth, he built seven small palaces for them and set each in one with his wife and servants, thus giving them free scope to enjoy that stage of humanity as they liked.

One night the moon was shining bright. The old king was sitting in the topmost court of his palace in company with his queen and enjoyed the pleasantness of the night, so much that he wished to see his sons and hear how they enjoyed their night. No sooner had this thought entered his mind than he got down from his palace and came to the first prince. The father asked the son to give out to him freely what he would like to be doing on that moonlight night. The first prince humbled himself before the feet of his father and spoke thus: "This moonlight night is a very cool and pleasant one; and I think this is the best time for conducting an army of men, horses and elephants into an enemy's country." The father now went to the second prince and wished to know what he would like to be doing. He replied that he would like to spend that pleasant night in irrigating half a dozen acres of land without undergoing any fatigue as in the day time. The father then went to his third son and asked what he would like to do that night. He said that he would like to plough half a dozen acres as that time would relieve the beasts and persons engaged in ploughing from their fatigue. The king Lokapâla now went to his fourth son and wished to know what he would like to be engaged in that part of the night. He replied that he would like to walk from one village to another without the scorching sun up above, as it would be in the day. The king after the receipt of the above answer from his four sons, went to the fifth and asked him what he would then like to be doing. He replied that he would like to go ahunting. The king now went to his sixth son and asked him about what he would be engaged in that night. He replied that he would choose to be a cooly then, than anything else, as he could do much physical work without great exhaustion. The old king now went to his seventh and last son and put him the same question. He replied: "My dearest father! I wish to be the sole emperor of the world, reclining on a sofa with the daughter of Indra [1] giving me betel-leaf rolls to chew, the daughter of Agni [2] shampooing my legs, the daughter of Varuna [3] singing sweet songs, and the daughter of the Adisêsha [4] (serpent king) fanning me with white chauries." The old king who was pleased with the simple answers of all his other sons was highly enraged with the imaginary happiness of his seventh son. "Thou vile wretch. Thy desires are imaginary. I do

---

(1) Indra is the Lord of the skies.

(2) Agni is the God of fire.

(3) Varuna is the God of waters or seas.

(4) Adisêsha is the first serpent—of one thousand heads that sprung from the ocean when the Gods churned it. He is represented as bearing the whole world over one of his heads; also as forming the cushion for the contemplation sleep (*Yôganidrâ*) of Vishnu, the preserver of the universe.

not know how long thou hast thus been building castles in the air. Before to-morrow morning these shall be an end to thy life which is attempting impossibilities." Thus threatening his seventh son, the old king flew to his palace and calling the executioners, gave them his signet ring to murder the seventh prince next morning. They received their orders and took leave of their king.

The mother of the princes (the old queen) overheard her husband's order to murder her last son. That son was, as usual, her pet, and she knew not what to do, when she heard the above order. "Has Jagatalapratâpa [5] done such a serious crime? Shall I go and speak to my husband about him?" thought she, but on second consideration she found that as the king was in very great excitement and her interference would make him still more enraged against their seventh son. She thought it prudent to send away her son to a distant place to avoid the execution of her lord's order. She hastily took a bag containing a thousand pagodas and flew to her son, who was thunderstruck at her unusual appearance in that part of the night. Not to keep him longer in amazement, his mother began to speak, "My dearest son, I do not know what great crime you have committed to deserve murder tomorrow morning. Your father has given the order to the execution-

(5) Jagatalapratâpa means literally the famous on the face of the world.

ers. Fly for your life, avoiding the common ways, lest they, the executioners, pursue you." Jagatalapratâpa received the money and blessings of his mother, and jumping over the walls of the town ran away. He, avoiding public paths, broke his way through a forest.

After several days of journey Jagatalapratâpa reached a cottage in a wood. He entered it and found there an old woman, whom he requested to take him under her protection. She gladly agreed to do so, aud in return asked him to graze her ten buffalos in the east, south and west directions, and on no account to go to the north. He was doiug accordingly and living in that wood.

At Udayagiri the executioners came and searched for the prince Jagatalapratâpa to do their duty, and not finding him, they fearing the anger of the old king, murdered a beast and produced its blood as his life blood.

After grazing the cattie for three days in the east, south and west of the cottage, the prince, notwithstandiug the order of the old woman, wished to try the north, and on the fourth day drove the beasts towards that direction. There was a big *Jambu* [6] grove under which he gathered the buffalo for the heat of the sun and himself getting up on a *Jambu* tree was engaged in eating those black fruits.

---

(6) *Jambu* a fruit tree *Eugenia Jambolana.*

Out of curiosity he cast his eyes roundabout him, and in the extreme north a most lovely sight met his eyes. He saw a golden tank in which a maid of exquisite beauty was bathing naked. She was the daughter of Indra and was used to come there daily for her bath. Persons that used to see her thus in her bath never returned again to their homes. Hence it was that the old woman of the wood warned Jagatalapratâpa not to go to that direction. Her garments, the maid had left on the shore and was playing with four other maids in the water. Jagatalapratâpa got down slowly from the tree, secretly crawled along the ground, and taking her garment away took to his heels. She came running behind crying, "See me, see my beauty." Jagatalapratâpa turned back to see her beauty and was by her incantations turned to a stone. The daughter of Indra then took her garments back and returned to her palace in the heavens with the four other maids. The buffalos too returned to the cottage in the evening without the person set over them. The old woman was greatly vexed at the disappearance of Jagatalapratâpa. That night, she tied the buffalos herself and gave them hay. As soon as it was dawn she went to the north, and to her great sorrow found her prince turned into a stone. She could not do without him. Necessity made her to use the powers of her incantations. She went to her cottage and returned with a cupful of water, and pronouncing some incantations over it sprinkled it on the stone, when lo ! it rose up as Jagatalapratâpa. She reprimanded him for having transgressed her orders, and asked him to relate what took place. He obeyed his protectress' order, and at last humbly said, "Grandmother, I do not think that I would live long though you have given a rebirth to me. For the figure of that maid, though she was cruel towards me, ever stands before me. You must use all your powers to get that daughter of Indra for my partner in life."

The pathetic way in which Jagatalapratâpa clothed his words, the sincere emotions of love which were plainly visible in his face, and the painful condition in which he was, all these produced their effects in the minds of the old woman. She agreed to stand by him and to get him his longed-for maiden. To that effect she spoke to him thus : "My dear son ! Go then as you did yesterday to that tank, and hide yourself in a place where the daughter of Indra could not see you. She will not look around her, and undressing herself, and after placing her garments on the shore, will enter the water. You shall slowly emerge from your hiding place, and taking up the garment shall shoot off. She will follow you uttering as she did yesterday, " See my beauty, &c." You had better never see back, for if you do you will be turned into a stone. Fly at once to me and give me the garment. I shall then show to you how I shall make her stay in this world." With these injunctions the old woman sent Jagatalapratâpa to the tank and returned to her cottage.

She had not long to wait when she found him come flying with the garment of the daughter of Indra to the cottage. She took it from him, and pouring water over him turned him into a child of three years, and gathering him in her lap was fondling with him. She tore the thigh of the child, and putting the garment into the cavity stitched up the gap. Indra's daughter ran naked into the cottage,and asked the old woman whether she saw a young lad, stealing away her garment, enter that place. The old woman, of course, denied all knowledge of having ever seen in her wood any such lad ; she also pointed out to the daughter of Indra one of her own cloth which, compelled by necessity,Indra's daughter wore for the occasion. Her sorrow knew no bounds. Her garment she lost and found it impossible to return to her father without it. So she made up her mind to stay with the old woman till she secured her lost clothes. Thus passed some days.

One day the old woman found a fitting opportunity to lecture to the daughter of Indra about the advantages of married life, and requested her to get herself married to some youth. She agreed to it,and the old woman converted the child agai to his former shape—Jagatalapratâpa. The marriage was duly celebrated. The pleasure that the parties felt made up for the want in the company of guests, &c. Thus by the favour of the old woman Jagatalapratâpa obtained what he was once, as he thought, only dreaming upon. For six months after the marriage the pair remained in the cottage, till one day the old woman spoke to them as follows:—"My dear children! Your company is always very dear to me. In fact in this wood where there is no sign of human habitation your company is a great welcome to an old woman-like myself. But you young people are not thus to be buried in this forgetfulness of a wood. It is time for you to go out and earn your own livings in an honourable way." These words seemed very reasonable to Jagatalapratâpa, and he at once started out with his wife, the daughter of Indra, to go to some town or other. The old woman showered her blessings upon the pair, and calling Jagatalapratâpa aside thus addressed him: "My dear son, one word unto your ears. Keep it confidential. Do not on any account give away the cloth that is hid on your thigh to the daughter of Indra. If once she has it, she will leave you for ever; and with her all your fortunes too will leave you. So take great care. But at the same time you must not have the garment with you, when you go ahunting or on any expedition. For if you do, you shall always only meet defeat. Therefore on these occasions give the cloth into the hands of some one dear to you as your life, and when you return again put it up in your thigh" Thus advising the prince the old woman sent him away from her cottage with his wife.

Jagatalapratâpa started that early morning with his wife and journeying day and night reached a town named Visvarañjitanagara the next morning. He saw a tank, in which he washed his hands and feet and sat down with his wife in a grove on the shore. The minister of the town of Visvarañjitanagara happened to be bathing in the tank then, seeing Jagatalapratâpa and the heavenly beauty that accompanied him, he fell into the following contemplations:—

"This beauty or the like of it we have never, in our life, seen till now. Our king has no such female in his harem. If we by some trick or other try to get this female in the harems of the palace the king will become our tool. I must try to do that." Thus thinking with himself he approached as an ordinary man and asked Jagatalapratâpa his name and history. Without relating anything true of himself the prince said that he had royal blood in his veins, and that he came out in search of employment. The minister went to the palace, and reporting what he had seen on the tank to his bad king, got his consent to take Jagatalapratâpa into his employ. The prince demanded ten thousand pagodas per mensem, and the minister agreed to give that enormous sum apparently for his services, but secretly to take away his lady on some day or other. They provided him with a palace to live in. From the day of his entertainment the prince was used to leave his bed in early morning, bathe and perform his ablutions, take his meals before the first watch of the day was over and wait in the royal presence as the bodyguard of the king with a drawn sword in his hand. In this attitude he stood before the king till it was dark, and then returned home to his wife in the night. The daughter of Indra was ever at home. She engaged a couple of maid-servants, and with them was managing the duties of the house. She was as chaste as she was beautiful. She never left her husband, and was always engaged in ministering to his wishes and comforts. Thus passed a full month. On the first of the second month the minister of the city of Visvarañjitanagara sent half a dozen peons with money bags on their head to the house of Jagatalapratâpa. These bags contained the ten thousand pagodas, the salary of the prince, for his past month's services. The minister sent these men to pay the money to the prince's wife, and let him know how she behaved herself towards them. These peons went to Jagatalapratâpâ's house and called out the lady of the house, saying that they had brought her husband's salary.

She received the money, in presence of her maid-servants and gave them receipt, and when they went out carefully bolted the doors. The peons found her very majestic, reserved and noble, and had nothing bad to report of her to their minister.

After this secret information which he received from the peons the minister went to the king and spoke to him thus: "Your supreme majesty, I have been watching by secret means the beautiful wife of the prince serving under us, and find her very careful. So there is no possibility of our taking her into our possession secretly as long as her husband is alive. We must devise means to kill him. A thought just occurs to me of how to do it. Your majesty must fain severe headache, for which I shall order him to bring serpent's poison. In the act of bringing the medicine he will die. We shall then without any fear take possession of his wife." The king consenting to it, feigned headache ande fell ill. The minister as pre-arranged called upon the prince-bodyguard and ordered him to bring the poison of the serpent, which alone he said would effect the cure; Jagatalapratâpa agreed to it and returned home early that day. But how to procure the serpent's poison! This thought troubled him. After having received such a princely salary his conscience dictated to him not to refuse any of the royal orders, however impossible it might be. Without knowing what to do, he came home and laid himself down on his bed with great uneasiness of mind.

The daughter of Indra was first startled to see her husband returning home early that day. She saw no cheerfnlness in his face. Her confusion was at its height when she saw him confining himself to his bed instead of conversing with her as was usual with him. So she approached him and requested to know the reason of his illness. "I am asked to bring the poison of the serpent" was the reply. "Is that all. Then banish my lord all your fears; I shall get you the poison without any difficulty. Kindly obtain leave for three days and come home with a peaceful mind." Jagatalapratâpa, the moment his wife assured him that she would procure him the poison, turned out quite a new man. His face glowed with joy. He ran to the palace, obtained leave for three days and returned home. The daughter of Indra asked him to rest for two days at home and never to harbour any doubt or anxiety about the poison. She told him that she would make all arrangements to get it and a wife to boot. On the morning of the third day she wrote a few lines on a palm leaf, and rolling it up addressed it to her uncle Kârkôtaka, and giving the note to her husband said, "My dearest lord. Take this please to the nearest wood and slip it down in the hole of any anthill there; wait for a couple of minutes, and you shall see what follows." Jagatalapratâpa flew with the note to the nearest wood and let it down in an anthole. That note happened to fall on the head of a serpent, and as soon as it found it addressed to the serpent emperor Kârkôtaka, he took it and flew to the royal presence in the infernal regions and handed it to his majesty. Kârkôtaka saw it, and sent a pearled palanquin on the heads of one thousand serpents to invite to his court the husband of his brother's (Indra's) daughter. In her letter she had asked her uncle to give his daughter in marriage to Jagatalapratâpa and also to hand him in a small casket some serpent poison. Kârkôtaka did everything as stated in the letter, and on that very evening sent Jagatalapratâpa with his new married wife to the world with a casket of poison too. So by the aid of the daughter of Indra our prince had not only the poison but another immortal daughter as his wife.

On the fourth day Jagatalapratâpa rose up in early morning, bathed, finished his ablutions, and after taking his meals attended the royal presence with his casket containing poison, and informed the king that he had brought the required medicine for the headache. They all in the palace, the king, minister, &c., were astonished at his powers and wanted to see the poison. Jagatalapratâpa told them that the casket in his hand contained the poison, that he could not open it there, for, if he did, the whole palace would burn down, and that he would show it to them in the neighbouring forest. They all wondered at the account that he gave of the poison, and followed him to the nearest wood. Jagatalapratâpa asked no one there to stand in the way of the wind and slightly took the lid of the casket. All the trees, shrubs, beasts and birds that stood in the direction in which the wind blew were reduced to ashes. The king of Visvarañjitanagara there in the midst of the whole assembly dubbed him as the most powerful man that he had ever seen, and they all returned to their quarters. Everything went on right there. The wicked minister being afraid of the great power of Jagatalapratâpa, never dreamt of any evil towards him. Thus passed one more month. On the first day of the third month the minister sent Jagatalapratâpâ's salary on the heads of the peons whom he sent on the former occasion, and instructed them as usual to examine what passed in his house. They came and delivered the money taking due receipts, and to their great astonishment they found two ladies instead of one as on the former occasion, and reported it to the minister.

He again wanted to try some means or other to do away with him, and going to the king spoke to him thus in secret: "My lord, I now hear that our body-guard Jagatalapratâpa has two beauties in his possession instead of one. We must somehow devise plans to kill him and get the ladies into our possession. Our plan of sending him after poison had no effect. I think now that I have a sure way of killing him. If your majesty feigns belly-ache, I shall send him to bring the fat of a whale from the ocean to cure it. This is not an easy affair like the killing of the serpent. He must perish in this attempt after the whale, and we shall have his ladies after his death." The king, whose stupid thoughts turned in all the ways the minister guided them, now feigned belly-ache and fell ill. The minister ordered Jagatalapratâpa to bring the fat of the whale to effect the cure of that sickness, and he returned home with a dismal face.

His wives saw his change of colour, and enquired of him the reason, and when that was explained, they assured him of their power to procure the fat, and requested him to obtain leave for five days. Jagatalapratâpa accordingly obtained leave for that period and returned home. They asked him to rest for four days in his house without any anxiety about the whale-fat affair, and that on the fifth day they would procure him that medicine. He acted according to their instructions. On the fifth day the daughters of Indra and Karkô*taka* wrote a conjoint letter to their uncle V*ârun*a, Lord of the Seas, asking him to give his daughter in marriage to their husband Jagatalapratâpa, and also to procure some whale fat for certain medical purposes. Giving the note addressed to Varuna to Jagatalapratâpa they asked him to throw it in the nearest sea and wait the results. He did accordingly; the note happened to fall on the head of a crocodile, and as soon as it saw the address, it carried it to the lord of waters—Varuna. He was extremely pleased at the contents of the letters, and inviting the bridegroom to his palace beneath the oceans, had the marriage regularly celebrated. That very night Jagatalapratâpa returned to Visvarañjitanagara and left Varuna's daughter, his newly married wife, with his other wives and returned alone to his new father-in-law's house.

On the morning of the sixth day, he got from Varuna a casket-ful of the fat of a whale, and riding on the back of a crocodile was approaching the coast of Visvarañjitanagara. Several people saw him while on the sea, and reported the matter to the king and minister who, when they saw that it was true, were thunderstruck at his great powers and sent word that they did not want the whale fat. Jagatalapratâpa reached the shore, and joining his duty discharged it most satisfactorily to all his superiors. Thus passed the whole of the third month too.

On the first day of the fourth month the minister as usual sent on the heads of the six peons the salary of Jagatalapratâpa for the third month to be given in his house. The peons as usual gave the money, and that time they were astonished to find three ladies instead of two, of the most charming beauty, and of course they reported this matter to the minister.

His envy knew no bounds. His main object was somehow or other to get possession of the ladies. So he approached the king and spoke to him as follows; "My sovereign. I have long been thinking of some plan or other to do away with Jagatalapratâpa; and at last found out one which must put an end to his life. It is this. We shall all write letters to our grandfathers, great-grandfathers and other relatives who have died long ago: and ask him to deliver these letters to their departed spirits in the other world. We shall also order him to bring us back their replies, implying thereby that we mean him no harm. He must die first to reach them. Then the fear of his coming back is over for ever, we shall take possession of his wives." These words of the minister fell like nectar into the ears of the king of Visvarañjitanagara, and he made arrangements to carry it into effect. Every one in the palace wrote letters to their departed friends and relatives, and the minister gave all their notes to Jagatalapratâpa and asked him to get replies, and as usual the prince returned home with his head hanging down.

His wives came to him and inquired the reason of his despondency, and when they heard of it they laughed and said, "This is a pretty thing. I see that by those tricks the king of this town wants to do away with you to enslave us. I now think that I must pay him in his own coins and kill him. Kindly get leave for eight days and ask the king to provide you with a big fire-pit with burning flames on the last day. Inform them also that you will jump into it and reach those ancestors." The husband agreed to it, and going procured leave for a week; he also wished them to assist him with a big pit containing flames on the eighth day, as by that means only he must reach the departed persons. They, as they wanted to promote his death, agreed to the fire-pit project easily and made the necessary arrangements.

The prince spent seven of the eight days in company with his three wives. During this interval, the daughter of Indra wrote up the replies, to the king, minister and others as their dead relatives in the other world would do. She gave them all to Jagatalapratâpa and asked him to take the replies also with him when he went to the god of fire,—Agni—to whom, she said, she would send him. On the eighth day she wrote a letter to Agnibhagavân asking him to spare Jagatalapratâpa when he jumped in the fire, as he was the husband of herself and the daughters of

Varuna and Kârkôtaka, to give his daughter in marriage to him. Giving the note to her husband, the daughter of Indra addressed him thus: "My dearest husband, this is my note to Agni, which you shall throw in the fire this evening before beginning to jump. Agnì will take you to his region, give his daughter in marriage to you. Kindly bring her away here this midnight that others might not see her. You shall again return to Agni and come back next morning, while the whole town is assembled to see you." Thus instructed, Jagatalapratâpa set out on his letter delivery expedition. The whole town was assembled near the pit to see the man that made it the road to reach the other world. Jagatalapratâpa appeared with his load of letters (and replies also,) showed them all to the spectators, and after throwing first into the fire his wife's note, jumped into it, asking them all to be present there next morning to receive their replies. They all concluded with themselves that he was no more, but still wanted to see till next morning, and so went to their respective homes.

gnibhagavân as soon as he saw the note addressed to him by Indra's daughter obeyed every word of it. He gave his daughter in marriage to Jagatalapratâpa, and sent her away that very night to join her sisters.

Jagatalapratâpa remained that night there, and addressed to each of the reply letters one or two sentences. These conveyed to the inhabitants of Visvarañjitanagara a consoling information of what happiness the dead persons were enjoying in the other world, and how they would like to have the company of their living relatives for a day or two, and how they would be enriched by their coming there.

On the morning of the ninth day the whole town assembled round the pit to see Jagatalapratâpa bring the replies. The king and the minister also were there. Some thought that Jagatalapratâpa might return as he on two former occasions successfully did after attempting the impossibilities of bringing in serpent poison and whale fat. Some thought that he must have died the previous evening. While they were thus speaking, the fire in the middle of the pit opened wide and through it there came out the man—Jagatalapratâpa himself, bearing on both his shoulders big bundles of palm leaf rolls. Not a hair of his body was injured. He wore over him most costly jewels, being the presents of his father-in-law, Agnibhagavân. He was not in the ordinary dress with which he jumped, but in a bridegroom's dress. To every one that gave him a letter he now returned a reply. "Are they all in such a good condition. If we go there, are we likely to meet them and return rich?" These and one thousand similar questions every one began to put him. He answered them all in the affirmative, and by his description of their happiness increased their curiosity. So, one and all determined to pay a visit to their departed relatives by throwing themselves into the fire, and asked Jagatalapratâpa to assist them in their transit. He promised to do so, and asked the king and minister to dig up a still larger pit.

That larger pit was blazing with fire and all the persons awaited the evening to fall into the flames. The evening came on. The king, the minister, and all the persons of the town taking their choice presents to the spirits of their forefathers approached the fire place. Jagatalapratâpa was waiting there to conduct these people down to their ancestors. He bore a note in his hand which was given by his wife, the daughter of Indra. She therein had written to her uncle Agni the following sentences: "My dear uncle, this evening shall fall into your mouth your son-in-law Jagatalapratâpa with all the inhabitants of Visvarañjitanagara. Spare your son-in-law only and burn every one else to ashes." The king, the minister and every one requested Jagatalapratâpa that evening to conduct them to their departed relatives. The conductor asked them all to hold each others hands. Every one on the bank jumped after him, and down they all went.

The God Agni or fire spared Jagatalapratâpa only and all others were burnt to ashes. Thus was the vile minister, the still vile king who was giving a ready ear to all his advices, and all the avaricious inhabitants of the town were consumed by the flames. Jagatalapratâpa alone rose up. He took possession of the kingdom of Visvarañjitanagara and ruled over it for sometime. He then gave it over to a poor man who had been waiting under him and set out with his four wives in search of new adventures.

They all journeyed for a few days and found themselves in the midst of a thick wood where there was not even a drop of water to drink. The daughter of Indra spoke to her husband Jagatalapratâpa as follows:—

"My dearest husband. We now see before us a vast forest in which we cannot find even a single drop of water. I shall by my powers turn this into a city fairer than Amarâvatî,[7] the capital of my father". Here she ended and her husband replied, "My dearest wife. As fate had so written on my forehead, I became your husband. You are a heaven-born woman. Nothing is impossible to you in this world. Do as you say and make me your lord, the lord of that city also". Indra's daughter was elated at the words of Jagatalapra-

(7) Amarâvatî—The capital of the divine world of Indra.

tâpa and remained dumb for a time, when lo! the forest was no longer a forest. Splendid mansions of several stories in height, palaces, bâzâr-streets, public roads, offices, elephant-stalls, horse stalls, shikârkhânas, hospitals, schools, temples and other requirements sprung up. Varuna's daughter to show her power enriched the new city with rivers, tanks, channels and fine wells. The serpent daughter by her magic power raised up flower garlands, parks, fruit-groves, villas, and other things. The daughter of fire created all the required subjects of the realm, the ministers, commanders, spies, subjects, &c. Jagatalapratâpa was consecrated as the emperor over this magic city, and all the kings of the world by the magic influence of the daughter of Indra, paid their homage to him. In the loftiest part of his palace Jagatalapratâpa had his bedroom and lived with his four wives. Thus what he spoke out in play to his father proved true to him.

Let us now enquire of what became of his father Lôkâdhipa, the king of Udayagiri. Some days after Jagatalapratâpa left him, his fortunes also abandoned him. An inimical king—the king of the Odda country invaded Udayagiri, and drove away Lôkâdhipa. He with his queen and six sons went into a wood and to avoid detection they dressed themselves like peasants. These eight, cutting fuel from the forest sold them in the nearest town for a slight sum, and buying rice with it made their living. One day these persons came to the magic town over which their seventh son Jagatalapratâpa was king. They appointed a place of meeting and separated in the streets to sell their fuel, crying, " Firewood to sell, who will buy my firewoods, fine firewoods." The mother of Jagatalapratâpa happened to pass through the very streets in which the palace stood, and having seen much of ease in her younger days, was not able to bear the severe midday sun. So, she fell down in a swoon in front of the palace, and Jagatalapratâpa from the top of his mansion discovered in the swooning woman his mother. He reported the fact to his four wives. They came out running, poured cold water over the face of their swooning mother-in-law ; one fanned her, another brought some breakfast, another brought a seat, and an another took her up. She now opened her eyes and asked the fair ladies round about her who they were. " Mother-in-law. It is only to-day we had the happiness of serving you. Come in. We shall tell your honour everything. Thus saying they conducted her in. By that time Jagatalapratâpa had come down, and seeing the sad condition of his mother, was moved by the sight. Though he recognised her, she could not do that easily, as she saw him only while young and not after he had attained his fixed growth and features ; she was not long in confusion,

Jagatalapratâpa himself related everything and enquired about his father and brothers. "They are engaged in selling their burdens in the streets of the town," said the mother. Jagatalapratâpa sent his ministers in search of them. They came in, and there was a great confusion of joy and sorrow at their meeting. The joy prevailed in the end. Jagatalapratâpa relieved the miseries of his parents and brothers, and they remained buried in an ocean of joy at the fortunate recovery of their lost relative—a murdered son to Lôkâdhipa. Jagatalapratâpa gave the sovereignty to his father and acted only as his minister ever afterwards. Thus passed on a couple of years. The father was astonished at the power of Jagatalapratâpa, especially at his having secured to his wives the daughters of Indra, Varu*n*a, Kârko*t*aka and Agni—the four maidens, for loving whom Jagatalapratâpa was first ordered by him to be murdered.

One day Jagatalapratâpa wanted to go a hunting in the neighbouring forest. Remembering the instructions of the old woman of the wood, whose aid got him the daughter of Indra first as his wife, he opened his thigh and took out the garment of his first wife which lay concealed in it, and calling his mother to his side gave it to her asking her to keep it carefully, and never on any account to part with it to any one. But he never told her that she must not give it to her first daughter-in-law, but only made a general statement to part with it to no one on any account. Jagatalapratâpa and his brothers went out to hunt in the neighbouring forest.

The daughter of Indra was watching her husband when he handed over the garment to his mother. She now for the first time knew that her husband had it in his own thigh. She was astonished at his devise, and now wanted to take possession of her cloth from her mother-in-law. The four daughters-in-law now approached their mother-in-law with sweet words, one fanned her, another combed her hair, a third placed before her nice fruits and betel leaves to chew. And the fourth, and that was Indra's daughter, cunningly asked her to show to them what their husband gave her. The mother of course never dreaming any evil intention in the words of her daughter-in-law, brought out the cloth and said : "This is all that he gave me. What do you trouble yourself about it." Indra's daughter praised the beauty of the cloth and wanted her mother-in-law to allow her to wear it for a few *ghatikâs*. The stupid mother never able to read the inward thoug hts of the daughter-in-law,gave the cloth to her.The daughter of Indra wore it. The mother-in-law admired her. The word Paramêsvara came out of the lips of the daughter of Indra ; at once they—the four heavenly maidens—were ascending the skies. Now it was that the old mother of Jagatalapratâpa discovered her mistake. True to the statement of the old woman of the wood, the prosperity of Jagatalapratâpa vanished with the vanishment of the garment. The magic city was again turned into a forest, its former state. The horses on which Jagatalapratâpa and his brothers rode disappeared, leaving them in the wood. He at once thought that his mother had been duped. Returning to his city, he found it no more a city. All the inhabitants had disappeared except his parents. His mother now stood sobbing before him, and explained her own mistake and the tricks of her daughters-in-law, and at last fell down in a swoon, stung by her conscience that she was the cause of all his calamities. Jagatalapratâpa found universal sorrow round about him, and so called up courage to his assistance then without yielding to the stroke of misfortune. He brought back his mother to her senses and spoke to her thus: " My dear Mother. No use of accusing yourself or any one now. We are all under the influence of fate and her minister, Time. No one could dream of having for his wives heavenly maidens. But my fate so ordered it that I should have them for a few years. Now I have lost them. If I have fortune still I may get them again" Thus he consoled his mother. He wanted to leave them all in a safe place, and himself to go again to the old woman of the wood and try to bring them back.

We have already seen how he consecrated a dependent of his as king over the city of Visvarañjitanagara. He now with his parents and brothers went to that town and sent word to the king about his arrival. That king having learnt from his peons that Jagatalapratâpa had come in a reduced condition, and had not his four, wives through whom he had all his fortunes, returned word that he had no leisure to see him. He also ordered his servants to push Jagatalapratâpa out if he persisted in seeing him—the king. The servant who had previously known Jagatalapratâpa well, and what a deal of good he had done to the then king of Visvarañjitaagara, was startled at the latter's reply to his former patron, and reported every word of it to Jagatalapratâpa. That servant to his great credit and future prosperity now added, "My noble lord, I have heard my father repeat the proverb, 'Never give up a dried-up chunam or a reduced king; I shall take your parents and brothers under my protection, and give them heartily what I have in my possession. You may follow your pursuit as you wish it without any concern about those people.'" These fell like nectar into the ears of Jagatalapratâpa. He thanked his gods for their having sent him a friend in the shape of that poor servant. He thanked that servant, left his parents and brothers under him, and started to the wood where the old woman lived, without taking anything to calm down his hunger. That poor servant pressed him to take food. Jagatalapratâpa begged excuse, saying that he had vowed never to taste a morsel of food without recovering his lost wives.

He went journeying on and on through woods, forests, thickets, and mountains. He spied a broad river before him in which several ants were struggling for their lives. The ant-king also was among the sufferers. He now called out to the king Jagatalapratâpa and said, "Passenger, whoever you may be, if you relieve me from my difficulty, I shall render you all that I can do for you, when you are in calamity if you would think of me for that moment. Pray help us." These words excited pity in the minds of Jagatalapratâpa. He now entered the river and extricated one and all of the ants from their difficulties. The ant-king praised him and took his leave. Going a little more distance he found a frog dying in the midst of a burning sand. He happened also to be the king of frogs. He called Jagatalapratâpa and begged him to take him into water, promising help in future to him. Jagatalapratâpa accordingly took up the frog king and threw him in the nearest pond. After this he proceeded a few more steps, when he found a *Pillaippûchi* 8 similarly suffering from want of water. That too happened to be the king of *Pillaippúchchis*. That too demanded help, promising future assistance in return. Jagatalapratâpa helped it; and after these three adventures and journeying for several days, he at last reached the old woman in the wood. She not happening to be at her cottage when he reached it, he fell down in a swoon, his strength which supported him till he reached that place having then deserted him. In the evening the old-woman returned, and to her surprise found the prince whom she once assisted lying at her doors in a swoon. She fanned him for some time, and poured down his throat some gruel. The prince Jagatalapratâpa recovered, and soon as he saw her sobbed into tears. She enquired the cause of his affliction. He related everything to her, and again demanded her assistance that time not to obtain the daughter of Indra alone but all the four heavenly ladies.

The old woman was moved much by the words of Jagatalapratâpa, which drew forth all her compassion. She consoled him and said, "My son,

---

8. An insect, the Gryllus, which going into mud is not defiled. This is often given out as a comparison to the spiritual man, who, in family life, is not contaminated by any attachment to it.

be not afflicted. I shall point you out a way by which you can obtain them again. I cannot myself act the part of bringing them. For then they will curse me. Go again to the tank where you once picked up the garment of Indra's daughter. Near that place stands a *punnai* 9 tree, under which you had better sit down, and be contemplating upon them. They daily pass and repass by that way while coming to and returning from their baths. They will pity you, after some days; you may then get them." So saying the old woman asked Jagatalapratâpa to stay in her hut for some days till the exhaustion of the journey was over. Jagatalapratâpa stayed only for that night, and on the next morning went to the side of the said tree.

He sat down there contemplating on the divine daughters. They saw him sitting there everyday while passing and repassing that tree, and never spoke to him. Thus passed full forty days. Jagatalapratâpa was at last disgusted and said to himself: "What I have been sitting here for forty days without food and water, and these, my former wives have not yet spoken one word to me. If I had served with as much faith my God for this period, surely he must have granted my boon. Hunger and fatigue overtake me. Be-

---

(9) *Punnai*, also written *pinnai*—The Alexandrian laurel—*Calophyllum Inophyllum*.

fore death comes on let me think on him." So pondered over Jagatalapratâpa and broke out "Oh! You God Paramêsvaras,[10] Mahâdêva, Govinda, Kêsva, Achyuta[11] I have sinned. I have sinned. Protect me at this point of death. Receive me in your abode." Thus crying out he fell down in a swoon as a tree cut in the root.

The four maidens who were bathing in the pond heard the noise. Indra's daughter broke her silence and said, "Our former husband is losing his life on account of us. We must not show our reservedness now. Let us hasten to assist him." The others too said that they noticed him from his first arrival, but did not like to take prominent part of first of all speaking on that subject. They all came to the tree and tried their best to remove the swoon of their former husband, who now spoke to them, "My dearest wives! Was it proper on your part to have thus deceived me. What crime did I commit to deserve such treatment at your hands." They then spoke to him no more to place his thoughts on them, that they were divine maidens never destined to marry men in the world, that as they had a curse they were obliged to live with him for a time, and that they cannot do anything for him. Jagatalapratâpa thus replied to

---

(10) Names of *Siva*.
(11) Names of Vishnu.

them: "Oh, you divine daughters, these your words are the same as raising a man on high and then throwing him down. If you had meant to give me this reply then, why should you have revived me. You might as well have overlooked me and allowed me to die than thus to have revived me only to make me undergo that death again. I beg of you all never again to abandon me." The heavenly ladies were now in a delicate dilemma, to leave Jagatalapratâpa there, or to make up their mind to marry him. At last a thought occurred to them, and they spoke to him thus: "We shall now take you to the divine world and leave you before Indra. Then it is your duty to plead before him your case and get us lawfully married to you. Jagatalapratâpa jumped up with joy and begged of them to do him that much of favour, and that he would try his best afterwards to press Indra on the marriage affair. Now the divine daughters converted him into a frog, and throwing him into the water in their pot carried him to the world of Indra and there giving him his original shape and beautiful and costly ornaments to adorn himself with, went to their places.

Jagatalapratâpa was naturally a beautiful prince. The divine ornaments which his former wives gave him, made him a thousand times more beautiful. Twisting up his mustaches and holding a naked sword in his hand he roared out like a lion and stood before Indra who was sitting in his council hall. The God Indra was highly pleased at his bravery, nay audacity, and wishing to know more of him asked him the cause for his uncalled for intrusion; and Jagatalapratâpa in sweet silvery tones broke out in the following harangue: "My lord, I have come here to lodge a complaint before you against your daughter as well as her three sisters. I fell in love with her by robbing away her garments while she was in her bath and thus enslaving her first married her afterwards. Through her kindness I married also the daughters of Agni, Varu*n*a, and Kârkô*t*aka. They, all in a sudden, when I was absent in hunting in a forest, left me and came away to this your world. They not only came away, but have done the greatest mischief that can be done to a king by destroying all my kingdom. I again sought them, and after forty days of penance through their kindness reached this place. The matters speak of themselves to you. Call your daughter with the others. Inquire into the case and give justice to me." The sweet and yet bold tone in which Jagatalapratâpa clothed his words, the visible anger, shame and mortification that came and went in his face, made much impression on the mind of Indra. He now sent for his daughter with the others, and on due enquiry found all Jagatalapratâpâ's tale to be quite true. He now replied to him as follows: "Young man and king of the world. I have no objection to give you my daughter in marriage. For you seem by your very appearance to be a man of many rare attainments. For getting the daughters of Varuna, Agni and Kârkôtaka for your wives, you must stand three tests, which if you succeed, these ladies are yours." "My life I shall give up in the attempt to win them than to lose them without attempting. Now for your test," roared out Jagatalapratâpa, who became almost a new man when the sweet promise of his sure marriage with Indra's daughter at least fell into his ears. Indra now sent all his servants to reduce to the finest dust an acre of land to scatter in it ten *kalams*(12) of sesamum and to plough it well one hundred times: and they accordingly executed the orders and informed him about them. Indra asked Jagatalapratâpa to heap up these ten *kalams* of sesamum seed without omitting even a single grain if he really deserved his daughters. The would-be bridegroom thought the trial was easy, and going into the field tried all his might, but was not able to gather even a very slight portion of them. His sorrow knew no bounds. He sat down on the ground, and resting his head on his left arm began to weep. Just in

---

(12) *Kalam*—A measurement of grain varying according to localities. At Trichnopoly 40 Madras measures make one *kalam*. At Tanjore 24 measures, &c.

front of him he observed a swarm of ants, in which he discovered the ant-king, whom he had assisted formerly. He now requested him to oblige him in return. The ant-king issued a general order to his army to gather all the grains of sesamum seed, and thus in almost the twinkling of an eye the ten *kalams* scattered were gathered and heaped up. Indra was much pleased and wanted him to try a second experiment. He now showed him a well inhabited by serpents and spoke to him thus: "I shall throw my ring into this well. If you by your powers get me back the ring, you have won a second wife." So saying, Indra threw the ring in it. Jagatalapratâpa saw the serpents and found no other way of getting down than by killing them all. He waved his sword and began to cut them down. But for every part cut down, there arose one thousand serpents in its place thus increasing the calamity the more. Jagatalapratâpa hung down and pondered over for a while, when he saw a frog croaking near the well. The sight of that poor reptile brought into his mind his assistance to the frog-king (*Mandûkârâja*) and having already seen how the ant-king was useful to him, he thought of his frog-king thinking that he too may do him some assistance. That king at once stood before him and demanded to know how he would be serviceable to him. Jagatalapratâpa spoke, "My dear frog-king! Indra has now thrown his ring into this well which is swarming with serpents; I must get that jewel back from the well through your kind assistance." The frog-king issued the order at once to his subjects, who entered the well in vast numbers. The serpents each one of them caught hold of a frog and were engaged in swallowing them. Then one of the frogs jumped into the middle of the water and brought the ring back to the benefactor of its king. Jagatalapratâpa got back the ring. Indra who was witnessing all that took place, was greatly elated at the success of his would-be son-in-law, and admired the faithfulness of the frogs. He gave them back their life, and blessing them all with immortality, placed them in a big tank.

Indra now brought his third experiment to test Jagatalapratâpa with it. It was a plantain tree in appearance, but really seven plantain trees joined together by magic into one. Indra placed the tree before Jagatalapratâpa and asked him to cut it into two by one stroke if he wanted to marry the daughter of Agni. That daughter admiring his success in two former experiments, and knowing the trick with the plantain tree thought of her Gods and prayed them to assist Jagatalapratâpa in his successfully coming out of his third test, and it accordingly proved so. Indra dived into the way in which Jagatalapratâpa succeeded, and found out that the maids also internally favoured him.

Last of all came the fourth experiment. In this Indra converted all the four daughters into one shape and asked Jagatalapratâpa to choose out his (Indra's) daughter. "How to do this. I have by some chance or other successfully withstood these three trials, but how to overcome this the fourth." While he was thinking so, he saw the insect *Pillaippûchchi* hopping before him and said, "My dear *Pillaippûchchi*. If you remember my assistance to you kindly hop up on the foot of the daughter of Indra. I shall choose her out by that indication." And the insect did it accordingly, and Jagatalapratâpa by tha means chose out the right daughter of Indra.

True to the proverb that an assistance even though it be rendered to a dog is not thrown away, Jagatalapratâpa, by the aid of the petty insects to whom he rendered help, got back his four wives. The marriage was regularly and publicly celebrated. Several presents of jewels and clothes were given to Jagatalapratâpa. After the wedding he returned with his four wives to the old woman of the wood, and after spending a few days with her, started to Visvarañjitanagara where he left his parents and brothers under the protection of a poor servant. They were all overjoyed at Jagatalapratâpâ's success. The old king who turned away his patron without helping him in calamity now flew for his life. The poor servant who protected his father was raised to the throne of that city.

After this Jagatalapratâpa went to the forest where by the magic of Indra's daughter, a fine country once rose up. Again, by the same powers, the forest was converted into a splendid city, but this time never to perish afterwards. He ruled there for a time and then invaded Udayagiri, his paternal realm. The usurper was defeated and driven out. The elder brother of Jagatalapratâpa was consecrated in that throne. He also procured other kingdoms for his other five brothers aud himself reigned over the magic city with his four wives. "And must not such a prince become ihy husband. Oh! Thou the gem of womankind." Here the minister's son Buddhichâturya ended the story. The sun was already up in the horizon. He and the princess went out of the bed room.

[MORAL.—This story shows that there is nothing in the world impossible for a truly persevering man. We here see how our hero successfully accomplishes what his father once thought impossibilities by persistently following his adventures without giving them up.]

SIXTH STORY.

On the night of the 6th day the minister's son took his dinner, and after chewing betel-leaf, entered the bed chamber. The second of the princesses putting all her choicest ornaments on her body, came into the room, and after a few love songs on her guitar, approached the bed of her lord. Buddhichâturya wishing to allay her desires by a pleasant story, began as follows: " Listen! Oh thou the gem of womankind. There was a city named Pirandanagara ruled over by a king named Pirandarâja. He had no son for a very long time. This was a great blot in his happiness. To avert the displeasure of the gods he underwent severe penances, distributed charities to the poor, was hospitable to all the strangers, and otherwise conducted himself in such a way as to secure the happiness of every one he saw about him. One day a venerable hermit paid a visit to that city, and of course Pirandarâja welcomed him with all hospitality. The sage spent a few days with the king. One evening, Pirandarâja extolled the hermit for his rightly discharging the duties of his stage of life, and made known to him his want of an heir to succeed him on his throne after his death. The sage with closed eyes contemplated awhile and spoke out thus: "Oh king, by my knowledge of astrology I divine that you are not to have a son in this part of life, *i. e.,* while you are a king.

A few years hence a terrible foe will invade your dominions, and you will then be driven out of the country after your defeat. The supremacy of Saturn in his mansion of your horoscope then will put you for a period of seven years in difficulty. During the first year of that star's supremacy you will lose your kingdom. During the second year your wife shall give birth to twin sons, who, in their proper age, will relieve you of your difficulties." Thus giving some hope to the king the sage went away. After a few years, as already prophesied by the hermit, a powerful enemy invaded the city of Pirandanagar and ousted Pirandarâja from his throne. In the expectation of twin sons the year after his defeat that king forgot the sorrow of this sad event. He went with his queen into a different country, and there got himself and his wife entertained as male and female servants in the house of a rich *Chetti*. The mistress of the house, after extracting full work from them till the evening, would give them the eighth part of a measure of rice as wages for the day's work. They would cook that very small quantity and eat it. Thus passed some days.

True to the statement of the sage, the queen became pregnant. The king, though he welcomed the change that come over his wife, was highly vexed. "It is all the will of God that I should have no children when I was in very affluent circumstances, and that my wife should be big with child now that I am in need. The ways of fate are undiscernible. Let me console myself as, the sage prophesied, my miseries shall end after a few years that there is now a prospect of sonbirth before me." These thoughts brought copious tears into his eyes. They calmed down his sorrow, and as the time of the confinement was approaching, he went into the neighbouring wood, and gathering some boughs and creepers, built a small room for his wife in the pyal of a deserted house. Having no means to pay for the midwives, he himself performed their duties while his wife was labouring. In an auspicious *Muhûrtta* or occasion the queen gave birth to a son. The ten days of confinement were over, and the queen came out safe, bathed and cleaned herself of her pollution. The king not wishing to make her work, as her body was much exhausted, himself did in the *Chetti's* house her work also. One day, while engaged in husking out the paddies, a few drops of tears trickled down his eyes. The *Chetti* who was sitting opposite to him saw his servant crying, and naturally being of a tender heart asked him the reason for his sorrow. "Nothing" was the reply, after which the master again and again pressed the servant, who now replied : " My lord. I had no son. Now in this stage of my calamities I had one by the favour of God. I think that under my meagre care he shall not live long. These thoughts brought on tears in my eyes, for which I beg your pardon. Every man must have his prescribed space of happiness or miseries in this world. You shall not trouble yourself about it." These words infused pity into the heart of the *Chetti.* He removed the anxieties of his servant by ordering his wife to take care of the female servant and her newborn baby. So, from that day, the prince was growing up in the *Chetti's* house. The king in return for the assistance of the kind *Chetti* served faithfully under him. Thus passed on three years, at the end of which time the queen gave birth to another son. The *Chetti* took that son also under his kind care. Thus both these boys were growing up in the *Chetti's* house. Their parents were doing some extra work also to bring something more for their children. In this way there passed several years till the princes attained their youth.

One day the second son spoke to his elder brother thus: "My dear brother! Our parents daily undergo so much of trouble on our account that, I think, it is now high time for us to be serviceable to them. We shall go out, somewhere or other, and after seeking some means to earn our livelihood, shall return to them." The elder agreed to it, and to have something in the way to eat when they started out, they went abegging in that town, and brought home two measures of rice; giving it to their mother, they spoke to her thus: "Dear mother, we have till now been mere children fed by your kindness. We have now reached our proper age. It is now time for us therefore to go out in search of adventures or any other means by which we can make our living. So, give us cooked these two measures of rice for our way. We must start tonight." The fond heart of the mother now dissuaded her sons from attempting such adventures. The sons persisted in going and spoke to her thus ;—"My dearest mother. No use of your dissuading us. We see no end to our poverty if we remain here with you. So give us leave. We shall find some means by which we can live a little honourably and then return to you." The mother was greatly pleased at her sons' words, and cooking the rice they brought, she gave them meals for the way, tied up in a small piece of cloth. They received the bundle and started. Journeying and journeying a long distance they reached a thick wood which the sun's rays had no power to pierce.

In that wood there was an extraordinary mango tree which yielded one fruit in every one hundred years. To get that fruit a sage was practising penance before that tree. The time the two princes entered the wood was the exact time for the falling down of the fruit. It dropped down from the tree before the sage, who was highly pleased at his fortune. For he thought the fruit to be almost his, and not suspecting anything wrong in that wood unfrequented by any beasts, birds, or men, he went to bathe, thinking it would be more religious to touch the fruit with a more clean body. No sooner had the sage left the tree than the princes happened to pass that way. The younger brother saw the fruit glittering like a gold ball, and going near it took it by, without being observed by his elder brother, untied his rice bundle, placed the fruit in the midst of the rice ball and tied it up us usual. They then proceeded on their journey.

The sage, after his bath, returned to the spot. His hundred years of attendance on the tree ended in nothing. The fruit was not there. He was in a confusion and did not know what to do. He saw some footsteps, and like a mad-man followed those marks, till quite out of breath he saw the princes. " My dear friends. Did you see a mango fruit on your way ? Oh, if you have it with you please give it to me. I shall give you in return whatever you want," uttered the sage to the princes, his speech faltering, his eyes whirling, and his whole body shaking as under the influence of ague. " My dear sir. Examine us. If at all we have the fruit you mention it must be with us. We stand here before you and are ready for any examination," said the princes. These very words removed the little doubt that the sage had about them. He now began to weep and wail and tear his long beard (which had not seen the razor for the last hundred years) as one who had lost some dear thing which he had no means of recovering. The princes pitied his distress. The younger pretended to sympathise with him, and separately asked him the reason for his sorrows. "My son. For this fruit I—after all—have waited for nothing. Oh wretch that I am, for having gone to bathe. I waited for full a hundred years. Not a day, a month or a year, but for full a hundred years, till after all it fell, but not to my benefit." " What speciality is there in that fruit that you should rue its loss so much," asked the prince. "My dear son. He who eats the cover of that fruit would at once become a king, and he who eats the seed shall drop gems from his mouth every time that he laughs," replied the sage. The princes seemed to take much compassion on his sorrow, and taking leave of him pursued their journey. At about evening time both the brothers were very much tired. They saw a stream running before them. The elder said to the younger to give him something to eat. The younger untied the bundle and gave him some rice and the cover of the miraculous mango fruit, himself eating the seed of it. After finishing their meals and drinking three or four handfuls of water they sat down in the sand to rest themselves awhile.

There was a city named Vîragha*ntâ*ma*ni*-nagara near that wood. The king of that city died childless, and in his deathbed called his ministers and spoke to them to send his crown-elephant with a flower-wreath in its trunk, and to choose him on whom the elephant throws the garland as his successor. The king, after giving these instructions, breathed his last.

The ministers, after finishing his funeral ceremonies, decorated the elephant and sent him out. Several went and stood before it, wishing to have the honour thrust upon themselves. That noble animal rejected them all and broke through the wood. Coming to the stream where the brothers sat, it threw the garland round the neck of the elder, and gathering him up by its trunk, placed him on its back and broke away. In the confusion of the sight of the elephant, the younger brother forgot all the powers of the mango fruit, and stood at a distance crying that his brother had been carried away by a wild elephant. The ministers of the Vîragha*nt*ânagara received the prince, their animal had brought from the wood, and installing him as their sovereign, obeyed him in all his commands. The elder brother never thought of his younger, and was leading an easy life in his realm.

Now to turn to the younger brother. He ran to a distance when the elephant approached his brother and carried him away. "Ah me. Did we avoid home and come to this wood only for this. There I see my brother being carried away by a wild elephant. Perhaps in an hour, I too must furnish the table of another wild animal." Thus thinking and shedding tears he walked fast and tried to avoid the wood before darkness overtook him. He at last reached an another town and went to the nearest house to beg his meals. That house was a dancing girl's, who seeing the features of the beggar, read royal parentage in his face. She welcomed him inside and requested him to bathe. Then she set before him the sweetest food to which the hungry prince did full justice. The dancing-girl had an old mother at home. That woman too discovering royal traces in the countenance of her guest secretly instructed her daughter never to leave the side of the prince and to be always acting obediently to him. The young woman did accordingly. One evening while talking pleasantly, the young dancing-girl applied her hands to his hip and he laughed. No sooner had he opened his mouth in laughter than lo ! there fell heaps of gems from out of it. The mother and daughter were astonished at what they saw, and enquired of their guest the reason of the phenomena. He now related everything connected with himself, and concluded that as the mango seed was in his stomach the gems fell out so very freely. These cunning women made the prince laugh again and again and filled every nook and corner of their house with these precious stones. Their avarice did not stop at this alone. They now wanted somehow or other to get out the seed from his belly, and that one of themselves should swallow it up. After a few days the old hag in very kind words spoke to the prince about his falling ill often and wished him to take a dose of purgative. He consented, not knowing the evil intentions of these women. They now gave him a very strong pill, powerful to purge out anything from his stomach. After one or two motions the seed too came out, which the woman took up, washed, and scenting it swallowed. The prince not being able to bear the severity of the medicine fell in a swoon. The wretched women after the attainment of their intention brought him out of their house and threw him on the pyal, shutting and bolting the door. At about midday the prince came back to his senses and knocked at the door. He knocked with all his might and tore his throat; for all that, no voice replied from inside. The neighbours came out hearing his call, and pitying his state gave him some gruel. After calming his appetite a little he went to the tank of that town to wash himself. While there, he saw at a short distance from him an old *Sanyâsi* breathing his last. That sage was surrounded by four of his disciples, to whom he was speaking thus: "My students. I have been keeping with me for a long time four objeets as dear to me as my life. They are a bag which yields to one whatever he may want, a cup which serves you new cooked meals whenever you request it, a cudgel which would belabour all your enemies if you aim it at them, and a pair of sandals which takes you to wherever you wish to go. First entomb me and then take these properties to yourselves." The sage breathed his last, and his students buried him near that very place under a tree. They then quarrelled over the four things as to which student should take which, and wanted to choose an umpire to settle their dispute. They all placed them in the hollow of an old tamarind tree and went to the town in search of an umpire.

The prince was observing from a distance what was passing near him, and as soon as the students went away in search of the umpire, he went to that spot and himself took possession of those rare articles; concluding with himself that unless he took the permission of the departed soul of the dead sage, these articles would produce no miracles to him, he went to that *Sanyâsi's* grave and there said, "My respected *Sanyâsi,* your students fought over these wealths and threw them away carelessly in the hollow of a tree, I have taken them up and with your kind permission wish to use them." And the following answer came out of the grave. "You did very well in taking possession of these rare objects, which will prove more valuable to you than to those envious fellows." The prince heard the reply in joy and thought that everything went on favourably with him. Wishing to test the truth of the cup he went into a grove and sitting down before it requested the cup to serve him meals. All on a sudden one thousand different curry stuffs, soups, pickles and varieties of rice were placed before him by unknown hands. He heartily partook of them all, and not forgetting his affection to the faithless dancing-women he approached their house. The old hag saw, even at a distance, the prince with his cheerful face. He also had in his hand a bag, a cup and other things. She therefore approached him with a pleasing face and spoke to him thus :—"My dear son. The pill that I gave you did not agree with your health. When you began to purge too much, I was afraid, and being a female left you outside locking up the doors. You must excuse us for it, and come again into my house. The prince who was young and hence blind in his attachment to the daughter of the old hag came in and began to live with them as before. One day while the prince was sleeping inside he found the room very sultry, and so going into the garden adjoining the house he placed the bag before himself and said, " May there spring forth a palace," and accordingly a palace came forth into existence. "May there be silver sofas with beds of silk." And accordingly these two sprang up. The prince went into his newly created palace and slept on the silk cushions created by himself.

When the day dawned the dancing-women were astonished to see a mansion in their garden. They saw nothing to that effect in the previous evening. Their joy knew no bounds. They ran in, and still to their greater joy found their prince sleeping in a rich sofa placed in the midst of it. They awakened him and requested him to tell them how he made the palace spring up. The prince who dreamt the whole world to be as true as he was, revealed to them the bag and its powers, as well as the other three rare objects—the meals-serving cup, the swift sandals, and the enemy-belabouring cudgel. The dancing-girls pretended to be extremely delighted, but ever since they heard the extraordinary powers of the four rare objects the prince had with him, their minds were devising plans within themselves to take them away without his knowledge.

One day when the prince was in a pleasant mood the old-woman came to his side and said: "My son, you know that I have an only daughter whose affection is wholly placed in you. Of late I have long been searching out the cause for it, till yesterday I heard from a soothsayer that we have not performed a vow to a certain god whose temple is situated in an island in the midst of the Indian Sea. If we go there and perform the vow, then, everything will go on right with my daughter and your dear wife if I may so call her.

She spoke only these words and put on a dismal face as if she did not know a way by which she could reach the island. The prince now replied "Fear not old woman ; procure all the necessaries for the vow. We shall go over tomorrow to that island." The old woman procured everything for the *pûjâ*. The morning came. The prince mounted his sandals and asked the dancing women, mother and daughter, to hold firm his hands on both sides. They did accordingly. The power of the sandals raised the three into the skies and flying, they reached a certain uninhabited island, surrounded by seas on all sides. The old woman spread all her vessels and provisions that she brought in a bundle in the preparation to cook. She asked the prince to fetch some fuel for her kindling the hearth.

The prince went away in search of firewood and was collecting some rotten timbers at a distance. With his usual confidence in those that speak kind to him he had left behind with the two women his sandals and other articles. As soon as he went to bring the fuels the old and wretched woman mounted the sandals and took hold of the other things belonging to the prince. She asked her daughter to hold her tight which she did accordingly. "May I reach my house with my daughter," thought she, and in a few *ghatikâs* she was in her home.

After they had left the island the prince returned with a big bundle of firewood over his head to see them. To his great dismay he did not find them there. "I must accuse my own foolishness in having trusted these cunning females even after knowing them once," thought he, and much overcome by hunger he got up on a mango tree to taste some fruits that hung on its branches and appease his hunger. That tree had four branches and four only; each of these branches was studded with fruits, ripe and yellow like gold; he tasted the fruit on one of the branches. He was turned into a black ape. He next tasted a fruit in the second branch. His monkey body disappeared and he all on a sudden became a kite. He tasted a fruit from the third branch. He became an old woman. Lastly he tasted the fruit from the fourth branch, and he became again a young prince. He was extremely pleased. He tied up in the four corners of his cloth some fruits of each sort. Praying God for having showed him the way to get out of that uninhabited island, he ate the fruit of the second branch. He was all of a sudden transformed into a kite. Catching the bundle in his leg, he soared into the sky, and flying all the way crossed the sea, and before evening reached the city of the dancing-women. He went to the old woman's house, and entering the garden in the form of a kite flew into the palace which he had formerly created by the powers of his magic bag. He tasted the fruit which would convert him to his original form and became a prince. Keeping under his head the heavy bundle with the four varieties of fruits, he slept in that palace for the night. Though he was hungry he never went to the dancing-women, wishing that they should find him out. He had not to wait till then ; for the old woman and her daughter came to sleep in that mansion during the first watch of that very night. They saw their prince sleeping there. Thinking that it was their imagination, and that the prince could not have come inside, they went near and satisfied themselves that it was their own prince whom they had deceived in the island that very morning. "This is a very powerful prince. I must somehow kill him," thought the old hag, and again she awakened him and spoke to him as follows;—"My dear son. May Paramêsvara be praised for having given you back to us. Just when you left us this morning in the island to bring firewood, we saw before us a fierce tiger, and being afraid of our lives, flew home in your sandals leaving you to your own fate. May God give you a long life even a year more than the full hundred years allotted to every human being in this world. What are those in your bundles ?" The prince put on a smiling countenance, as one who sincerely believed the accounts the old woman gave him and replied, "My dearest mother. What of that ? Life is dear to every one. It was well in your part to have escaped the claws of the tigor. My one thousand *Namaskâras* for to the god Paramêsvara for his having rescued you. I am not at all sorry for your having left me in the wood. I saw a fine mango tree and in collecting fruits to give you I was late. Now let us eat some of these fruits. You shall see how nice they taste." So saying he gave an ape fruit to the young dancing girl, and a kite fruit to the old woman, and himself took the fruit of the fourth branch. The three were tasting their fruits when lo! the young woman became an ape and the old woman a kite. The prince remained in his own form; he now caught hold of his ape and kite and searching their house took back his bag, cup, cudgel and sandals. Overcome by hunger he placed the cup before him and asked his dinner. The cup now served him all rare dishes. He ate his bellyfull and slept in that house that night. Next morning he rose up, and assuming the disguise of a beggar went to town after town begging his meals and performing tricks with his ape and kite. After a few days he reached a big town, and meeting with a cabbage seller enquired the name of the king of that place. He said that he did not know his name, nor that any one there knew it, and that the crown elephant brought an unknown person from the wood a year ago who was consecreated as a king. Intending to see him by force and not dreading any punishment from the royal hands, he turned out a stubborn beggar and began to demand five pagodas from each *bâzâr*. The *bâzâr* men would not give, and the beggar would not go without his money. This matter reached the ears of the king, who sent his ministers to bring him the beggar. But he would not come. "What has a beggar to do with a king. Go away," was the reply to those that came to call him. They returned with this reply to the king who was greatly astonished at the beggar and came to see him in person. Even from a distance he found it to be his younger brother. Not liking to see him in the middle of the immense crowd that had already gathered round him, he ordered from a distance that the bâzârmen and others should give the five pagodas as the beggar demanded. The beggar too recognised his elder brother and shed tears of joy in secret. Collecting his due from the shops, the younger brother went to a choultry, finished his bath, ablutions, &c., and presented what he collected to the poor Brâhmans. Then placing his extraordinary cup before him he demanded meals and finished his dinner. Then he laid himself down to sleep a little.

In the palace the king could not rest quite after he met his long lost brother. He explained his birth and adventures to his minister, and sent him to bring to his side his younger brother. The minister found him sleeping, and rousing him from his slumber, told him that he had come from his elder brother to take him to the palace. The younger shed tears of joy again and followed the minister, taking along with him his ape, kite and bundle. The brothers met and recognised each other. They flew into each others arms and remained silent for a time. Each related his adventures to the other. The younger brother showed him the ape and the kite, saying that they were the young and the old dancing women. The elder brother was so highly pleased at this younger brother's adventures that he called forth an assembly and made him again to relate them there. Before them all he gave two fruits of the fourth branch to his ape and kite and converted them back to their former shapes. On the next day he gave a strong doze of purgative to the young dancing girl and took back his gem-shedding-mango-seed from her stomach. He then drove them away to their native country.

The elder ruled over that city. The two brothers thought of their parents, and by the power of the sandals reached them. They were in extreme want and were cursing their sons for their not having returned to them. What was their joy then when their sons reached them. The sons related their adventures to their parents, who were extremely delighted at them.

The elder took them to his kingdom. The younger marched to the country of Piranda, his paternal dominions that had been taken away by an enemy. He sent his cudgel against his enemy and conquered the country. He ruled over it. His brother reigned over the kingdom in which the elephant consecrated him, and the parents lived sometimes with their first son and sometimes with their second son. "Must not a prince resembling one of them marry thee my dear !"

Thus Buddhichâturya finished his sixth story. The day dawned,, and they both went after their respective duties.

[MORAL.—This story illustrates that the right shall always go to the right and greedy hunters after impossibilities shall meet with disappointment. The sage who after having renounced the world sought after the mango fruit, and the greedy disciples of the sage, who fought about their master's property lost them to the deserving prince. There is also another moral in this tale. The treacherous dancing-women being punished in the end, proves that treachery shall always be punished.]

SEVENTH STORY.

On the night of the seventh day the minister's son as usual finished his supper at an early hour, and with his bridegroom's dress, scents and ornaments entered the bed room. The elder of the princesses who had her turn for that night came after him chewing betel-leaf and carrying in her hand a platter containing sweetmeats and fruits for her lord. She was ornamented with the choicest ornaments and dressed in the finest silk. As was her custom she sang some love notes on her guitar, and being overcome by love approached the bed of her lord, who, wishing to put down her desire by a fine story, began as follows :—

"Listen thou the gem of womankind! I have a short story to tell thee, and soon as that is over we shall retire to rest." The princess consenting, the minister's son thus commenced :—

There was a city named Amarâvatî in the extreme north. The king of that city was called A*l*akiyasingarâja. He had a minister named *S*ubhamantrî. Both these had reigned over their kingdom in peace and prosperity for a very long time, enjoying all the happiness of a good rule; but, unfortunately, both of them had no children. But they had made this agreement that if God favoured them with children they should have them married to each other if one of them happened to be a male and the other a female. Several months passed away after this.

One day while the king and his minister were sitting in the council hall, a maid servant from the harem came and told them that the queen and the minister's wife had shewn signs of preguancy in their body. Their delight knew no bounds, they thought that their repeated vows had at last their intended effect; after the usual course the queen and the minister's wife underwent their confinement, and the former brought to bed a tortoise and the latter—the wife of the minister —a beautiful daughter, splendid like a hundred suns in her bodily lustre. The news of the birth of such a child to the king spread throughout the town, and throughout the world. The king, though vexed at heart, considered it as the result of his sins in his former life. But he never lessened his care towards his tortoise son. The minister also brought up his daughter with all the cares due to an only child born to one in his position in his old age. The minister afterwards had two daughters more in course of time.

The tortoise prince was now thirteen years old as was also the first daughter of the minister. She had attained her maturity in her eleventh year, but lived as a virgin in the harem of her father's palace. One day when the king was in conversation with his queen, he heaved a deep sigh and said, "Alas! Our misfortune! Had we been blessed with a son instead of a tortoise, we would have been in a different state of circumstances, than that in which we are now. Of what use can a tortoise be to us in this stage of our life—our old age. In our younger days, I had taken an oath from the minister to give his daughter in marriage to our son. There is his first daughter who is now fit for wedding, spending her virginhood in her harem; how can I go and demand her hands on behalf of our tortoise son?" Here the king's sorrow overcame his strength of mind, and he sobbed into tears which would have struck pity even into the heart of an unfeeling stone. The tortoise prince who overheard the conversation of his parents by their side, and who had never till then opened his lips, began now to reply in human voice, striking amazement into the hearts of his father and mother.

"My dear and respected parents, if such an agreement as you were now speaking of, had taken place between yourself and the minister, why should you be in suspicion whether he should keep to it or not, because God has favoured you with this unhappy me—a tortoise son. Better now to go to the minister's palace and request his daughter to be given in wedding to me." The king was filled with wonder at the human voice and sound reasoning of his tortoise son, and concluding that some wonder must underlie all these prodigies, went to the minister's palace to make the said demand. He pointed out at length the original agreement of the minister, who in return only laughed and exclaimed, "My lord, true that there took place such an agreement between us; and I would be the greatest fool on earth, if I did not agree to keep to our engagement, if you had given birth to a prince; may Brahmâ be cursed and become temple-less for his having given you a tortoise. What would the world think of me if I were to give my daughter in marriage to a tortoise prince?" The king hung down his head, overcome by sorrow and shame at the birth of an unnatural son to him.

The first daughter of the minister who overheard what passed between her father and king, came out of her room and in sweet and silvery words thus humbly addressed them:—"My dear father. Why should you thus incur the displeasure of his majesty the king by refusing my hand to the prince? Just hear my vow; eversince I came to know myself I have taken an oath to marry only him who would fetch me the divine *pâri-*

jâta[1], be he a tortoise or a prince, I do not care much for it ; if he only brings the flower, he wins my hand ; if any other brings it, the prince must give up all hope of me ; therefore kindly send word to the prince, that if he succeeds in fetching me the *pârijâta* I am his wife."

The king returned home admiring all the way the sweet and respectful words in which the minister's daughter clothed her argument. He intimated her vow to the prince, who seemed to be much pleased at it. The son wanted his father to ascertain whether she would have any objection in case he successfully brought the flower. Again the father went and again he returned, with his repeated promise that she would surely marry him, if he only brought the flower.

The prince now asked his father to take him to the nearest sea and throw him in it. The father though fond of his son, was compelled by confidence to act according to his wish ; accordingly the tortoise prince was set afloat on the waves of the nearest sea ; he went on swimming and swimming for days and weeks till he crossed the seven mighty

---

(1) *Pârijâta*—The coral tree. Erythrina Indica. These flowers, blossom always in the early morning between two and four o'clock. This tree is therefore always planted by Hindu gentlemen on any open space near their bed-rooms.

oceans and reached the *Udayagiri* [2] mountain on the other side. There on the way of the sun, he laid himself down for rest.

The day was just dawning. Aru*n*a [3] had then taken up the whip to conduct the sun's chariot through its wonted diurnal course. The green steeds [4] yoked to the car suddenly, most unaccountedly stopped at the sight of the tortoise in the way. The charioteer in front and Sûrya-bhagavân inside were greatly amazed and came down to examine the cause. The presence of a tortoise in the road made their wonder doubly great. The Sun-god now asked the tortoise the reason of his barring his way, who most humbly thus began :—" My most respected God who gave me birth in this world. Was it proper on your part to have made a tortoise in the woombs of a human mother. I have come all along the way

(2) *Udayagiri*.—The rising mountain. In Hindû mythology the East mountain behind which the sun rises.

(3) Aru*n*a—In Hindû mythology the charioteer of the Sun-God. He is the brother of Garu*d*a and is human above his hip and stone below, by reason of his mother having broken the egg in which he was born before the embryo reached its development.—*Mahâbhârat.*

(4) The sun's horses are supposed to be seven in number perhaps representing the seven days of the week and to be green in colour perhaps representing his morning rays.

to lodge my complaint in your holy-presence, and it is now your holiness's duty to point me out a good course for this wretched life of mine." With these words the tortoise closed its eyes and shedding tears of joy for his having met the Sun-god broke into one thousand and eight praises of that deity of the day.

Sûryabhagavân who was greatly pleased at these spontaneous praises in his honour, thus replied: "Tortoise, you once committed a great crime in your former life by placing a tortoise shell on the head of a *Rishi* (sage) practising penance in a secluded forest. He in anger cursed you with a tortoise birth in this life: but we are now much pleased by the one-thousand and eight praises you have just uttered in our honour. We have now given you the boon of a human-body splendid and beautiful like ours. Stand aloof from our way." No sooner were these words uttered than lo! the tortoise prince was no longer a nasty reptile. His body shone like Cupid's, and he rose up with his palms joined over his head, and humbly prostrating himself before that god, again begged—"My most benign God, I request of your supreme holiness, to give me the power of my assuming or renouncing the tortoise shape whenever I like it; and your holiness's assistance in conducting me to the divine *pârijâta*." The Sun-god granted him his first request and said; "At a short distance from this place is a fine little garden near which there lives a hermit. If you go to him and secure his favour, you may get the flower." Thus saying, the Sun-god drove off hastily, and our prince went in search of the sage whom he easily found out. That sage was used to open his eyes for every (*yâma*) watch. The prince waited before him to see him opening his eyes which he did in his usual time. He was astonished to see in that forest where there was no sign of human habitation, a beautiful prince standing in front of h ima nd questioned the latter as to who he was.

The prince now prostrated himself before the sage with the eight members of his body touching the ground, and informed him that he had come in search of the *pârijâta* flower, and that he must oblige him by pointing out the course to it. The hermit was astonished at the address of the person that stood before him and said, "My son, I know nothing of it; at a short distance before me there sits another sage who opens his eyes once in every two watches: if you go to him you will gain your desire. The prince accordingly went and stood before the second sage; he opened his eyes in his turn and was astonished to see like the first sage, a prince before him in that forest, untrodden by human feet. The prince explained to him the cause of his coming there, to which the second sage replied: "My son, like the first sage who conducted you here, I too do not know how you may obtain that flower ; but at a short distance before me is a third sage undergoing penance ; if you go to him you may attain your object.

The prince went again to the third sage who was in the habit of opening his eyes in every third watch. That hermit too was equally astonished at the prince's daring and admiring his boldness thus spoke: "My friend, I am sorry that I cannot do much for the fulfilment of your desire. But I can point out the way by which if you are skilful you can attain it. At a little distance from this place there is a bathing tank beautifully situated in a fair garden. Far off from the tank is a mango tree and a Ganésa [5] temple. The divine maidens are used to come and bathe in that pond every day. You must go there in advance of them, and hide yourself in a place where they will not easily see you. The maidens will take off their dress and leaving it on the shore, go into water ; you must slyly emerge from your concealment and taking up the cloth of one of them, fly towards the direction of the temple. The maiden to whom belongs the garb will follow close at your heels, uttering "Look behind, my beauty in front,

(5) The lord of *Ganas* who are the bodyguards of Siva. The first son of *Siva* and Parvati, and always invoked at the commencement of all rites and prayers.

my beauty behind, turn back and take a look at." Do for heaven's sake, never turn back and look at her, for if you do, you will be turned into a stone; but fly towards the Ganêsa temple and bolt the door behind. Unable to follow you in, she will come and knock at the gates, and request you to give back her cloth; you had better request her in turn not to curse you and to bring you the required flower. She will agree to it. Then only open the door and give her her cloth."

The prince followed the sage's advice to the very letter and ran away with her cloth to the temple, where, after extracting several oaths from her as to his safety and to the *pârijâta* flower, gave back her garment. The divine maid was won over by the beauty of the prince when she saw him giving her back her cloth; and she had every reason to be bewitched, for we saw the Sun-god gave almost the whole of his beauty and lustre to the tortoise prince. She took a hasty embrace of him, and requesting him to wait in the temple for the flower, returned to her sisters. They enquired into the fate of the thief. She satisfied their curiosity by telling them she converted that dishonest individual into a stone. They then went to their respective abodes in the heavens.

The maid who had met the prince constructed a (*Vînâ*) guitar with the assistance of the divine carpenter; she also gathered a basketful of *pârijâta* flowers to be given to the prince. Taking these in her hand with all delicious dishes for a sumptuous supper, she approached the Ganêsa temple. The sun had already set. The prince overcome by fatigue and hunger fell down to sleep. Just at midnight, he was awakened by the maiden whom he had seen that morning, who now spread before him all sorts of divine dishes for his supper, to which the prince did full justice. She then raised up by her powers a sweet bower in the wild moonlight, where they both slept during the remaining part of the night. Just before sun-rise, before leaving him, she gave him the divine guitar and the basketful of flowers and addressed him thus: "My dearest prince. Instead of a flower which you asked me to bring, I have here a basketful, which you may give to the minister's daughter. And this guitar is the means of communication between us. Just play upon it, whenever you are hungry, and wherever you may be, I shall be with you with all the dishes for your dinner; only do not forget this poor me." Thus instructing, the divine maiden returned to her celestial abode.

The prince, in addition to the accomplishment of his object, won the heart of a divine damsel, and returned successfully with the basketful of flowers and guitar to the third sage. The sage had just closed his eyes; it was nearly midday when the prince reached him: so hunger was pinching him severely, to appease which he played upon the guitar. The divine damsel with celestial viands for his dinner, came to that hermitage and served him meals. The third sage, when he opened his eyes, saw what passed before him at a little distance, and spoke to himself thus,—"This prince must be a clever youth; in addition to the accomplishment of his object, he has brought the love of a divine damsel. The guitar seems to be the means of her company. I must by some means or other secure it. Enough of this penance which keeps me away from all worldly pleasures." Thus thought the sage, and his vile desire at once took away from him all his high powers. For what man can aim at sublimity after once becoming feeble in his mind. So, the powers of closing his eyes, for three watches were gone. The prince, after finishing his dinner, approached the sage, and in the sweet conversation that followed, related to him his adventures, taking care not to speak a word of his guitar affair and his having won the love of the divine damsel. The worldly passions reigning supreme in his mind, the hermit thus spoke to the prince: "Dear son, of what use is this guitar to you. You are a prince commanding several carpenters who could give you finer musical instruments than this crooked one. I have in my possession a club of extraordinary powers that would put to death a vast army of enemies in the twinkling of an eye. That club I procured by my several years of penance, and would much like to exchange it for your guitar. In my opinion we would both be gainers by such an exchange. As a prince the club would do you mighty services in the army of your enemies, and the guitar would be the best companion for my weary hours in this solitary forest." The position of the prince was most delicate. The question of giving the guitar or not, the prince found it difficult to solve. If he refused, the sage must think him to be most ungrateful; if he gave, he gave away with it the love of a divine damsel. These thoughts passed over his mind for a few moments; and at last by necessity of self-respect, he parted with it for the club. With a heavy heart and a mournful face, the prince took leave of the sage, and with his basket and an awkward club instead of a lovely guitar in his hand, he slowly pursued his way towards the direction of the second sage.

When he was just out of the sight of the third sage, the club jumped down on the ground, and in sweet words addressed thus his new master: "My most noble lord! That old beggar, my old master, has given me no food for the past generation. To wreak my vengeance, I must now go and murder him first." These words fell like nectar into the ears of the prince. He at once ordered it upon its dreadful duty pronouncing over it the requisite *mantra* (incantation) in which he had been duly instructed by a third sage. The club set out with great anger and in one stroke smashed the head of the old hermit into a jelly and cleaning itself in the nearest tank of the blood, returned to the Prince with the guitar. Thus by the kindness of the club, the prince secured again his guitar, and with all these acquirements, pursued his way to the second sage. This hermit was in meditation and so had his eyes closed. The prince not to be idle meanwhile and suffering from hunger, tuned his instrument. The divine maid as usual appeared there with several varieties of dishes, to which the prince and his cudgel companion did full justice. While they were in their feast, the second sage opened his eyes, and to his wonder and amazement, saw the prince had successfully returned with the divine damsel. Thinking in his mind that the guitar must be the cause of it, he wanted somehow to induce the prince to give it up to him. By this time they had finished their dinner, and the divine maiden, after her business was over, left that place for her heavenly abode. The prince now approached the sage, and related to him all his adventures in which, as usual, he omitted all mention of the guitar and the heavenly maid. And the sage too, not to awaken any curiosity, never touched on the subject. Now the second sage, whose fate was drawing near, addressed the prince thus—"My dear son! I have a magic purse with me which, if you handle with a certain incantation, supplies you with everything and anything that you want. From the time that you first met me, I had thought of giving it to you, and I would now much like to exchange it for your guitar." The prince who laughed with himself at the evil passions of the old age, and thinking that he had not much time in the world, received the magic bag and took leave of him. Soon as he walked a little bit, he sent his club after the sage, who was duly belaboured and transported to the sufferings of the horrible hell for his evil intentions. The club, after washing itself in the nearest water, returned with the guitar to its master who welcomed it with inexpressible joy. The prince now went to the first sage, and finding him with his eyes shut, wanted to summon the heavenly maid to give him something for his stomach. He tuned the instrument. The sage on hearing music in that forest, opened his eyes; wonder of wonders, he saw a most beautiful damsel of divine origin serving meals to the youthful prince, who had left him but four days ago in search of the divine *pârijâta*. It was easy for this sage to conclude that the guitar was the means of summoning the maid. So when the damsel disappeared and the prince came to him, to relate his success, the sage wanted by sweet words to get possession of his *vînâ*. "My dear son, for a prince like yourself, a *vînâ* is no luxury ; when you will it. you would get it; but for a hermit, like me, living, in a wilderness unknown to the human world, it is a rarity. I have with me a pair of sandals, over which if you place your feet and think on the place you wish to go to, you will reach it in the twinkling of an eye ; if you would like the exchange, I will give them to you, taking back in return your *vînâ*." Thus the cunning sage, as if he did not quite like the exchange, spoke to the prince who, as he never feared the loss of his guitar as long as he had the club, readily consented with sweet smile and courteous words The sage sipped water thrice,[6] taught him the proper incantations and gave him the sandals, receiving the *vînâ* in return. The prince proceeded a few steps and gave the commission to his ever-faithful club to fetch him back his guitar, which it did after sending the usurper of it to the other world. Thus the tortoise prince in his adventure of bringing the divine *pârijâta*, exchanged his nasty shape for a most lovely human form, won the love of a divine damsel, got from her a guitar to summon her when he wished it, and made himself master of a dreadful club, a magic purse, and a wonderful pair of sandals. With

(6) Before beginning any prayer Hindû high caste persons have always to sip the water thrice.

these he reached the shore, and before commencing his voyage wanted to take leave of the heavenly maid; he tuned his instrument, which brought her at once to him. It was just the time of sun-set. The maid as usual had come with all sorts of delicious viands, that the celestial world is rich in, to feed her affectionate lord. The prince to show her that he was not inferior in his own supply of delicate dishes, opened up his magic purse with the proper incantations, and commissioned it to serve before them dishes unknown in this as well as in the other world. Sweetmeats, puddings, curry-stuffs, varieties of cakes prepared in varieties of ways, were placed before them by unknown hands. The maid now discovered that her lord was no ordinary person; after their meals they retired to rest in a flower pavilion that sprung up by the power of the divine damsel. There the prince related to her everything about him—his extraordinary birth, the vow between his father and the minister, the vow of the latter's daughter, his starting after the *pârijâta* flower, his adventure with the Sun-god, his acquaintance with the three sages, his cloth theft, his acquisition of herself and of the club, purse, and the sandals, after dealing death to their respective possessors who unlawfully coveted her: every one of his adventures awakened her admiration for the prince who now spoke thus—"My dear love! I must leave all these objects in your care for a time. I intend keeping all these, except the basket, in the hollow of the baniyan tree, over which I place you, as the guard. I will return in my original shape with this basketful of flowers to the minister's daughter, and celebrate my wedding with her as a tortoise. Till I come here and take these back, you must oblige me by taking care of them." She consented. The prince taking leave of her assumed the tortoise shape. He had power to do this by the boon granted to him by the Sun-god. Holding up the *pârijâta* basket in his mouth, he patiently swam across the seven oceans and reached the shore nearest his father's kingdom.

The tortoise with his heavy weight reached Amarâvatî, and placing the basket before his father spoke to him thus : "My dearest father. Here is a basketful of *pârijatâs* instead of one which the minister's daughter wanted. Take these to her and return home after fixing the wedding day."

The king went to the minister, and placing before him the basket which his tortoise son had brought from the divine world, reminded him of his daughter's vow ; and she, quite amazed at the successful accomplishment of a most difficult undertaking by a tortoise, took it no longer to be such, though it appeared so ; she consented full willingly for her marriage with the prince. An auspicious *muhûrta* was fixed ; bridegrooms for the other two daughters were settled to be married on the same day; wedding cards flew in all directions. Thousands of royal guests assembled in Amarâvatî, some to grace the feast, some out of close relationship, some from pure formality, and several out of curiosity to see a human maid being wedded to a tortoise prince.

The wedding hall was most splendidly decorated as befitting the occasion. Three planks had been spread with three sacrificial fires in front of them. All the necessary *mantrâs* (incantations) were undergone in their order. The priest now asked the three bridegrooms to tie up the marriage badge round the necks of their wives. The two younger did their duty with no difficulty; but how could a tortoise do that while it had no human hands; but to the amazement of all it took the marriage badge into its mouth, and climbing up to the shoulders of the minister's eldest daughter, and passing the cord round her neck, secured one end of it in the back part of her gown (Tam. *Ravikkai*—Hindi; *Chauli*) and knotted up the ends most neatly. The whole hall was astonished. "Surely that is no tortoise, see how systematically it knotted the ends of the cord of the marriage badge," said one to the other; some said that the tortoise must be a prince in that reptile shape. Thus went on the chatting in the hall. Then the Brâhmans celebrated the marriages. The minister rewarded all the guests who graced the marriage occasion with suitable gifts. Three bed-chambers were kept ready for the three pairs. The last two daughters of the minister rejoiced in the company of their husbands; the eldest—the wife of the tortois prince—pined away in sorrow at her unnatural lord.

The tortoise prince, after finding his wife sound asleep, left his room, crawled to the coast, and fell down into the sea and reached the baniyan tree on the other side where he had left his instruments. He there called upon his club and asked it to remove his tortoise shell, which it did accordingly. He then played upon his violin, which brought him at once his divine damsel. She, the heavenly maid, came to the baniyan tree with all sorts of delicate dishes, fed him well, and slept with him. Before morning the prince left his sweet tree and returned to his marriage bed-chamber in the shape of a tortoise and pretended sleep in his usual place. Thus there passed some days.

The two brothers-in-law of the tortoise prince, *i. e.*, the two husbands of the minister's two younger daughters, wished to start on a hunting expedition and made great preparations for it. They chose the swiftest horses from their father-in-law's stalls. The best hunters of the kingdom were summoned. The sharpest weapons were chosen. The nobles of the country made up their mind for a gay hunt with the royal son-in-law. The tortoise prince too was not idle. He called his wife to his side and ordered her to bring him from her father a horse and a sword. She replied, "My dearest husband. The world will laugh if you start also for the hunt. Some puny creature would crush you down, and you would be of no use in the world. So kindly give up the idea and take pity on the cries of a poor and faithful wife." These words, though they came out most sincerely from the heart of the wife of the tortoise prince, were enough in themselves to provoke him. "Go as you are bid; and never open your lips," vociferated the enraged husband, and the wife accordingly went to the minister and made the demand. He was extremely disgusted at the mockery of his unnatural son-in-law, and with an avowed object of ridiculing him sent a lame bandy-legged horse and a blunt sword.

The dutiful wife brought these to her husband, who now asked her to tie him up on the horse with cords. She did as was ordered. The whole gentry of the town went out to hunt. The tortoise prince too went bound up on the horse tight by a rope. He followed the party to the wood. After showing himself in the crowd he escaped by a thick avenue to the sea shore, and there by the powers of incantation, he with his limped horse crossed the ocean and reached his baniyan tree. There he called upon his club, who now undid all his knots. Leaving the horse there, he took hold of his club, and mounting his miraculous sandals returned to the wood where the hunt went on. He strewed white ashes most profusely over his body and stood in the midst of the amazing crowd, who took him to be the great god Sâmbamûrti himself. Nor had they any reason to think him to be otherwise. His sudden presence in the midst of a thick forest with sandals down his feet, club in his hand, and the divine holy ashes over his body gave him the true majesty of the great god Mahêsvara. The other two sons-in-law of the minister were extremely pleased at what they saw, and mistaking their disguised brother-in-law for the Great God fell down at his feet. The tortoise prince in his divine disguise freely blessed them all, and asked them in return the tip of their last fingers of their hands, and they in their devotion had no hesitation to give the demanded bits ; with much game and a proud heart that they had seen in the woods Mahêsvara they returned to their father-in-law who welcomed them with great joy. The tortoise prince too returned in the twinkling of an eye to his baniyan tree, where he concealed his treasures. Before putting on the tortoise shell he collected in the saddle of his horse the birds that fell down dazzled at the lustre of his body to produce these sylvan subjects as his game before his father-in-law. Then he resumed his tortaise shape and called upon his club to knot him up tightly which it accordingly did. After these preparations he slowly crossed the sea and returned home where his wife was very anxiously waiting, perhaps with even more anxiety than her sisters.

What was her joy when she saw her husband coming up slowly on the back of his lame horse not empty handed but with such game as was in his power to gather as she thought. She slowly freed him from his knots, enquired into his health and took in with a cheerful face the birds he had brought. "Take them to your father and place them before him as what I have brought," said the husband, and the wife did accordingly. But the minister most humbly asked his eldest daughter to cook that game for her husband only. So, she returned vexed and ashamed; but this never lessened her love towards her husband, however unnatural he may be to others. So she prepared several varieties of dishes out of the game he brought and fed him most sumptuously.

After some days again the two sons-in-law of the minister started for a second chase. Again the tortoise prince went and appeared before them like the God Mahêsvara and returned with their rings.

After a couple of years after the marriage all on a sudden a fierce enemy invaded the kingdom of Amarâvatî. A*l*agiyasingam had no son except the tortoise prince whom he thought quite useless for coping with the enemy. So he came to the minister and addressed him thus: "My dear *mantrî*. A fierce enemy has now come to break our neck. I have not been favoured by God with a son to stand by me on this occasion. So I request you to send your two sons-in-law to the battle-field. Them I regard as my own sons." The minister agreed to it and made all the arrangements necessary for it. The tortoise prince wanted also to enlist its services. The king and the minister laughed at the idea; but it would not yield, and so they left it to its own fate. There was a great consternation throughout the town. A fierce enemy with a vast army extending like the ocean had invaded Amarâvatî. The two latter sons-in-law of the minister mustered their pretty force, relying on the assistance of their favourable deity Mahêsa. The tortoise prince too marched on towards the enemies. Every one laughed with himself when he saw the tortoise prince. And he, before he started, gave notice to his wife to have seven tubs of very hot water for his bath on his return from the troubles of the day. A fierce battle ensued. The tortoise prince disappeared all on a sudden, and in a minute returned to the side of his brothers-in-law with his club, which understanding the sumptuous feast in preparation for it elated with joy. They now fell before him and said, " Most supreme Mahêsvara ; we are all your dogs. Grant victory to us and save us this time also " The tortoise prince now gave the orders to the club, which did most horrible work in the phalanx of the inimical army. In a minute the whole army lay dead on the ground. The enemy ran away. The brothers-in-law sounding their drums of triumph returned in glory to the immense joy of the old king and minister. But the tortoise prince did not return at that time. Some thought that he must have been cracked to pieces by the belabourings of Mahêsvara's cudgel ; joy of joy he also was seen slowly returning. His wife welcomed him. He got down from his horse, and after a brief rest wanted the tubs of hot water to be kept ready for his bath. He also asked his wife to leave the room bolting the door, and to allow none inside till he finished his bath. She obeyed the orders of her husband. But curiosity, especially to a female, is very great. A tortoise to bathe ! and that in seven tubs of hottest water thought she, and watched what went on inside the room through a slit in the door.

The tortoise now removed its shell. The wife was stunned by the lustre that issued from the body underneath and fell down in a swoon. She rose up, and again saw whether she had not been deceived; what was her joy to see her husband no more a repulsive tortoise, but the most beautiful young man that God ever created in the world. She flew secretly to the spot where the shell was kept, and cracking it to pieces burnt the bits.

The husband had by this time finished his bath. He looked for the shell. It was missing. He called upon his wife, who stood trembling at her mistake, begging pardon for her haste. He excused her, and overcome by fatigue took his dinner and fell into a deep slumber.

The joy of the wife knew no bounds. She flew to her parents, and in hot haste related to them the change of their tortoise son-in-law. They all flew to her abode, and joy of joy, instead of a tortoise they were dazzled by the lustre of a most charming youth. The old king and his queen, the parents of the tortoise were informed of the glad news. They came running and found the report to be true. By this time the prince had finished his slumber. Every one round him was questioning him as to his change. His brothers-in-law recognised in him their Mahêsvara of the wood and hung down their heads. The tortoise prince related his adventures from the beginning. A propitious day was fixed for his remarriage with his most affectionate and dutiful wife. The club, the sandals, the bag, and the guitar were brought from the baniyan tree. In the presence of all, the prince played upon his violin when lo! the divine damsel appeared. The assembly stood in amazement. With the permission of that maiden he remarried his wife. The brothers-in-law stood a little ashamed at their having lost their finger tips and rings which the tortoise prince now produced to them to prove that he was the same Mahêsvara. For all the sorrow at her having married an unnatural husband, the first daughter of the minister was now in the topmost point of her joy at the turn of events and was ever sending up prayers to God. The old king now gave the throne to his son and retired. The new king our tortoise prince afterwards reigned over the kingdom in great prosperity.

"And must not such a prince marry you my dearest love?" Thus Buddhichâturya finished his seventh story; the sun was rising already. The princess left the bed room for the harem.

[MORAL.—This story demonstrates that true merit shall always be rewarded, that pride shall always meet disgrace and that evil intentions shall end in calamities. We see these illustrated in the tortoise prince, his twin brothers-in-law and the three sages respectively.]

EIGHTH STORY.

On the night of the eighth day of the marriage the minister's son, after his supper and betel-nut chewing, reached the bed-room. And the younger of the princesses soon as evening approached, finished her bath and meals, and scenting her body with the most choice scents and flowers, approached the bed of her lord. Taking her seat in front of him, she played for a short time on her guitar some sweet love-notes, and overcome by love, she laid down the instrument and sat beside her lord, who, wishing no longer to give any room to her desires, thus spoke—"My dearest gem of womankind ! I have today also a short story to relate to you, and soon as that is over, we will go to sleep." The princess consenting, Buddhichâturya proceeded.

In the fertile kingdom of the Kâvêrî there lived a very expert gambler named *S*ûdan.* He was the most skilled in his calling. He had not even a pie to depend upon. Daily he was used to rise up very early, finish his religious duties of the day, and call upon any one whom he chanced to meet to gamble with him. In the end *S*ûdan would always come out successful and win the

* Which in Tamil means gambler.

game. Whatever he earned he spent that day. Thus he went on practising for several years, till the whole country round became afraid of him: whenever any one saw *S*ûdan walking in the streets, he shuddered, ran in and bolted the door behind him. Nor was *S*ûdan unaware of the terror with which every one began to regard him.

One noon after the duties of the day were finished, the gambler *S*ûdan started out to find some one to play with. He went street by street and door by door. He was not able to meet with any one. Thinking that the *pûjâ* (worship) performer would be staying in the temple, we went to that place. The *pûjâ* performer seeing him from a distance and reading his thoughts, ran to the innermost part of the temple and concealed himself behind the image of the god. To his great disappointment *S*ûdan saw none there, and after all resolved to gamble with the god. "You must be the second party to my game my god. For why did you create me and instruct me up in this profession. To-day no one has yet turned up to gamble with me, you therefore must be the second party. If I lose the play, I give you a damsel, and if you lose, you must give me a damsel. I shall turn both our dice." So saying, the gambler *S*ûdan sat down in front of his village-god and spread the sheet for the play. He conducted the game most impartially. At first he threw the dice in honour of Ga*n*apati, then in honour of the very god before whom he was playing. The play continued for a long time, till in the end the gambler *S*ûdan succeeded. "What say you now to the bet," said *S*údan to the god. The god remained silent. "I shall teach you to speak now." So saying, *S*ûdan rooted up the goddess that was placed below the god and ran off. The god was amazed at the audacity of the gambler, and calling him out by his name, told him to leave the goddess behind and that he would give a damsel to him the next morning. The *pûjâ* performer, who from his place of concealment had seen all that transpired, determined with himself to stay there that night and watch what occurred. In the middle of the night several damsels from the divine world came to that temple to worship the god, and in the end of their prayer asked that god's permission to go to their world. That deity allowed every one except Rambhâ[1] to depart. She alone remained behind, without knowing the cause. The morning dawned. The gambler came to make his demand. The god gave him Rambhâ for the promised damsel and sent him home.

*S*ûdan returned home with a triumphant face bringing a divine damsel with him. He showed her his hut. She was ashamed to live in it, and

(1) Rambhâ—a courtezan of the divine world.

so asked her husband to describe a square in a spacious waste land adjoining the village. The square was described, when, lo! by her magic powers, Rambhâ raised up a beautiful mansion. *S*ûdan brought before her his first wife, and Rambhâ by a touch of her hands converted her ugly body into a most lovely one. Entering the new-sprung house, they (*S*ûdan, his first wife and his newly acquired Rambhâ) lived in great happiness there. Thus passed the first week.

Once for a week Rambhâ had to dance for a night before the celestial lord, Indra.[2] Her appointed day arrived and she wanted to go to the heavens for that particular night. *S*ûdan would not permit her unless she carried him also to that place. She, finding her arguments vain, agreed to it and converting her lord into a garland, wore it round her neck. She then climbed to the skies and there gave human form to the wreath. *S*ûdan as soon as he came to himself sat down in a corner of Indra's hall to notice unobserved what passed on there. *S*ûdan's wife, Rambhâ appeared before Indra in her finest apparel and ornaments and danced before him. She did her art so very well that all the *Dêvas* assembled there paid every respect to her accomplishments. The nautch ceased. The morning dawned. Rambhâ converted

(2) Indra—The God of the Heavens.

*S*ûdan again into a garland and came back to the world. When near the river of her husband's village she converted him to his original shape; and he, asking her to go home first, stayed on the river to take his morning bath. That river was the most famous water in the mortal world for its sacredness. Hence, the *Dêvas* too, now and then, used to come to its *ghâts* to take a holy bath. On the morning that *S*ûdan stayed there, the *Dévas* visited the river and engaged in their baths. Some of these very people he had seen the previous night doing respect to his wife Rambhâ. "*A for tiori* must they do me respect as I am her husband," thought *S*ûdan with himself and assuming the dignity of a divine bridegroom placed himself before them. The *Dêvas* mistaking him for a fop left him to himself and were engaged in their duties, which being over, they prepared to start. When *S*ûdan saw no more respects were forthcoming from the *Dêvas*, he rose up, and rooting out the wild rushes on the shore thrashed them right and left, abusing "You meanest *Dêvas*, you who had so much respect to a female and that to my wife, bear these blows in return for your having insulted me, by not doing the proper respects due to my position as Rambhâ's husband." The *Dêvas* received the blows on their back and were astonished to hear that Rambhâ had a husband in the human world

They flew hastily to the heavens to report their case to Indra.

Meanwhile *S*ûdan returned to his house. His wife and Rambhâ welcomed him. On seeing them *S*ûdan laughed. Rambhâ pressed him to explain the cause of his laughter, and he revealed to her everything. She was extremely vexed at the stupidity of her husband, and begged permission to go to the world of Indra, and the gambler fearing his own error allowed her to depart.

Now the *Dêvas* had finished their complaint to Indra about their troubles that morning from mortal hands. That celestial monarch burned with anger at the thought that a divine maiden had united herself to a man of the world. It was at this time that Rambhâ reached the (celestial) Council. Indra was for cursing and reducing her to ashes. All the *Dêvas* interfered in her favour, and begged Indra to visit her with only a moderate curse, and he thundered as follows: "Since you have insulted your exalted birth by causing yourself to be thus lowly connected in the mortal world; since you went to the most atrocious act of bringing a mortal into the divine world to show him the celestial nautch; since your affection to your mortal husband gave him the audacity to thrash the innocent *Dêvas* on your name, we curse you. Be you—." Here at this point, notwithstanding Indra's anger, all the *Dêvas* in one voice begged their lord to visit Rambhâ with a moderate curse, and after this slight interruption the Dêvêndra proceeded as follows :—"Be you turned into a fierce devil till the seven big spires at Bânâras which are each eleven stories high are reduced to powders and rebuilt in their original shape." Rambhâ knowing her mistake, and fearing that any request on her part might only aggravate Indra's anger begged him to excuse her the curse till she revealed the matter to her husband Sûdan ; and he allowed her her request.

Rambhâ came to the human world, reported her curse to her husband, and said, "My dear husband I shall now go to Bânâras and take possession of the princess of that country. If you travel up to that place and proclaim yourself to cure her of her malady and begin the treatment, I shall also begin to leave her little by little. You should then demand the demolition of the seven spires and their rebuilding. I shall possess the princess till the accomplishment of the said avoidment of the curse. Then we shall happily live together after your supposed success in driving away the devil of the Bânâras princess." Soon as Rambhâ revealed this to her husband, she was turned into a devil, flew to Bânâras in the twinkling of an eye, and possessed the princess of that place. That damsel, an only daughter of a great sovereign, tore her garments and ran naked in the public streets, uttering nonsense peculiar to insane minds. The king of Bânâras was struck with sorrow at the change that came over his daughter. She now lived in a cave near the town in a nude form, pelting every one that approached her with stones. All the devil dispellers were called in. No remedy was effected. The king proclaimed that he would give his daughter in marriage and half the kingdom to him who would effect the cure. No one could succeed.

Soon as Rambhâ ran away, *S*ûdan started to Bânâras. It took him six months to reach that place. The king of Bânâras had hung up a bell, at which every new physician proclaimed himself to have come into the town by striking it. *S*ûdan sojourned with an old woman of that place who, in the course of her conversation, informed him of the insane princess. *S*ûdan then told her that he was a great proficient in incantations, having studied much of them during his younger days at Malaiayâ*l*am.[3] She then gladly conducted him to the bell at which he struck.

---

(3) Malaiyâ*l*am—The present Malabar was supposed by the ancient Hindûs to be the best place for learning devil charms. Even today more devil-charmers or supposed devil-charmers exist in that part of India more than in other parts.

The king came running and welcomed him. *S*ûdan proclaimed himself a great proficient in incantations, powerful to drive away any devil. The king threatened to hang him in case he failed to effect the cure to his daughter. With all these formalities the gambler began his treatment.

To make much fuss in the beginning, he ordered for a great quantity of *ghî*, rice, &c., to begin the ceremony for the driving out of the devil. No pain was spared in supplying him all he wanted. After a couple of *ghatikâs* during which he continued to call up the goddess Châmu*ndâ* by several names of *Kâlî, Mahâkâlî, Bhadrakâlî*, &c., he started with the king, ministers and others to the mountain which the princess had chosen for her abode. "Come out all you evil spirits," vociferated the gambler. The princess bearing on her head a big piece of stone with her body, naked as nature made her, came out of the cave; some fled away fearing that she would throw the slab on their heads. Some ran, not able to bear the sight of her nakedness. *S*ûdan only dared to approach and shake hands with her. Soon as he touched her, she came to herself, threw down the stone, and ashamed at her nudity, ran to hide herself in the cave." Well done *Mântrika* (charmer) exclaimed the whole assembly around. The king was greatly pleased, and admired the skill of *Sûdan* who now returned from the cave. The *Mântrika* asked the princess's garment to be sent up to the cave. It was accordingly done, and what was the joy of the father to hear that she had it put on. Though a great change for the better was plainly perceived, there was still a slight lingering of the devil disease. The king showed all kindness to *Sûdan* and requested him to leave nothing undone to effect a perfect cure. *Sûdan* pretended to do a good deal of ceremony for a couple of days, and at last exclaimed, "My most noble king. The devil that has possessed your daughter is a divine devil. It appeared to me last night in my sleep, and exclaimed that unless the seven big spires, each of which is eleven stories in height, are demolished, reduced to fine atoms and rebuilt in their original shape—that unless this is done, the devil will not entirely leave the princess." "I will issue the orders now only, if you promise that the devil will by that means be entirely off," cried out the king. "Do you ever doubt it," thundered the *Mântrika*, and at once the king made the necessary arrangements for the demolition and erection of the seven spires. When a king for the cause of the restoration of his own darling daughter to her senses issues the order, is it even necessary to say that it was most hastily executed? The whole of the Bânâras kingdom was in the business, and lo ! in the course of a month the seven spires were rebuilt. After the re-erection of the *gôpuras* *S*ûdan boldly went up to the hill where the possessed princess was lurking. He called her out and she now showed signs of shame—a clear indication that she had come to herself. Nor was there any doubt of it. For Rambhâ, soon, as the she saw the seven *gôpuras* re-erected after their demolition, left the Bânâras princess, and in her original shape ascended to the skies. At Bânâras the king's joy knew no bounds to see his daughter perfectly recovered. He, true to his promise, married her to the incantation master—*S*ûdan, and rewarded his son-in-law with half of Bânâras kingdom. He sent for his first wife, and with the Bânâras princess lived there in happiness.

Rambhâ, who went to the world of Indra, fell down on his feet and intimated to him the erection of the seven *gôpuras*. Indra wondered at the rapidity of the execution of the vow and enquired the cause of it. She pointed out the gambler, her husband *S*ûdan, and his stratagem to attain the reversal of the curse. Indra was astonished at the power of that person, and sent down the messengers of Yama(4) to bring the gambler to the divine world. Before they start-

(4) Yama—The God of death.

ed Rambhâ had rejoined her husband, and began to live happily with him.

By this time the servants sent by Yama reached the house of *S*ûdan. The fire cf the chastity of his wives was burning so very bright that Yama's messengers found it unable for them to approach the gambler's house. They waited out of doors for a long time till he came out, and on seeing him said, that Yama had sent them to bring him to the world of Indra. *S*ûdan putting on an authoritative countenance, replied," Who is that Yama that has wanted me in the other world ? Is it the old Yama or the new Yama ? Till I know him exactly I cannot come. Bring me reply soon, as to the exact personage." The messengers of Yama were starlted at *S*ûdan's reply. They had all along thought that there was an only Yama—the Yamadharmarâja in the whole universe. Now that the gambler had asked whether it was the new or the old Yama that had sent them, they began themselves to doubt whether there were more than one Yama and ran to their lord to know that and report to *S*ûdan about it. Soon as they went away *S*ûdan called his wives and addressed them thus : "My dearest wives. The lord of death, his majesty Yama has sent for me. That shows plainly that I have not a long time to live in this world. In a couple of days they are sure to take me away to the other world.

But you must not be sorry for my death. For it will last only for a short time. As soon as I die my corporeal remains will stay here, and I in my spiritual form will fly to the other world. You must then carefully scent my corpse and preserve it in an air-tight box without allowing it to corrupt. One of you must ever continue to sit by the box and watch it day and night wide-awake. Soon as I reach the world of Indra, I shall fight with the gods there and try to return here soon as I can. I shall then reappear in my corpse and call one of you by her name. She who watches then by the boxside must open it and take me out. When I am again in this world we shall continue to live happily for a long long period of several tens of years." Thus the gambler insturcted his wives and continued to spend that day most joyfully in feasts in company with them.

Already the messengers of Yama had reached the world of death and asked their lord as to whether he was the new or the old Yama. He was puzzled at the question and unable to give a precise reply, went to Indra to have his doubt cleared up. Indra was equally confused, and they both went to Brahmâ, the lord of creation, whom they found in no way better off than themselves. So they all now went to Vish*n*u who was equally unable to clear the doubt. There was a general amazement and a feeling of shame among all the gods for their not being able to clear a simple question raised by the lowest mortal of the world—a petty gambler. So they all went as their last resort to the God of Gods Mahêsvara and stood before him with their question. The great God admired Sûdan for his having thrown the gods in confusion and calling Yama to his side, thus ordered: "Oh you Yama. How bold is this mortal for his having caused such a great stir by an unmeaning question to the gods. No use, hereafter, of sending your messengers to him. You must yourself go direct and bring him away here without any delay. If he asks you, as to who you are, whether you are an old or a new Yama, tell him that you are both in one." Yama on receiving the order flew to the world to bring the gambler and took his seat in the horns of the cow of Sûdan, who happening to come near it, was bored in his belly. The gambler died; and his wives remembering his injunctions, carefully preserved his body by scenting and enclosing it in an air-tight box and watched the contents ever by its side.

Let us see what happened to Sûdan after his departure to the skies. Yama, the lord of death, brought Sûdan (his spirit) to the celestial region and made him stand before the God Mahêsvara' Vishnu, Brahmâ and Indra. The great God, soon as he saw the gambler, called Chitraputra, (the registrar of the general character and death of individuals and the agent to his majesty the god of death) and ordered him to take out his account and see what he had written about *S*ûdan. Chitraputra examined his lists and read out that *S*ûdan, the notorious gambler, was one of the most sinful men the world has ever produced. Soon as he heard this, *S*ûdan joined both of his hands, and in great anger gave a blow on the cheeks of Chitraputra, who stood stunned by shame at the insult he had received from a man. Mahêsvara in great anger demanded *S*ûdan the reason for his rashness, to which he replied, "My most holy God. If a person, however notorious a sinner he may be, only happens to see one of the three gods.—Brahmâ, Vishnu or Mahêsvara he at once becomes the holiest of the holy in the world. I now see before me the three gods. Then are not my sins washed away ? Am I not now the most holy ? While such is the case this fool of a Chitraputra calls me a sinner. And why should he not be more sensible, The blow that fell now on his cheeks should teach him better manners." Thus reasoned *S*ûdan, and Mahêsvara in his admiration of the gambler's audacity, forgot his anger towards him. Surely this man deserves to be a Yama for some time for his sensible answer, and let him be so for a *muhûrta*, ordered Paramêsvara. And Yama at once vacated his seat and went home for rest during that time—a luxury which he had never enjoyed since he succeeded to the death dealing authority. Isa with others went to his abode after issuing the necessary orders for the new appointment he made.

*S*ûdan sat now on the throne of Yama. The first thing he did was, to call Chitraputra and to ascertain his age. "Your age, my lord, ends with this day in the world," replied Chitraputra; "And how many years have each of my wives in the world" asked the new Yama—*S*ûdan.

"Your first, my lord, has three years, three months and three days. Your second is immortal, and your third, my lord, has twenty more years," answered the divine accountant. "Scratch the old numbers out and write one hundred years before each of our names. Do it at once," ordered the gambler, and it was accordingly done. Chitraputra cannot refuse any of the gambler's orders for one *muhûrta*; for it was Mahêsvara's peremptory order that during that period the gambler should be Yama. After getting the age of himself and his wives thus altered, *S*ûdan now set the elephant of Indra against the old Yama to tear him to pieces. It could not do otherwise and so ran against the old Yama who, unable to oppose it, ran to Indra. And Indra ran to Brahmâ, Brahmâ to Vishnu and

Vishnu to Mahêsvara. Mahêsvara called Yama behind him and asked the elephant the reason for his rashness. "It is the order of *S*ûdan" said the elephant. By this time one *muhûrta* had expired and Mahêsvara, perceiving it, uttered: "He is no more on his throne. His period of rule is already past." The elephant stayed its ravages and returned. *S*ûdan came to Mahêsvara pretending great anger and said, "What is the use of your having given me a power with no prerogative to exercise it. Let me go away to my world. Be pleased to give me permission. The elephant of Indra, though I ordered it, did not after all kill the old Yama." The more *S*ûdan spoke, the more Mahêsvara admired his audacity and said, "You are a very extraordinary man. Notwithstanding all your impertinence I admire your courage. From this day I give you the title of the *Yamapurattan* the Yama-confuser and send you to your world. Go you in happiness and live there till you are destined to live." *S*ûdan returned with great joy to his house and infusing his spirit into his body which his wives were carefully preserving in the box called one of them out by her name. They flew to the box, and on opening it found their husband in life. General joy prevailed. They put him a thousand questions as to his adventures in the other world. He reported to them one and all the points he said, and did in the divine world and lived for one hundred more years with them all.

"And must not such an able individual marry you my gem of womankind?" Thus saying Buddhichâturya concluded his eighth story. The creator of the day,—the sun had already risen. So the minister's son and the princess retired to their separate duties.

[Moral—This story conveys the moral to a Hindû shewing how much his wife's chastity governs his own fate and how that good quality in her can set a naught the messengers of death even, for a time at least, from taking away the husband, however great a sinner he may be in himself.]

NINTH STORY.

On the night of the ninth day, the minister's son entered the bed chamber after his supper and betel-nut. And the elder of the princesses bathed in the evening, adorned herself with the choicest jewels and entered the bed chamber with *vînâ* in hand, on which she played some love notes near the bed of her lord, who seemed to listen to it pretty attentively. Overcome by love, she now approached the bed of her lord, who perceiving her turn of mind and wishing to subdue her desires by a story, began as follows:— "My gem of womankind, I have a short story to-day to relate to you, and soon as that is over, we shall retire to rest." The princess consented: and Buddhichâturya thus began:—

There was a city in the world named *Senpakâpura*. The king of that city with his ministers, commanders and councilors ruled over it for a long time, according to the Code of Manu, collecting only one-sixth as tax from his people. After a long time he had the fortune to be the father of two daughters. These were born to him in his advanced age when he had almost given up all hope of getting any children. Of course these children were brought up with all the care due to their exalted birth. In their proper age, the king got his two daughters married to two princes. The first son-in-law staid in his wife's house. The second started out on an expedition, and no news reached anyone of his safety. The two sisters attained their puberty. The elder daughter's nuptials, as her husband was near, were celebrated with all pomp, while the younger had to wait for the arrival of her husband. Couriers were everywhere despatched to search out the son-in-law. In the end, one messenger came back to the king and informed him that his second son-in-law was no more in the world, and that he had died. The old father-in-law, though vexed deeply at heart, hushed up the matter for sometime at least, and always pretended to be expecting his second son-in-law's return.

The two sisters who were called Tûngâvi*l*akku and Kuttuvi*l*akku were used to spend their days in each other's company. During the nights, the elder Tûngâvi*l*akku retired to her husband's bed-room. Thus passed some days till after a time Tûngâvi*l*akku too happened to know about the death of her sister's husband.

One day Kuttuvi*l*akku adorned her body with all choice ornaments and like a swan in its youth came on slowly walking in great pride from her garden. Her elder sister when she saw her thus coming smiled a little, and afterwards began to shed tears. The younger who had never before any occasion to see such a change in her elder sister approached her in great anger and asked her to give out the reason for her smile first and tears afterwards. Said Tûngâvilakku with tears in her eyes ;—"My dearest eye, my sweet sister. I pity you. With what great tenderness our parents brought us up and married us to suitable husbands. Most unfortunately your husband who started out on an expedition has never yet returned. Rumour says that he breathes no more in this world and that he is dead and gone. And when I saw you with all these ornaments I admired your beauty and the thought that your husband is no more, brought tears to my eyes." The elder had scarce finished speaking, than the younger threw down her ornaments tore her beautiful clothes, and attiring herself in pure white went to her father ; spoke she ;—" My dearest father. You gave birth to us in your old age and brought us up most tenderly. Heaven ordained that I should so soon become a widow. I cannot live for one moment hereafter in this world. I must throw myself in fire and give up my life to follow my dead husband to the heavens. Kindly order the funeral pile to be spread for me. I can live no more." The father who saw his daughter weeping there could not contain his sorrow. He sobbed till his throat began to burst and replied, "My daughter I do not know what great sins I committed in my former life to be made the sufferer of such calamities in this old age. The inevitable has come upon us. Let us bear it patiently. And I beg of you not to leave me in my old age. The whole kingdom with the treasury and everything is yours. Spend the money in charities and remain in this world." These soothing words of the old father could not turn the determination of the strong-willed daughter. Finding her obstinate and determined to die, the king ordered his ministers to prepare the pile, which was accordingly done.

When the fire began to blaze and burn high, the second princess Kuttuvi*l*akku bathed and dressed herself in pure white. She circumambulated the fire thrice, gave all the ornaments on her body, and all the wealth belonging to her in donation to the Brâhma*n*s and jumped into the fire pronouncing, "Hara! Hara! Hara! Gôvinda, Mâdhava!"

Soon as she jumped, the sky, in the twinkling of an eye, began to change. A heavy downpour commenced; the fire died away, and a fierce flood washed down the embers, and the princess to a big river. A few minutes after jumping, the princess was carried away headlong in a high flood. No one was able to rescue her. After great difficulty the freshes launched her near a garden, and catching hold of a reed that grew near, she got up on dry ground, in a flower garden. Her cloths were off. She was quite naked. So she hid herself in a bower of jasamine creepers without knowing what to do.

Now that garden happened to belong to an old woman who lived in an adjoining town; she used to come there every morning to gather flowers which she made into wreaths and nosegays for the ladies of the palace. That morning as usual she came to her garden, and to her astonishment found a female pure as nature made her resembling Rati in her beauty. Mistaking her to be the goddess of that garden, the old woman fell down at her feet and began to extol her. Now the unfortunate princess removed her suspicions by saying that she was a human being as herself. She concealed her true history, her royal birth and every thing, and only said that as she was crossing a river with her husband, a sudden flood washed down both of them, and that she managed to get into the garden and did not know what had become of her husband. These words, the old woman believed, and taking pity on a young female in distress, spoke thus to her: "My daughter, for so must I call you henceforth. I send praises to god for having sent you here. Iam an unfortunate old woman with no children; come to my house and remain my daughter."

So saying, the old woman gave half her cloth to the princess. She received it and dressing herself, followed the woman to her abode where she continued to live as her daughter. The old woman was very kind towards the princess. She never allowed her to work. Daily she would rise early in the morning, and go to the gardens to fetch flowers. On her return, she would first arrange and tie up the flowers in wreaths and then go to cook. This was the old woman's daily routine.

One day when she returned from the garden, the princess felt herself unusually hungry, and wanted her mother or adopted mother to cook first. "The flowers must first be arranged and tied up," replied the old woman. "Never mind about them to-day. I shall do that for you at least for a day," said the adopted daughter and began to arrange and tie up the flowers. The old woman engaged herself cooking in the kitchen. Soon as the dishes were ready, the old woman invited her daughter to meals. She in return produced her basket containing her new made wreaths. The old woman was extremely pleased at the fineness of the garlands, and, after serving her daughter took, the garland to the queen of that city to whom she was used to sell them. The queen who had never before seen such fine garlands in her life, asked her who the maker was for that day. Now the old woman related to her the adopted daughter's history. The queen was delighted to hear it. She herself had two stupid daughters. So, she sent for the adopted daughter of the old woman and rewarding the latter, took the former under her own protection, and requested her to teach the two princesses. Kuttuvi*l*akku as a nurse to the two princesses of that town, began to live in the palace. The queen too, to her great praise, treated her most kindly.

Once upon a time, the king and the queen wished to perform a great ceremony in which they had to give in donation several pearl garlands. They gave a measure of pearl to each of their daughters and Kuttuvi*l*akku too—the instructress wished to have a measure of pearl for her share to be made into garlands. The queen gladly gave it, and the three ladies engaged separately in making the garlands. Before they finished their work, the dinner time came on. A maid servant came and requested them all to come to their meals. Kuttuvi*l*akku placed her pearls with the unfinished garland in a niche behind the belly-god before whom she was sitting engaged in her work. The belly-god swallowed the pearls during her absence. When she returned and saw the niche, she was startled not to find her pearls there. The old queen now demanded back her pearls; and when Kuttuviḷakku failed to produce hers, she broke out in anger thus:—"I never came across such an insincere girl like yourself. You eat my salt and prove faithless to me. Would anyone believe that the basket of pearls you left here in the niche have gone amissing in my palace. So saying the old queen wanted to punish her for her insincerity and sending for the barber, ordered him to shave Kuttuviḷakku's head clean. Horror of horrors her head was in a moment's time shaved bare for a crime she never knew the cause of. To add insult to injury, the old queen placed a cake of wet cow dung on the barehead of Kuttuviḷakku and fixing a small pan with oil over it, lighted up a lamp and asked her to walk in her threshold like a moving lamp in bodily shape. Thus, by misfortune Kuttuviḷakku left her kind adopted mother and coming to a queen was, by her, thus most shamefully punished. In this punishment she passed one full year.

Now the country in which Kuttuviḷakku was undergoing her punishment happened to be her aunt's country. The husband of Kuttuviḷakku who was reported to have died, was still living. He had conquered several countries and was returning in great haste to see his wife and old father-in-law. On his way he halted in the house of the sister of his mother-in-law. The old queen welcomed her sister's son-in-law who was reported to have died long ago and celebrated a great feast in his honour. After the pleasures of the day, the victorious son-in-law retired for rest. Now the old queen asked Kuttu-*vilakku* to go and sit in a corner of the room in which her sister's son-in-law was sleeping. Of course she had no reason to know these relationships as she did not move closely with the members of the palace after her punishment. So as she was ordered to do, she sat up in a corner of the room in which the son-in-law slept.

After the first watch was over the sleeping prince got up and finding a human lamp as it was in a corner of his room, seeing the lamp-stand to be a beautiful female possessing royal marks in her face he asked her who she was and how she came to serve in the mean position in which he found her. She, overcame by shame, remained silent. He again and again pressed her to relate her history and when she continued silent rose up and taking down the lamp on her head pressed her to open her lips. She, finding her silence more pernicious in rising the curiosity of the prince, began to speak and in sweet and pathetic words related her history from the beginning up to her punishment. When the princess was through half the story, the son-in-law found out, that she was none other than his own wife. For be it known now once for all that Kuttu*vilakku* was serving in her own aunt's house though the aunt, as well as herself, had no reason to know it. The prince subdued his anger till the princess had finished her story, and soon as she ceased to speak, he rose up from his bed, and with his eyes full of tears made the poor princess to get up, told her that he was her husband, that her calamities had ended that very day, and that he would never taste a handful of meals in the house of the mean aunt who had thus cruelly punished a female and cared not for her ignorance of relationship. At that very moment, he called his servants, ordered them to bathe and adorn his wife as became her position. Soon as morning dawned, the prince departed to his father-in-law's, country. The aunt shock with fear when she saw the angry countenance of her sister's son-in-law. He now related everything to the aunt's husband, who cursed himself and his wife for her thus having cruelly treated a female. "I would never have done it had I known her to be my sister's daughter" said she; to which the son-in-law asked her to shut her mouth. "A *female*—it matters not who she is—ought never thus to be punished." Thus vociferating the son-in-law went away with his army and his rescued wife to his father-in-law's dominions. He despatched messengers to intimate to the old king, who had given up all hopes of seeing his daughter or her husband in this world, that his son-in-law and daughter were coming to him. The old king's joy may be more imagined than described. He walked out a mile to welcome his long lost son-in-law and daughter, and was extremely pleased at their safe arrival, though the punishment of the latter vexed him extremely. In the joy that followed, past sorrows were forgotten. A second marriage was performed, and the nuptials of Kuttuvi*l*akku with her victorious husband were celebrated on the same day. The old king gave a separate palace for his second son-in-law to live in; and there, he enjoyed his honeymoon with his wife.

Thus some time passed, after which the husband of Kuttuvi*l*akku became enamoured of a beautiful dancing-girl in that town, and began to spend a greater portion of the day with her. But he also exercised a due portion of his love over his own affectionate wife. As the dancing-girl did not like this and wanted him, except in the time of his meals, to be always by her side, she entirely brought him under her influence by a secret medicine. The power of this drug acted most triumphantly, and Kuttuvi*l*akku's husband was always in the house of the dancing-girl. The princess, thinking it all to be the perversity of her own fate, remained alone in the house. Thus passed three years. Now there lived an old woman next to Kuttuvi*l*akku's house. She paid a visit to the latter one day, and in the course of the conversation that followed, she took the princess to task for her thus allowing her husband to go astray, for which she replied that it was all her own fate. Said the old woman: "It is all bosh to speak of fate in such things. Have you not in you, your fresh youth and charming beauty to attract your husband? Listen to what I say. I have a certain medicine with me, which if you mix with soup and serve him, he shall, soon after he tastes it, be ever in your possession. Do that and live happily with your husband. You are a princess born to live happy, and your husband a prince more fit for your company than that of a dancing-woman." Thus advising, the old woman went to her house and brought in the drug. The princess mixed it in the soup and found the dish turn all red. A doubt, as to whether the drug in the soup would affect her husband's life, began now to confuse her mind. The more she thought of it, the more it confused her, till after all she determined with herself not to serve that soup to her lord. For, "What is the use of living a a widow in case this drug puts an end to my husband's life. If only when both of us live in the world I could have an opportunity of being one day reconciled, if fortune so turns, to my husband," thought she, and emptied the dish containing that soup mixed with the drug in the backyard of her house, and in no time prepared another and kept ready for her husband.

The drug that was poured out in the backyard happened to fall in the cavity of a hole underground and touched the head of a five-hooded serpent, that was living there. By the influence of the medicine the serpent took the shape of Kuttuvi*l*akku's husband, and approached her house in the night and knocked at the door after she had bolted it behind her real husband, who had a few minutes only before that time left for the dancing-girl's house. Who must he be that knocks now at my door! after my husband has left the house, thought she, and with a throbbing heart removed the latch. Wonder of wonders! she saw her own husband (which we know to be the serpent transformed) in her threshhold. With herself, she praised the power of the drug, and thought that by some unperceived particle of it, which must have been sticking to the pan, her lord was brought back to her. And never suspecting the person who appeared to be none other but himself, she from that night began to live most happily with the serpent-prince, who, be it said to his credit, acted most skilfully as not to give even the least room for suspicion. Thus passed some time till Kuttuvi*l*akku became pregnant.

The serpent-prince now wanted no more to keep himself secret. He wished to disclose to her his true origin and enjoy her with her own confidence. So, he spoke to her thus: "My dear love, scatter on me a little of the holy ashes. I shall then assume a strange shape at which you had better never fear, and if you again scatter on me a small quantity of holy ashes, I shall come back to my human shape and reveal to you some secrets." Thus instructing, the apparent husband of Kuttuvilakku and the father of the embryo in her womb stood at a distance of ten feet from her. She scattered the ashes on him, when lo! he was no longer man; five hoods and the body of a serpent with its natural hiss graced the place where he stood once. In short a five-hooded serpent and not a man seemed to have been her lord. But as instructed she, without any fear, threw something more of the holy ashes on the reptile, which at once assumed its original human shape. The wife broke out, "My lord, I never till this time knew your extraordinary powers; was it proper on your part to have so long kept them secret from me?" Thus expressing her amazement, she began to praise him, to which, he, the apparent husband, thus replied: "I beg your pardon. Oh you gem of womankind! I am not your husband; your real lord is in the dancing-girl's house; but who is then this lord that stands before you? To be no more in the secret, know me henceforth to be the five-hooded serpent-king living in the backyard of your house. That drug which your kind old neighbour gave you, and which you fearing to administer to your husband, upset in the backyard, reached my head, and has thus transformed me to the most welcome shape of being your lord, for which I shall never be grieved. You now have become pregnant through me, but better not fear that this will in any way affect your honour. Now has come the time for you to live happily with your real husband ; and I shall so manage it that that dancing-girl shall ever after become your enemy." Thus, the serpent-prince consoled Kuttuvi*l*akku, and as usual was regular in his visits to her ; she too never disliked it and lived happily with her serpent-lord. The signs of pregnancy becoming more and more developed every day, the real husband grew suspicious and reported his wife's conduct to her father, complaining that she had become pregnant when he had not slept by her side for the last few years. The old king was much vexed at the ill-report of his daughter, and sent maid-servants to fetch her to the palace. But as the princess did not like to do anything without consulting her serpent lord, she sent word through them that she would see her father next morning, which of course was duly reported to the old king.

That evening the real husband of Kuttuvi*l*akku had his supper, and before his hand dried, reached the dancing-girl's house. And, of course, as usual, the serpent was in the bedroom of Kuttuvilakku to sleep with her. She disclosed the whole matter of her husband's complaint to her father, to her serpent-lord, and consulted him as to how she should behave herself the next morning. The serpent-lord smiling, thus replied: "Now has come the good time for you. When you stand before your father to-morrow morning, a council will have met there already to enquire into your conduct. When they question you as to the cause of your pregnancy, you had better without any fear give out the name of your husband. If they doubt it, proclaim before the assembly that you have become pregnant through your husband and by your husband alone, and that if this fact is doubted by your husband and father, you will be ready to undergo the hardest ordeal of taking out a flower-pagoda from a pot containing a serpent in it, after bathing and dressing yourself as befitting the serpent-ordeal occasion. I shall be the serpent that shall be in the pot to-morrow, and when you plunge your hand boldly into it, for the flower-pagoda shall do you no harm." Thus instructing the serpent-prince went away that morning a little early to prepare himself for the pot.

The morning dawned. An assembly of the nobles of the town had already gathered in the palace to inquire into Kuttuvilakku's conduct. Her husband and her father sat there with their faces hanging down at the certain guilt which they thought, the princess of the palace had committed. Kuttuvi*l*akku was sent for, and she without any fear stood most composedly before the assembly. When she was accused of her guilt, she denied it most solemnly, asserted that she became pregnant through her own husband, and then if they had any doubts about it, she would undergo the serpent-ordeal. The council thought that the best course, and at once sending for the serpent-charmer, ordered him to bring one of the best serpents. He, by his incantations, described the boundary, and taking a pipe in his hand began to blow at it most melodiously. The shrill music brought forth several serpents, but putting them all down, the five-hooded serpent stood to the front. The charmer took hold of it and brought it before the assembly. The king and the other gentlemen there were greatly astonished at that extraordinary serpent with five hoods which they had never, in their life, seen before. They rewarded the charmer most amply and sent him away. A new pot with a flower-pagoda in it was already waiting to receive the master of the ordeal, who was made now to go into it. Kuttuvi*l*akku now bathed and attired herself in a solemn way, and circumambulating the assembly, thrice prostrated herself before that august body, and advanced towards the pot. Standing before it, she in a most solemn voice, which appeared to be the breath of innocence itself, vociferated: "The husband whom I touched on that day is my husband, as the serpent that I am going to touch to-day is a serpent." Thus uttering, she undauntly plunged her hand deep into the pot, and taking hold of that five-hooded enemy of mankind, wore it as a garland round her neck. Then she took out the flower-pagoda and placed it in the midst of the gold tray in front of the assembly. One and all the people assembled there were thunderstruck at her boldness, and exclaimed in one voice that she was the most chaste woman they had ever seen in their life. Our heroine now prostrated herself a second time before the assembly, and uncoiling the serpent which had entwined itself round her neck, she let it into the pot, the mouth of which she closed. The old king, her father, and her husband, who suspected her after seeing her coming off successfully from the ordeal, not only gave up their doubts, but began to venerate her for her acknowledged and most supreme kind of chastity. The assembly dispersed and each went to his own quarters.

After the due development of the pregnancy, Kuttuvi*l*akku brought to bed a male child who shone in splendour like a *karór* of suns. For this confinement, the very five-hooded serpent assumed the shape of a woman and acted as midwife. It also brought several ornaments prepared of serpent-gems and made a present of them to the new-born baby. And after the ten days were over, the serpent-midwife spoke in pleasing words to Kuttuvi*l*akku's old father, and asking him to take care of his daughter and her young one took leave.

The old father left no stone unturned in bringing his weak daughter back to her health. In one month she was all right. The child also grew up with all care due to its position. It reached its third year and was sporting in the cradle with all the ornaments that were presented to it by the serpent-midwife-and-father. The real husband of Kuttuvi*l*akku, the supposed father of the child, now happened to see his son when he returned home from the dancing-girl's house to his dinner. The lightninglike lustre of his son's body stunned the father's eyes for a time, who, though he much longed to take him in his hands, did not like to do it there, without the company of his affectionate dancing-woman. So, washing his hands he returned to her house, and from thence despatched a maid servant to Kuttuvi*l*akku, requesting her to send their child to the dancing girl's house for a few *ghatikas* as she wished to see it. Kuttuvi*l*akku, not liking to do anything without the order of the serpent, sent back the maid, requesting to be excused till the next morning, when she would without any hesitation send up her son. Great was the wrath of the dancing-woman and her keeper-prince, and this of course was duly communicated by the latter to the old king. He satisfied his son-in-law by saying that he would enquire into the matter in a regular assembly the next morning, and made arrangements accordingly.

When in that night the serpent came as usual to sleep in its human shape besides Kuttuvi*l*akku, she duly reported the matter to it and asked as to how she should conduct herself in that affair. The serpent listened very attentively to what she said and thus replied: "My dearest love, now has come the time for you to enslave that dirty dancing-woman. Tomorrow your father may enquire of you the cause of your refusal; you had better say boldly that you feared to trust your son with the jewels into the hands of a bad woman, that you would be ready to send your son with the jewels to her on the condition that she would weigh and take them and bind herself to return them weighed, and that if there was any deficiency she would bind herself to make up the loss out of her own property, and that as a punishment for her guilt she would serve you as (your) maid-servant ever throughout life." Thus instructing the serpent-*râj* went away early in the morning.

Before the day broke maid-servants from the palace came to call the princess to the assembly. The old king was already sitting there with his son-in-law by the side. The due enquiry went on, for which our heroine gave the reply in which she had been already instructed by her serpent-lord

One and all in the assembly seemed to approve the reasons, and made the dancing-girl agree to her conditions. She fully consented to it, and received the boy and the jewels weighed before the assembly itself, promising to return them the next morning similarly weighed.

Though this dancing-woman guarded the jewels most carefully, the fivehooded serpent made its appearance most stealthily by a secret hole into that house, and glided away with a portion of the jewels. This, of course, she had no room to suspect, and so when she brought them the next morning she was unconsciously caught; the scales on the ornament side rose high, and according to the contract of the previous day she had to give up all that she had to cover but a very small portion of the missing jewels and to bind herself to serve her. For the jewels having been of serpent-gems were very valuable. Her object was accomplished. Her true husband came to her. Her great rival, the dancing woman, was made her slave.

Joyfully she returned home, and forgot in her extacy the serpent-king who had done so much for her. That night when she was sleeping sound with her husband, the serpent-lord came to her side, and finding her deep asleep was much vexed at heart for her great forgetfulness. "Shall I remove now my enemy—the true husband by a poisonous sting?" thought he. However on second considerations he did not like it, as that would make Kuttuvi*l*akku a widow. And not wishing to kill her who had been his object of affection for the past four years and more, and much grieved at heart for the disappointment, the serpent gave up his life by strangling himself by a lock of Kuttuvi*l*akku's hairs. Thus passed away in a moment's time the five hooded *Nâgarâj* who did so much for the princess.

When on the morning the husband awoke, he was startled by the sight of a dead serpent in the head of his wife. Slowly asking her to get up, he stood dismayed. Of course Kuttuvi*l*akku understood everything within her mind, and was extremely vexed for her forgetfulness. For the serpent seemed to have warned her never to forget him before going to bed. Now that it was too late to repent, she cursed herself internally and said to her husband that the boy must perform all the funeral ceremonies of the dead snake. "And why should he do it?" said the husband, who knew nothing of it. And the wife then replied: "This is the serpent of our house to whom I had vowed to perform *pûjâ* in case I got you back. And after recovering you I entirely forgot it; in vengeance for which the serpent has thus given up its ghost. So, it is but necessary that our boy should perform its funeral ceremonies." The husband accepted this explanation and allowed his son or supposed son to do the necessary rites to it, which the boy ought to have done, as the latter was his father. Then Kuttuviḷakku, her husband, and the prince lived for a long time.

Thus Buddhichâturya ended his ninth story, remarking in the end that we can never keep great faith in our wives. The sun began to rise, The princess retired to the palace and the minister's son too went after his duties.

[Moral.—This story shows what a mild lady, an affectionate husband or a dutiful wife may not do when under the mighty influence of anger, tender passion or conscious guilt respectively.]

TENTH STORY.

On the night of the tenth day the minister's son entered the bed chamber after his supper and betel-nut with scents smeared all over his body; and the younger princess adorning her body with the choicest ornaments and decorating her head with sweet scented wreaths, with guitar in hand, entered the bed chamber. After playing for a while on that musical instrument, she approached Buddhichâturya's couch overcome by love but he, wishing to calm down her amorous desires by a story thus addressed her:—

"My dearest love! To-day also I have a short story for you which being over, we shall go to rest." The princess consenting, the minister's son thus began:—

"Listen! Oh you gem of womankind! There was a city named Tiruma*nd*alam ruled over by a a king called Tirurâja. He had an excellent minister named Tiruvilâsa. Both these happened to be sonless and were performing austerities to obtain children. God seemed to favour them after all and the king and the minister had each a son. The son-birth festival was most grandly celebrated in the palace. The prince was named Mahîpati and the minister's son Bhayamkara. Both these were sent to school at their fifth age, and as they advanced in their years they advanced in their studies too, till they became proficients in the four *Vêdas*, six *Sástras*, sixty four arts and sciences, &c. When they reached their proper age the prince Mahîpati turned out to be a brave, intelligent and noble warrior of charming beauty while the minister's son Bhayamkara, quite in appropriateness to his name, became unfit to face an army. But for all that, he had a capital head for learning and study.

On a certain day the prince Mahîpati thus addressed his minister Bhayamkara: "Dear friend Our fathers exercise authority over this town; what is the use of our calmly remaining here without any work. This is the age for us to go after adventures; if you are willing, let us start this very evening and go away to some other country." Bhayamkara agreed and after dinner each supplied himself with enough of money for the way and started on the expedition. They journeyed through woods, forests, mountains and wilds and reached a city named Kalingapa*ttana* where they sojourned in an old Brâhma*n*î's house paying the lady a pagoda per day for meals to them and grain and grass to their horses. On the fourth day of their sojourn, prince Mahîpati asked the old woman whether there was any adventure in that town to which she replied : "My dear friend. The king of this city of Kalingapa*ttana* had an only daughter who was sporting one day in her pleasure garden with three maid-servants, when a mad elephant broke through the place and ran away carrying the princess on his back. The king sent several of his warriors in search of the daughter and they all brought word that the elephant had placed her in the midst of a thick forest adjacent to this city with four circles of armies round her. The first and outer circle is formed, said they, of jackals, the second of leopards, the third of tigers and the fourth of elephants. Our king has proclaimed long ago that he would give his daughter in marriage to him who brings her away from the midst of these several armies. He has also promised to give his kingdom to him.

The prince communicated these thoughts to his young minister Bhayamkara, and told him that it would be improper on their part not to take up the adventure. He also agreed to it.

Early next morning, both these friends had their dinner and started for the palace. There they saw the king of Kalingapa*ttana*, told him that they intended to try the rescue of the princess in the wood and requested his permission. The king gave them betel-leaf and nut, in the act of allowing them to try the adventure, and with his kind permission they started to the wood. After a hard journey of a day and night through mountains, wilds, forests and jungles, they reached the wood of the elephant next morning. With sword in hand, the prince Mahîpati fell on the army of jackals; they all in a great pack attacked him. The minister's son Bhayamkara fell in a swoon on his saddle, and so Mahîpati removed him to a great distance and there made him rest while he was engaged in the battle. Returning again to the army of jackals, he attacked them on all sides and killed not less than ten for every wave of his sword. This kept him engaged till midday, when a few of the jackals that remained howled out, that he was the greatest of all the warriors that had come to them, and that he would rescue without failure the princess. Then they took to their heels for fear of their own lives.

Then, Mahîpati returned to the tree under which he had left Bhayamkara with a small bundle of eatables. He partook of a portion of them, giving the remainder to his timid friend. Near the place where they sat ran a fresh stream from which they took each four or five handfuls of water.

The prince did not like to give up the good turn events had taken that day. So he wished to continue his battle with the leopards: the mention of the name of this enemy of mankind made Bhayamkara to swoon away. And Mahîpati consoled him and left him under the very tree where he took rest during the former part of the action. Sharpening his sword, the prince entered now the second circle composed of leopards. These ferocious beasts began to attack him on all sides. But undaunted, the prince by his sharp sword did a very great havoc among them, so much so, that before the sun began to set that day, there was not even a single leopard that lived.

Thus, in the course of one day, our brave warrior with the assistance of his single sword destroyed entirely the two outer circles of jackals and leopards that were watching the Kalingapa*tt*ana princess. The sun was already sinking, and the prince himself was greatly exhausted. So intending to try the other portion of his adventure next day, he returned to the side of his timid minister, to whom he related every portion of his exploits. They both saw a twinkling light at a short distance from that place, which seemed to come from a village. Already hungry, they started towards it praying God to grant them a sumptuous supper there in the house of some hospitable and kind gentleman.

On their way, Mahîpati saw an old and respectable tiger, deep-entangled in a thick mire. Owing to several days of fasting, the tiger was dying of hunger, and when it saw a prince on the road, it kindly called him to its help. The prince too pitied the famished state of the tiger but pointed out to it that it would make him the first morsel of its hungry mouth, in case he took it out. The tiger in reply quoted several examples, by which even ferocious beasts observed oaths on several occasions. The prince not wishing to lose much time on the way in discussion and trusting to his sword in case matters turned against him, released the old tiger from the mud. Soon as it came into firm ground, the tiger-king circumambulated its protector thrice, and thus addressed : "My life giver. I am the king of tigers. Demand of me any boon that is in my power to give you. I shall readily grant it. Also think of me whenever you are in trouble. I shall come there and oblige you. These words fell like nectar in the prince's ears. He requested the tiger-king to speak to his subjects, who formed the third circle round the Kalingapa*tt*ana princess and take them away, leaving only the elephants for him to battle with the next day. The old tiger consenting to it, the prince rode in haste to the village. There, he gave one pagoda for an old Brâhma*n* woman who gave very good meals to himself and his minister.

Next morning the prince rose up early, finished his bath, ablutions and meals and leaving Bhayamkara in the village itself came to the wood. Joy of joys the tigers had already melted away. "That is a very faithful tiger-king," thought he and marched now deep into the elephant-herd. This was the hardest job to him. But his great agility in the wielding of his sword gave him complete success and before noon all the elephants had fallen before his sharp weapon.

Thus the prince destroyed the three circles of jackals, leopards and elephants by pure might and had the tigers removed by the friendship of their king which he so well secured. After destroying the elephants he found himself in a big meadow planted by fine avenues of trees through which even the god of the day was not able to penetrate. He traversed that dark meadow. In the midst of it he espied a small hill which he went round. Something like a cave appeared to him in the eastern side of the hill. It was very dark. But undaunted, the prince entered. A big and stout elephant was lying across the way snoring in sound sleep. With one blow of his sharp sword, Mahîpati killed that elephant, and on going further discovered a most charming female on a raised dais in the extremity of that cave. "This surely must be the Kalingapa*tt*ana princess" thought he and thus addressed her. "Do not fear anything from me, my dear lady. I am a prince that has killed all the four phalanxes set to protect you by the wretched elephant. Him also I have murdered a few *'nimishas* (minutes) ago. Take courage and follow me. I am your protector." Need it even be said that those words, charming as they were, fell like nectar into the ears of the Kalingapa*ttana* princess. She followed with a cheerful countenance in which the pleasure of her delivery from the tearings of a ferocious elephant and the still greater pleasure of a blooming royal warrior following her as her protector through the wood and throughout life were plainly visible. Mahîpati returned to the village where Bhayamkara was staying and taking him also with him, pursued his journey to Kalingapa*ttana*.

The whole night they three journeyed through the woods and reached that city next morning. Before going into it the prince wanted to answer his calls of nature. So, he asked the minister's son to watch the princess very carefully for a few minutes that he would be absent and went to a decent distance and hid himself out of sight. The minister's son with sword in hand watched the princess.

A tall hobgoblin now stood before Bhayamkara with a huge body and matted hair all over his head. The courage of our minister's son we already know. His body shook, his sword dropped and he himself fell on his face in the ground. The hobgoblin now took possession of the princess, in the bringing of whom Mahîpati had taken such great trouble, and vanished away to his abode in the nether-world where he had already kept in slavery another princess, the daughter of Kâlakanthâpura king. The fears and shrieking of the Kalingapattana princess may be more imagined than described. The absence of that brave warrior prince for a few minutes brought to her so much fresh calamities that she thought she would never recover. Cursing her fate and consoling herself to her new condition she continued to live from that day in that hobgoblin's abode. But she had this comfort at least that another princess was her companion there.

Let us return to Mahîpati. After his business he returned and to his great bewilderment did not see the princess. The minister was lying on the ground almost lifeless, on his back. He ran to the spot, took up the fainting Bhayamkara and asked him what was all the news. " The moment I missed seeing your head, a hobgoblin stood before me with a huge body and fearing him I fell down on my face. And I do not know what happened afterwards" replied the minister's son.

The prince was highly vexed. When God's will is so I cannot accuse you or myself. We are not so fortunate as to secure the princess to ourselves. There is no use of our going again to the king of this city. Come, get up on your horse. Let us go somewhere or other in search of some other adventure," said the prince. The minister's son agreeing to it, they both rode on their horses, leaving it to the beasts themselves to choose their course. In the middle of a wood which they were passing, the prince again met his old tiger-king who now made kind enquiries of him. "What is all the matter with you. The day before yesterday when I met you in the other wood and when you rescued me from that thick mire, your face was as bright as the moon. And now it is lustless like charcoal," said the tiger-king. Our prince explained to him how his efforts had all become vain, now that a hobgoblin had thus walked away with that fair prize. The tiger-king now smiled and said, "Do not fear for anything, my dear protector. I know that hobgoblin. He is an old rogue. If you follow my advice, you can reach him and rescue not only your princess, but another—the daughter of the king of Kâlaka*nt*hâpura. That hobgoblin long ago took away that other princess to his abode in the nether world. You must now go to the king of Kâlaka*nt*hâpura and tell him that you intend starting in the adventure of bringing back his daughter. He will ask you whether you will require any kind of help from him. Only say that you want a thick iron chain of a hundred *yôjanâs* in length. He will oblige you with it. Bring it here to this place where we stand and think on me. I shall come and tell you then what course you ought to adopt." Thus saying the tiger-king went away. Mahîpati in obedience to his tiger-friend's advice went to Kâlakan*th*âpura, saw the king, returned to the spot in the wood with that iron chain of a hundred *yôjanâs*, and thought upon his tiger friend. The tiger-king again made his appearance, and writing a couple of lines in a palm leaf, rolled it and tied the note to the neck of a bloodsucker who happened to be then passing by that side. The bloodsucker ran with the note to the midst of the wood and climbing upon an anthill shook his head. Vast herds of tigers, jackals, leopards, bears and other beasts of that wood came running at the bloodsucker's nod, and were duly conducted by it to the place where stood the tiger-king. He now issued a command to them to make a hole through the earth to the nether world sufficiently spacious to admit a man freely into it. The order was no sooner issued than the act was performed, and lo! in the course of a few minutes Mahîpati saw a deep hole by which the tiger-king said he could with the help of the chain descend and go into the world beneath. He asked the minister's son to sit up in the entrance of the cavity carefully watching the chain which was now suspended into the hole by the tiger-king with the assistance of his vast army. "Dear prince. The minister's son will watch the chain which I have carefully nailed to the earth in this end. The other end of it is now in the nether world. If you descend by this chain carefully holding it, you will safely reach the lower world; near the spot when you get down, you will see an old baniyan tree, in which lives that hobgoblin with the two princesses. By your power which did such wonderful work in the herds of elephants even, you must kill the hobgoblin and rescue the princesses. Conduct them first by this way and then come up yourself." So saying, the kind king of the tigers vanished away.

The prince Mahîpati again and again instructed Bhayamkara to watch the chain with the utmost care, as on that depended his life as well as those of the princesses. Descending and descending, he at last reached the nether world, and to his great joy found without difficulty the baniyan tree so accurately described by the tiger-king. The princess—the daughter of the king of Kalingapa*ttana*—was delighted to find her rescuer again in that lower world. The hobgoblin, most fortunately for them, had then gone out in search of provision. The princess of Kâlaka*nth*â-pura had also already heard the story of Mahîpati and his great valour, and how he had formerly rescued her companion from the elephant. They both welcomed him to their hole in the tree and concealed him in a pot, till the hobgoblin had come and had his meals and rest. After Mahîpati had safely concealed himself, the huge monster made his appearance. Already the princess had kept ready a very sumptuous dinner for his greedy stomach, which he now swallowed dish after dish and fell down in a profound sleep. The prince Mahîpati now came out of his pot, and with his sharp sword killed the snoring monster. When the monster breathed his last, a great joy prevailed. The ladies danced with pleasure. They three hastily partook of what remained in that place, and soon came to the hole by which they should ascend into the upper world. Carefully instructing them as to how they should ascend, the prince Mahîpati sent them first, and they very bravely traversed all the length of the dark hole and reached the other end, where the minister's son was sitting carefully watching the chain-end. The ladies soon as they reached safe, shook the chain that the prince down may know of it. When he saw the shake in the other end, he was sure that the princesses were already safe and began to ascend.

The minister's son, when he saw the two fair princesses, lost his moral courage and wanted to play a trick to his faithful friend the prince. In a word he resolved to kill him, which he could easily do if he could only cut the chain which he was watching, and by which his friend was coming up. And according he rose up in the act as it were of welcoming the ladies and cunningly managed to unhook the chain. Down went the chain, and the prince in the lower end of it fell down in the nether world with the weight of the whole chain over him. We may even say that he was almost dead. The ladies saw at once the trick and the vile intention of the minister's son. They threw themselves on the ground and wept and wept for a long time. The minister's son too wept or rather pretended to weep, and consoling them after all thus addressed: "Our brave prince is gone. What is the use of our remaining in the wilderness where we may again be haunted by some hobgoblin or other. Come, let us go to Kâlingapa*tt*ana and continue to live there in the palace." So said the roguish Bhayamkara, and the ladies in their sad plight in the wood did not know of any other course. So, they followed the minister's son, though they hated him from the very bottom of their hearts.

Bhayamkara with the two princesses reached the outside of the city of Kalingapa*tt*anam, sent one of the citizens to the palace to inform the king of the arrival of a prince who had a few days ago left for the wood to rescue his daughter. When this news reached the king, he came running with his vast army and other royal paraphernalia to do respect to the brave warrior, and his future bridegroom and successor to the throne. The minister's son now pretended to be the prince himself, and without any shame spoke to him of all his exploits with the elephant and the hobgoblin, and how instead of one adventure he had successfully accomplished two adventures. So great was the joy of the father at the rescue of his daughter that he believed in whatever the minister's son then said and took him to be the very prince himself. The princesses too did not like then to expose the treachery of Bhayamkara till they knew for certain the fate of their brave protector. So they left everything to take its course.

The king of Kalingapa*ttana*, now welcomed his brave future son-in-law, the self styled prince Bhayamkara with his daughter and the princess of Kâlaka*nt*hâpura. So great was the joy of the old king that he wished to celebrate the marriage of Bhayamkara with the two princesses on that very day. But they pleaded to excuse them for six months, pretending they were under a vow to some goddess. As the matter was religious the father allowed them their request. Of course, on that very day Bhayamkara became the king of Kalingapa*ttana*.

Let us turn to our prince and see what happened to him after his fall in the nether world. Most fortunately for himself he was not dead. He rose up after the great swoon and thought over his own fate. "Alas! Is this the way how my kindness has been repaid by my minister's son. No other god in the world but *Sankara*. It is his will that I should undergo this misery. Let me contemplate upon him. He is my only hope here. So thinking the prince Mahîpati sat on meditation. Without food or drink he propitiated the good-conferring deity,—*Sankara*, till he came in person before his dying devotee and asked him what he wanted. Mahípati danced with joy on one foot when he saw *Sankara*, and broke out in loud prayer of him, " O Thou Hara, Thou Hara, Thou Sâmbhâ, Thou Chandrachû*da*. Thine art the whole world, thy servant am I as well as everything animate and inanimate in the world. Grant thy servant's request. Thou lord of all!" The prince then begged the kind God to give him the power to assume the shape of a kite (*garuda*) whenever he wished it. The kind God granted it and disappeared. With the new acquisition Mahîpati assumed the shape of a kite and flew by the hole to the world above him. Thus by the favour of Mahêsa, Mahîpati reached the earth and went at once to the city of Kâlaka*nth*âpura, of course, hiding his ornaments and dress which would proclaim his princely birth to every one that saw him. He boarded in an old Brâhma*n*î's house, and enquired of her whether the prince who some time ago came to that city and took from the king a long chain to go to the nether world to rescue the princess had returned. She replied in the negative. Mahîpati now concluded in his own mind that Bhayamkara had gone to the city of Kâlingpa*tt*ana.

Without waiting even a minute longer at Kalaka*nt*hâpura, our hero Mahîpati started to Kâlingapa*tt*ana, and reached it after ten days' journey (night and day) without meals, except fruits and berries that he could secure in the woods. On the tenth day morning, he reached a small village very near Kalingapa*tt*ana and fell down in a swoon opposite to a Brâhma*n*'s house. The house-owner ran to the spot and found in the face of the traveller royal marks. So he received him into his house, and finding that the swoon was owing to hunger, he fed him sumptuously. Then the prince without informing the Brâhma*n* who he was, asked him whether the prince who started to fight the elephant in the wood, had returned successfully with the princess. When the Brâhma*n* replied in the affirmative, he concluded that the minister's son was reigning there. The Brâhma*n* also informed him of the six months vow of the daughters in the palace, and of three months more remaining still unaccomplished in the vow. Now everything became plain to Mahîpati the unmarried state and the faithfulness of the princesses to himself. After a short rest the prince took leave of the hospitable Brâhma*n* and entered the city.

But he was not destined to enter the city so soon. The treacherous Bhayamkara, suspecting that Mahîpati might return, had given a description of him to the guards in the gate, and had ordered them that if they ever saw such a person, to take hold of him, to carry him to the wood, and there to maim off his left leg and right hand. Accordingly, most unfortunately for our hero, the guards caught hold of him, took him to the wood and there lamed him as ordered. Thus again our prince most unfortunately met another calamity when he was at the point of recovering from all his former calamities.

Mahîpati had no other friend in the world now except his tiger-king whom he thought of now. That faithful animal-monarch came running to him, and seeing his sad state asked him all the reasons for it. With his eyes swimming in tears Mahîpati related to him every point of his adventures ever since he took leave of him at the time of his departure to the nether world. The tiger-king was astonished at the treachery of the minister's son. Still he advised Mahîpati to pluck up courage, and that he would soon return to him with some remedy for his lost limbs. The tiger flew to his priest Vyagramahârishi (the great sage of tigers) and represented to him the calamity of his human friend. That great sage taught his disciple, the king of tigers, an incantation, by the pronouncing of which in one intonation one would get his lost limbs, and in another intonation would lose his acquired limbs. The tiger-king carefully got by heart this incantation with the due peculiarity of pronunciation, and came to Mahîpati, whom he regularly instructed in it. The prince at once saw the effect of it by his getting back the lost limbs by pronouncing it in one way, and by his losing them in pronouncing it in the other way. Mahîpati fell down before his tiger-friend in deep veneration and said, "You alone are my friend. Thank the day in which I assisted you and got your friendship." The tiger requested him to make no mention of it, but to go at once to the city of Kalingapa*ttana* in the disguise of a beggar and win the objects of his affection.

Accordingly, with the blessings of the tiger-king, the prince in the disguise of a beggar started to Kalingapa*ttana* and safely entered the town this time. He engaged himself as a servant to a flower selling woman of that town, and performed his duties most satisfactorily under her. One day he asked her to whom she was selling the garlands she daily made. "To the princesses in the palace," replied she. "If so, I also know how to make fine garlands. I shall do it this day," said he, and that woman consenting, he made out of sweet-scented flowers two fine gowns for the two princesses. The work was done very nicely, and when the old woman presented them to the ladies, they were extremely pleased and rewarded her with a hundred pagodas. "Who is it that does this fine piece of work" asked the ladies. To which the old woman mentioned the lame servant that engaged himself to her. On the next day Mahîpati made two pu*d*avais (garment) out of flowers, and sent in one of them his ring in a small flower case unknown to the flower-woman to the princesses. The Kalingapa*tt*ana princess saw the ring, and recognised in it her valorous protector on two occasions. Calling the Kâlaka*nt*hâpuram princess to a separate place she showed her Mahîpati's ring and said, "Our brave protector is after all in our flower-woman's house. We have no objection now to give permission for our marriage." So thinking, the princesses ordered their flower-woman to take every kind care of the servant under her and by no means to give him any work. She agreed to do so.

The princesses gave permission for the celebration of their marriage, and every grand preparation was made by the king of Kâlingapa*tt*a*na* to make the festivities most splendid. The king of Kalaka*nt*hâpura and several other kings were invited for the occasion. This king of Kâlaka*nt*hâpura shed tears of joy when he heard that his daughter was rescued from the hobgoblin and was going to be married soon. He hastened to Kâlingapa*ttana*.

The marriage day came on. The princesses avoided in every preliminary ceremony the company of the minister's son, who was calling himself and making the world believe that he was the prince. This strange behaviour of the ladies struck amazement into the hearts of all the assembly. When the marriage ceremony was about to be completed, when the band was to be tied round the neck of the princesses, they rose up from their seats and thus addressed the assembly. " This vile wretch is no longer our husband. This is a timid beggar who gave us up to our enemies and never tried in any way to rescue us." They then related as far as they know their adventures, and how Mahîpati assisted them and how the minister's son behaved treacherously towards his own protector. The kings and the whole assembly were amazed and at once sent for the prince, who was now said to be in the flower-woman's house. He came in with his royal dress and related to the assembly whatever remained to be finished by him. The whole matter was now plain. Bhayamkara fell down in a swoon. He was at once removed to a room to be taken care of. To show the reality of his story to the guests Mahìpati took the form of a kite and flew before the assembly. Then taking his original shape he resumed his seat. He pronounced an incantation and his limbs disappeared. Again he pronounced the same in a different way and had them back. The whole assembly was amazed. Among the kings present were also the parents of Bhayamkara and Mahîpati. Both of them came to the prince, and on the recognition of his father Mahîpati flew to his embrace. One universal joy prevailed.

Mahîpati would not marry the princesses without the permission of his tiger-friend. So asking the assembly not to be afraid he just thought on him, when to the amazement of all, he made his appearance. Mahîpati in the presence of the assembly extolled the assistance of the tiger to him. The tiger in return extolled his supernatural sanctity in having seen the good conferring God, *S*ambhu.

Then, with the permission of the tiger-king, the prince Mahîpati in the presence of his father and the fathers of his wives married them and lived happily for a long time. He excused the minister's son and made him over to his father. And must not such a prince marry you, my gem of womankind ? Thus Buddhichâturya finished his story. The sun began to rise and the princess retired to her own apartment.

[MORAL.—This story proves that ungrateful wretches, though they may prosper in the world for a time, shall always be punished in the end for their ingratitude, and that pains shall always be crowned with success notwithstanding the several hardships and disappointments met with in the beginning. We see the former exemplified in Bhayamkara and the latter in the prince, his master.]

ELEVENTH STORY.

ON the night of the eleventh day, the minister's son took his supper and entered the bed-chamber, adorning his body with garlands of sweet scented flowers. And the elder of the princesses as usual bathed in the evening, and putting over her body the choicest ornaments, entered the bedchamber and soothed the ears of her lord with sweet songs for a short time, after which, overcome by love, she began to approach closer to him. Buddhichâturya perceiving her inclination, thus addressed her : "Oh.! You gem of womankind ! I shall relate to you a short story, which being over, we shall retire to rest." The princess consenting, he thus began : There was a city named Kalingapa*tt*ana. Near it, in a small village, there lived a poor beggar-Brâhma*n*. He used to go from house to house daily and beg his rice. The villagers obliged him with enough to eat and more, which he carefully preserved, and thereby had means sufficient to marry himself to a Brâhma*n* woman. In the course of time this pair had a son. His name the father fixed as Sundara. He was put to school in his fifth year, and before the eleventh was completed, had attained a very great proficiency in the four *Vêdas*, six S*âstrâs*, sixty-four

---

Com. Similar story p. 311. *Ind. Antiquary*, Vol. XIV.

sciences, the Codes of Manu, &c. At that age his father died and Sundara performed all the funeral rites duly recommended by the *Sâstras*, and began from that time to live as an orphan under his mother. She was daily used to go out to beg and return by about mid-day with enough of rice, *ghî*, *dhâl*, &c., for five persons to eat. She cooked rice sufficient for three in the morning, and never took her meals without feeding one poor Brâhma*n* in charity. Whatever remained she divided between herself and her son. This duty of giving food every morning in charity to a Brâhma*n* she continued doing every day.

Her young and intelligent son could not understand the reason for this. "We are very poor, so much so, that my mother has daily to go out to beg. Without reserving a handful of rice even, she is very particular in feeding some beggar Brâhma*n* or other. I have never seen such a careless woman anywhere else in this village." So thought Sundara to himself, and one day asked his mother the reason for her feeding one Brâhma*n* every day, To which she replied that she knew of no reason except that all the Codes recommended the charity of feeding to be the greatest of all the sixteen kinds of charities, in accordance with which she did so, and that Isvara (God) must clear his doubts. "Where shall I meet Isvara," asked Sundara. "My son. He is supposed to appear to the eyes of those who practise penance in the Himâlayas. And if you become one of those great men by such practices, you shall also see him," replied his mother. "Then give me something for the way to eat for one or two days. I shall go to the Himâlayas and there try to meet him," continued the son. The mother tried her best to prevent the son from carrying out his wishes; but he persisted. So, she gave him whatever she had for his use for a day or two in his journey, and with her manifold blessings started him out.

Sundara with his small bundle of one or two cloths on his head, which also contained a few eatables, continued his journey towards the north for a couple of days. On the third day he entered a dense forest in which he saw no signs of human life. What he had in his hand for refreshment was exhausted. He walked on very fast with the hopes that some village or other would be seen on his way. He was soon to be disappointed. There was no village anywhere in that part of the forest. The day was almost spent. The sun was sinking down to set in the west. At this time a hunter of the forest perceived the Brâhma*n* boy from a distance. Of course as a hunter he knew the forest to be unpassable during the night as beasts of prey were rife throughout that wilderness. So the hunter ran to the boy, and taking hold of his hand, thus addressed: "My dear boy. You seem to be too young for this travelling business. If I were to see your parents, I should abuse them much for their having allowed you thus to start out. However, we have no time for such discussions here. This wood is infested with bears, tigers and elephants, which will all come out of their dens in a few *ghatikâs*. Follow me to-night to my loft. It is very high and far above the reach of the beasts of prey. Sleep with me after eating, whatever you can get to eat in my hut." Thus spoke the most hospitable hunter, and Sundara found no other course but to follow him.

The hut was reached. The wife of the hunter, a very inhospitable woman, was waiting anxiously to see her husband, and when she saw him with a guest, her anger knew no bounds. She abused her lord most profusely, which he calmly bore. He requested his wife to give to the guest one-third portion of her honey and *tenai*-flour, promising that he would do the same out of his own portion. She firmly refused, on which the husband gave half of his portion of honey and *tenai* to his guest. This food, which the forester gave, was most sweet to Sundara, especially as he had tasted nothing since morning that day.

There was an only loft in the wood which had in it room for only two persons to sleep conveniently. Some arrangement must be made for the sleep of Sundara. The guest being a stranger to sleep in lofts, the hunter feared to leave him in the sides, and so requested his wife to allow the boy-guest to sleep between them. Said she, "I won't give him an inch of my portion of the loft. You must contract your body and sleep only in half of your portion of the loft, leaving the other half between us for the boy." "The God shall bless you for your charitable bent of mind" thought the hunter to himself, and safely made the boy to sleep between himself and his wife in half of his own portion of the loft. But this arrangement cost the hunter his life in return for his hospitality, for unaccustomed to sleep in such a restricted portion, he fell down from the loft in the midnight unnoticed by his wife and guest, who where then sleeping sound. A tiger was watching that night below the loft, and when it saw a human body dropping down it, pounced upon it and carried it away. The night was over. The sun began to rise in the east. Sundara was the first to get up. He did not see the hunter, but never dreamed that such a hard calamity could have befallen him. Thinking that he might have left the loft a little early and gone out on his morning duties, he started to resume his journey. The wife of the hunter next awoke, and not finding her husband she was extremely startled. On jumping down from the loft she found signs of some human being having fallen the previous night a prey to a tiger ; and perceiving at a distance her boy-guest safely continuing his journey, she ran to him and fell down with a great woe before him. "What is all the matter with you?" asked the boy. "All the matter with me! You murderer, you executioner! you are surely the God of death himself in human form. My husband fell a prey to a fierce tiger last night in return for his hospitality to you. Restore him to me before you go on your journey," bawled out the huntress. Though the fate of his hospitable host entered deep the bosom of our Brâhma*n* boy, he could not understand a bit how it was possible in him to restore a dead husband. So he explained to her its impossibility, which she persisted in not believing. At last, extricating himself with great difficulty from her hold, the boy Sundara ran away.

Walking through forests, wilds, mountains and hills, our young traveller reached a village. Now there lived a rich landlord owning immense areas of lands in that village. His fields, if properly cultivated, would furnish him several thousands of *kalams* of paddy. But whatever income he got was only sufficient to repair a big tank in that village, which was the source of cultivation of all the fields of that place, and which broke its banks every year by some reason or other.

Our hero Sundara now reached this landlord's house and became his guest. And at dinner time when the host asked his guest who he was and where he was going, Sundara related to him the object of his journey and everything about himself. The landlord was highly pleased with the boy, and requested him that if ever he happened to see Paramêsvara, he should, after getting his own doubts cleared, ask that God about the great calamity that occurred incessantly every year in his village. He then related to Sundara the tank affair, and how all his income was spent every year in the mere repair of it. Sundara promised to ask Paramêsvara about the reason for that also, and resumed his journey.

In the wood through which he passed after leaving the village, he met a cripple without hands and legs greatly suffering from his want of limbs. The cripple made kind enquiries of Sundara, and when he came to know that he was going to Paramêsvara, requested him to ascertain from that God the cause of his sufferings. Sundara agreed to it, and with his permission resumed his journey.

At a little distance more our traveller met with an old beautiful serpent having both its eyes blind. The serpent was lying on the road, and when it heard the footsteps of some person passing, it enquired of the passer-by as to who he was. Again our hero repeated his story of going to the Himâlayas to meet Paramêsvara. The serpent too requested him to beg of that God if he ever appeared before his eyes, the cause of its blindness, and consequent inability to find its prey. Sundara agreed to do so, and taking leave of the serpent, began his journey. After walking a long distance, he was much exhausted. The day was very hot, so he sat down under a very fine mango tree to rest awhile. That tree was full of fruits from head to foot; but most strange it was, no bird or beast approached it, sat in its shade or tasted its fruits. He was curiously observing t, but not long, for now the tree in human voice thus addressed him: "You friend, whoever you may be, you are the first being that ever sat under my shadow. Kindly tell me first who you are and where you go, before I relate to you my own sad history." The pitiable words in which that son of the forest clothed its words moved the pity of Sundara who, without omitting one single word, related his history to the tree. After hearing him in full the tree thus began: "I shall then think that that great God it was who conducted you here under my shadow. Listen then to my words. I have been standing here for the last several hundred years. Other trees there are round about me which bear fruits only at certain seasons, during which they are crowded by all sorts of birds warbling sweet notes. But though I, by some reason or other, which I am unable to see myself, bear fruits throughout the whole year in the same way as you see me now doing, no dwellers of this wood—beasts or birds—approach me. If you would kindly ask Paramasiva the reason for it, a great portion of my anxiety would be removed." The boy agreed to do so, and took his leave of the tree.

Thenceforth Sundara had no disturbance in his journey. So he safely pursued his pilgrimage day and night till he reached the Himâlayas. There, subduing his five senses, he sat in contemplation of Paramasiva, who appeared before him after two years. Sundara danced and capered with joy, and broke out in a thousand prayers of Paramasiva. That great God was much pleased with his young Brâhman devotee and wished to know what boon he wanted. Our hero gave out that he wished to know the meritoriousness of distributing rice gratis to Brâhmans as well as the cause of the disaster to the tank in the village of his second host the landlord, of the lameness of the cripple, of the blindness of the serpent, and of the unfrequentedness of the mango tree by beasts or birds. He also wished to know the manner in which each of the hardships could be removed. And Paramêsvara thus replied: "My son. To know the meritoriousness of the distribution of rice you must wait some time. There is a country called Virâta at a great distance from this place near to the place of your second host, the landlord who entertained you and reported to you about the tank disaster. The king of that country has no son. If you go to that place and give holy ashes, his queen will become pregnant. On the tenth month of her pregnancy while she is confined, ask the king to request the midwives to receive the newborn baby in a gold platter covered over with tender plantain leaf. When the baby is thus received, get it out of the confinement room and put to it the question, "What is the meritoriousness of the distribution of rice," and the baby to the amazement of all shall answer you. And as for the tank breaking in the village of your second host, he has two daughters in his house as yet unmarried. As soon as he gives them away in marriage that disaster shall cease. As for the suffering cripple, he is a great man of learning, and as he is averse to distribute his knowledge to those that came to him, he has become a cripple. If he hereafter leaves off that bad habit, he will have his limbs back. As for the serpent, it has a ripe gem in its hood. If it gives that jewel away to any one, it shall regain its sight. And as for the mango tree, it has a rich treasure-trove of seven jars of gold below its root. And as soon as they are taken and presented to any one, beasts and birds shall approach it and live under its shadow. Thus I have dispelled your darkness, and you may go now to Virâ*t*adê*s*a. Thus ended *S*iva, and Sundara now asked his God to grant him back the poor hunter who fell a prey to a tiger in return for his hospitality, to which Parama*s*iva said that he would learn everything about him from the baby and disappeared.

Sundara now returned. He reached the mango tree first and reported to it the reason for its being thus unfrequented. It presented the seven jars of wealth to him. He received them, and asked the mango tree to keep it on his account till he again came to take it. Now that the wealth was no more with the tree, beasts and birds began to frequent it, and eat of its fruit from that time. Sundara next went to the serpent, who, soon as he heard the cause of his blindness, presented his deliverer with the gem in its hood. Next Sundara went to the cripple who, knowing his own bad nature, and on being ashamed and convinced of it, taught to Sundara all the knowledge he had acquired. Sundara now reached the house of the rich landlord of the lake disaster. That gentleman, when he knew that his unmarried daughters were the cause of all mishaps, at once married them to Sundara. The disaster stopped, and Sundara leaving his wives in their parent's house for some time went to the country of Virâ*t*a.

There he saw the king, and said that he would give holy ashes to the queen by which she would become pregnant. The king had no hopes, but still not wishing to disappoint the new comer, allowed him his way. Sundara was not an ordinary man come down merely to try a chance. So, the holy ashes he gave had effect, and in a couple of months after he began the distribution the queen became pregnant. The king's joy knew no bounds. The new Brâhma*n*, our hero Sundara, had every honour. Month after month passed till the tenth month came on. Sundara now requested the king to make arrangements with the midwives to receive the new-born child on a gold platter with tender plantain leaves spread over it without the baby touching the ground. He also told them that the child shall disclose a secret which would amaze them all.

These words were enough in themselves to make the assembly astonished. The king made every arrangement for fulfilling Sundara's request.

It was accordingly done. The new born boy was brought before the king, and a large assembly which had gathered when it was made known in that town that a child was going to reveal some secret. " What is the meritoriousness of the performing of the charity of the distribution of rice," asked Sundara, after most respectfully bowing down before it. Silence reigned throughout the whole assembly to hear the answer of the baby, and amazing all a thousandfold it thus spoke : "My dear Brâhma*n*. I am quite unable to describe it in full, nor could Ádisêsha the thousand tongued do it. But listen please to my short experience, and judge from it yourself. Know that I am that hunter who met you first on that wood when you were proceeding towards the Himâlayas. Because I gave you honey and *tenai* flour and a little room to sleep in, I am born in this life a prince, after falling a prey to a tiger on the very night of my hospitality. My wife who refused you meals and place to sleep in, died on the next day after me, and is to-day born a pig in the *Paraiya* quarters of this town. That pig you can distinguish by its four legs being white and its forehead being spotted. From this you can imagine the meritoriousness of rice distribution yourself." Here the baby closed its mouth, and though several persons put to it several questions, it never answered them. All the persons in the assembly (and there were several kings also come from several countries) were amazed, and asked Sundara his history and the reason for the baby having spoken to him only. Sundara without omitting even a single part, related to them everything. An ocean of admiration for the excellent Brâhma*n* who had seen Paramêsvara rolled throughout the assembly. The king of

Virâ*t*a, who owed his son to Sundara's meritoriousness, made arrangements for the removal of his patron's mother, two wives and several jars of wealth to his own town. Sundara had a rich palace to live in. His mother and wives joined him soon, and with these he lived happily for a long time.

"And must not a prince like the Brâhma*n* youth Sundara marry you? Oh! You gem of womankind!" Thus ended Buddhbichâturya his eleventh story. The sun began to rise, the princess and the minister's son retired separately after their business.

[Moral.—This story contains the grand moral that the highest charity in the world is the giving of food to the hungry, and the masters of such charity shall be rewarded with princely birth in their next life in this world.]

TWELFTH STORY.

On the night of the twelfth day the minister's son, after his supper and decoration, entered the bed-chamber: and the youngest of the princesses as usual bathed in the evening and ornamented her person with her most costly jewels. She sang for a short time to her guitar, and afterwards, overcome by love as it were, at last approached the side of her lord, who now wishing to calm down her love by a fine story, thus addressed her: "My dear gem of womankind. This day also I have a short story to relate, which being over, we shall retire to rest". The princess consenting, he thus began :—

"Listen! Oh you gem of womankind! There was a country named Kalingadêsa. The king of that country was named Gauravarâja. He was a most just and benevolent king, and ruled so well that one and all his subjects liked him. This king had a son named K*r*ish*n*a. Gauravarâja had his son educated regularly, and when he came to his proper age married him to a beautiful princess of an adjacent country. Thus passed some months.

One day the prince K*r*ish*n*a started on a hunting expedition with hunters, hounds, &c. After spending the greater portion of the dayin the wood, the prince returned home late in the afternoon, and on his way happened to pass through the north street of that town where the oilmongers lived. In front of a certain oilmonger's house a charming beauty of that caste, a girl of ten to fifteen years of age, was sitting on watch over some sesamum seed spread in the sun for being dried. Wishing to talk to her, the prince K*r*ish*n*a thus addressed her: "Oh thou beautiful lady that wert born in the sesamum seed, that art bred up now in sesamum seed, what is that leaf that is smaller in shape than even the sesamum seed?" The oilmonger's daughter, who was more intelligent than the prince, made her reply a question as it were to K*r*ish*n*a, and thus addressed: "Oh thou prince that wert born and art bred up in a flower, what is that flower which has only two petals?" "It is the *Vattadârai* flower that has two petals," said the prince. "Then it is the same *Vattadârai* flower that is smaller in shape than the sesamum seed," said the girl. The prince was much ashamed at the device of the maid, in giving for her reply a question the reply to which formed the reply to his question also. The shame turned out in anger and the prince said: "Oh thou maid, now that thou hast put me to disgrace without patiently answering my question, I shall marry and imprison thee for thy whole life.'" The girl calmly received the sentence, and with a smile replied: "Oh, thou prince, if thou happenest to become my lord and imprisonest me as thou sayst, I shall by some secret way or other become pregnant to thee, and shall bear a son to thee and make him chastise thee with a cord after tying thee up first in a gunny bag."

Thus took place in fun an agreement between K*r*ish*n*a the prince and the oilmonger girl, who was named Rukma*n*î The prince returned home, without taking his bath and meals and confined himself to his room. This fact was very vexing to all in the palace. "There must be something wrong in K*r*ish*n*a today; for why should he not take his bath and meals after the tiresome hunt," thought they, and reported the matter at once to the old king. And when Gauravarâja came and saw his son he found him lying in his bed with his face disfigured by sorrow. "What is the matter with you my son," said the father. "Marry me to the oilmonger girl in the north street. She lives in such and such a house," replied K*r*ish*n*a, and exactly described the house, intimating to him at the same time that unless the match was settled he would never leave his bed.

The old father was extremely vexed to see his son in such a great sorrow. Away he flew to the north street to arrange that the oilmonger girl should marry the prince. When a girl of such a poor caste was courted by a king to become his daughter-in-law what objection would her parents have to it. The day of the marriage was at once fixed, and Gauravarâja returned to his son and informed him of the settlement of the match. Then it was that the prince rose up from his bed and had his bath and meals.

Letters were sent by the old king to all the kings of the world inviting them to the marriage. Before the day came off Rukma*n*i, the oilmonger girl, informed her father of what had taken place between herself and the prince, and what sort of treatment she would undergo under the latter's hands. "What if he is a prince? I shall then not give my consent to the marriage," said the father. "No," replied the daughter. "There is no use of your refusal at this stage. You must ascertain where I am imprisoned, and construct a subterranean passage between our house and the place of my imprisonment. I shall tell you little by little what we should do then." Thus was the old oilmonger instructed by his intelligent daughter. The marriage day came off and the festivities were celebrated with all pomp. After all the ceremonies of the marriage were over, the guests took leave and returned to their several countries. And the prince, true to his vow to his new wife before she was married to him, imprisoned her in a snug room of a sequestered house situated in a pleasure garden. He appointed a maid servant to assist her. In the house he left all provisions, &c., for several years, and locking up the door kept the key of it in his possession. Thus was Rukma*n*î imprisoned.

Her father, according to the instructions he had already received, after knowing the place of his daughter's imprisonment, readily made a subterranean passage between her room there and his house. Rukma*n*î was extremely pleased at her father's success, and bolting the door of the room on the inner side, she went through the passage and found it leading right to her house. As the way had been made, she spoke to her father thus: "My dear father. Now that the way is successfully completed, I may say that my object is almost gained. I request you now to look out for the best rope-dancer you can see and bring him to my house and promise to pay him any reward he demands. The father agreed and started to fetch the rope-dancer. Meanwhile Rukma*n*î returned to her room, called the maid who was set to assist her in that house, and addressed her thus: "I do not wish to be disturbed by you every now and then; when I call you by your name give me through the usual window whatever you keep cooked for me, to eat. At other times you may do whatever you like and watch the locked door." The maid agreed to it. Here it is necessary to explain the relation of the room in which Rukma*n*î was imprisoned to the house in which the room was situated. That room was one of the several apartments in the house in which Rukma*n*î was confined. The prince kept the key of the room with him. In that house, with no connection whatever with the imprisoned. Rukma*n*î the maid lived with all the necessary provisions to supply the imprisoned lady. When the food was to be served the maid handed it through a small hole in the window through which only a small hand could pass. Inside the rooms, the lady made her appearance at the time when she should receive her meals and after receiving them returned to her father by the subterranean passage. This sort of affair went on daily ; and except during the time she received her food Rukma*n*î never lived in the dungeon.

At her house her old father brought her a very clever rope-dancer under whom she spent her time in learning all the arts of dancing on ropes and playing other tricks of that profession. Said she to him : " My dear Rope-dancer. You are as it were another father to me. You must teach me all you know and taking me out as your daughter, make me to dance before the public. After short trials in one or two places we should all go to the palace and dance before the king.

I shall reward you with whatever you want if my object is only successfully accomplished." She then explained to him everything between herself and the prince and earnestly craved the old rope-dancer's assistance. This man taught Rukma*n*î all he knew with heart and soul. She too being very intelligent and having at heart a great object in view learnt everything most excellently, so much so, that she became a great proficient in that art. In dress and outward appearance she changed herself quite like a rope-dancer's daughter and with the old man of that art appeared before the public and successfully performed her tricks, on several occasions. She then asked her old friend and master to go to the palace and make arrangements to show their arts before the members of the royal household. The next day was fixed for it; and the old rope-dancer with Rukma*n*î disguised as his daughter and a number of other performers came to the palace and made a splendid display of his proficiency before the royal party. The supposed daughter performed almost all the tricks on the rope, and all the assembly especially the prince K*r*ish*n*a were greatly pleased. The latter went even beyond that. The young and brisk appearance of the female performer in addition to the proficiency of her art aroused in the mind of K*r*ish*n*a amorous desires towards her, so much so, that he desired to live with her for some time. He sent for the old man and he came. Krishna after praising for a long time his daughter's attainments secretly hinted the objects in his mind. The old man made very great objections or rather seemed to make them till he had to be rewarded amply before he consented. He then arranged a small hut outside the town where he asked the prince to pay his visits. The supposed daughter of the old rope-dancer, but the real wife of the prince —the oilmonger's daughter Rukmanî met her husband in the hut though the latter never dreamt that she was his own wife whom he had regularly married. The visits continued severa days, till at last Rukmanî became pregnant. During these visits the supposed daughter of the rope-dancer managed to get from the prince with his own consent, his pearl garland, diamond-garland and signet ring. Now that her object was accomplished, she asked her old master to take leave of the prince that he must go to his own native place for sometime and that he would return soon. The prince was not able to refuse the oldman's request though his affection for the daughter was very great. And the old man pretented that he would be back with his daughter soon. So they all separated. Of course, the old rope-dancer went to his own village with all the rewards he could get from the prince and the oilmonger's daughter and never returned.

Rukma*n*î too, we shall find never to see the prince again, till she had successfully performed her vow through her future son.

She no more wanted to take herself to the profession of dancing, now that she had become pregnant. She lived most conveniently in her father's house and only presented herself in the room of imprisonment during meal hours, and took away to her father's house whatever the maid servant gave her. So, there was not even the least room of doubt as to what was going on inside. When she was receiving the prince in her assumed form of a rope-dancer's daughter, she lived all the day in her room of imprisonment, and when the prince came there to see whether the criminal was all right she gave him attendance and thus calmed down his suspicious mind. At the end of her pregnancy, she brought to bed in her father's house a beautiful male child. The baby grew old, and began to display great intelligence. He mingled with the boys of his age and began to sport with them. His mother as usual waited in the room of her imprisonment for her food and lived in her father's house all the rest of the time and continued to bring up her son most tenderly.

One day, when this son of Rukma*n*î, who was named Ratnam, was playing with his companions, one of them accused him of being a bastard and as one having no father. The boy being very sensitive was extremely provoked, came running to his grand-father with his eyes swimming in tears and asked him who his father was. That old man instead of himself revealing the secret to him pointed to a hole and asked him to proceed by its way and ask that question of any one whom he met. The boy at once took to that way and reached the prison room of his mother. He prostrated himself before her and asked who his father was. She was extremely pleased at the curiosity of her son which she thought would open up the way to the fulfillment of her vow. Taking her son on her lap she related to him her whole history from the time she first met the prince up to the time she met her son. Ratnam was delighted at all that he heard, and encouraging his mother thus replied: "My dearest mother. I am very sorry that you should thus undergo imprisonment. I shall soon so manage that your vow shall be accomplished, and we all live together with the prince in his palace instead of this dirty room or my grand-father's house." These words fell like nectar in Rukma*nî*'s ears, and again kissing her son, she blessed him and sent him away.

Ratnam, soon as he came to his grand-father, took sufficient money from him and started to an adjacent wood, where he met with an old woman. "Grandmother, I am ready to become your servant and do whatever duties you assign to me, if you would only give me so much of rice," said Ratnam to her, spreading out the fingers of his right hand which he pointed to her face. She was much pleased with the boy's physiognomy, and willingly agreed to feed him if only he would graze her ten buffalos. Ratnam readily consented, and from that day lived in that wood. The buffalos he would drive out in the morning and collect them under a tree near the house of a notorious robber, from whom he learned all the arts of thieving. Thus he passed on several months, till he became himself a first-rate robber, both in open and in secret robbery. To put his knowledge to test, he wished to rob his father in his bed-chamber.

Accordingly one night after his duties to the buffalos were over and after his supper, he supplied himself with four plantain-tree stumps, and concealing himself by means of a *tilaka* (a spot applied to the forehead) entered his father's bed-chamber; there he found him sound asleep. By sprinkling a little powder over his body, he mesmerised him totally. After this Ratnam removed the four coral legs of his father's cot, supplanting them with the four plantain stumps and walked away with them as well as with all the jewels on his father's body. These he buried in the sandy bed of the river near the house of the old woman in the wood and went and slept in her house in his usual place without arousing the suspicion of any one.

In the palace the prince rose up in the morning from his bed when his cot tumbled and brought him down most awkwardly. On examining his body he found he had been robbed of all his ornaments. The legs of his cot had likewise been plundered. "What must be the dexterity and extraordinary ability of the thief, who thus in the dead of night boldly entered my very sleeping room, and without in the least shaking my cot or body, plundered the coral legs and ornaments"—thought the prince, and at once reported the matter to the old king. The news that a most daring sort of theft had been committed in the palace spread throughout the town. The head night-watch was called in. When he presented himself, the old king abused him in a severe way and threatened to have his head cut off from his body in case the previous night's thief was not detected before the next morning. He promised to do his best and went on his business.

Ratnam, our young robber in the wood, came to the town the next morning and heard people talking about the arrangements made to catch the thief. He also came to know the fact that the head night-watch had been ordered to produce the thief before the next morning, and that in case of his failure he would lose his head. On enquiring everything about the head-watch our robber Ratnam came to know that a young son-in-law of that watch had several years ago gone to Bânâras and never returned, though his people were expecting him every day. As the headwatch had only one daughter, his grief for the disappearance of that relation of his was unbearable. Our hero Ratnam now disguised himself in the shape of a pilgrim just returning from Bânâras, and took with him enough and even more of very valuable presents in the shape of valuable cloths, jewels, &c., to his parents-in-law and wife. With these he returned at about evening to the house of the headwatch. The sight of a pilgrim from Bânâras in their threshold brought on a cheerful countenance in the face of one and all the house. Ratnam had carefully learnt the name of the missing son-in-law, which name he temporarily gave out. The rich presents he brought, the coincidence in name and the several particulars which Ratnam carefully got up and gave out, made the night-watch, his wife and daughter think that the pilgrim was their very son-in-law. So many years had already passed that the parents-in-law were not able to find out any dissimilarity in the face of the present son-in-law when compared with the faint recollections they had of him when he, more than ten years ago, left for Bânâras. There was a grand feast. The costly presents caused greater respect to be shewn towards the son-in-law. The only anxiety the headwatch had internally working in his mind was the duty he had for the night to watch, and catch the thief. So heartily the son-in-law was entertained and sent in to sleep with the daughter in her bed-room. There he gave her all the presents and talked most affectionately to her. In the course of the conversation, he asked her the reason for his hasty entertainment. And when she told him about the duty her father had that night and the responsibility of it, he quickly embraced her and came out of the bed chamber. Then it was his old father-in-law or supposed father-in-law was starting out on the thief-catching-expedition. "Where do you go out, respected father, at this time of the night," said Ratnam to the head-watch. "My dear son, of late robbers have increased in this town and are doing a great deal of mischief," said the watch, and wished to go away soon. The son-in-law said that he would also accompany him. This old-watch could not refuse the first favour of his son-in-law and so took him along. On the way Ratnam saw a pair of stocks in the road, and as one who knew nothing about them asked his father-in-law what they were. "There are holes in the timber in which any rogue or thief has to put in his hands and legs till they are driven in and screwed as a sort of punishment for his offence. He would have to stand in that painful posture in proportion to his crime," said the head-watch, in explanation to the question which his son-in-law in a sort of pretended amazement asked his father-in-law. "This sort of punishment I have never met with in all my travels. Let me see how it is. I shall send in my hands and legs. You had better screw in the latch," said the amazed son-in-law to the head-watch, his father-in law, who, not liking the former to undergo the experiment, himself undertook to shew it to him. So the head-watch put his hands and legs into the holes and asked his son-in-law to screw the latch. Ratnam glad at heart that his trick had such good effect, screwed the latch so well that when he wanted or rather pretended to unscrew it, he found himself unable to do it without the requisite instruments for it. "What shall I do. I have screwed it so very tight that my bare hands cannot unscrew it now," said Ratnam to his supposed father-in-law, who now asked him not to be vexed at it. He then asked Ratnam to go home and fetch the proper instrument to take out the latch. And he accordingly went.

And did he fetch the instrument? No. He went to his mother-in-law crying most sorrowfully and stammering, "My father-in-law is in great jeopardy. He has incurred the royal displeasure and tomorrow he may lose his life. All his property is to be confiscated to the state. So he asked me to speak to you and make arrangements to conceal as much as we can of our wealth." That poor old woman took him for his words, and immediately gave him all the valuables she had in her house, with which our hero bolted away, pretending to conceal them in some safer place beyond the reach of the king's servants.

Thus Ratnam again most cunningly walked away with all the property of the very person who was ordered to catch him. He buried these near his first booty and returned to the house of the old woman of the wood before dawn. The head-watch continued watching at the stocks without dreaming of the trick that has been played upon him by his supposed son-in-law. He patiently bore up his miseries till dawn, and then finding no hopes he bawled out.

A great crowd began to gather near the place where the head-watch was put in the stocks. The old king, the minister, the prince and the minister's son came also to that place. The people of the head-watch too came to the spot and related to him what his son-in-law did to his property. The amazement of all knew no bounds. It was now perfectly clear that the disguised son-in-law was the thief himself. Every one assembled, even the king praised, the thief, and released the watch from his excruciating pain.

So great was the amazement of all, that the minister's son himself vowed to catch the thief that night. The king gave him an army of one thousand cavalry with which he started to the adjacent wood to trace out the robbers. Now we all know that our hero was living in that very wood. He came to know by some secret way that the minister's son was in duty that night to catch him. Our readers already know hat there was a small stream there in which our hero always buried his booty. He now disguised himself like a poor washerman, and with one hundred dirty rags placed in a huge tub, began to wash in that stream. After searching the several parts of the wood, the minister's son happened to pass by that way in the dead of night. When he heard a washerman engaged there in the dead of night, he came and asked him what reason he had to work in that part of the night. Our hero answered, "Sir, daily several robbers pass by this way. They give me dirty clothes to wash while going towards the town and take them back from me when they return. As I get good wages from them, I am engaged in my work even in this untimely hour." The minister's son was extremely delighted at this report, and thought with himself to have caught the robbers almost. He asked the supposed washerman whether he would assist him in catching the robbers. "How can it be done when these soldiers are round about us. We must both remain here: all these soldiers ought to go away to a great distance and conceal themselves. And they must not go to sleep in their place of concealment, but be ready to join us when we give the signal," replied our Ratnam, and the minister's son made arrangements accordingly. After their disappearance our young robber told the minister's son that the thieves would be rather chary in coming if he thus sat outside exposing himself. He told him that he would cover him over with his big tub, and when the robbers come up would let him out with the pretence of opening the tub. The minister's son agreed to it and removed from his body all ornaments and costly dress. After placing a stone over the tub that the minister's son might not escape, he took his ornaments and buried them near the two former booties and ran away to the old woman's house. The minister's son in the tub waited till he was suffocated. He then bawled out when his men came and relieved him from his misery. It was now as clear as broad daylight that the robber was no other than the washerman himself. The minister's son was much ashamed of the trick that was played upon him. He instructed his men to keep that night's shame a dead secret, and excused himself the next morning before the king and the prince saying that he was not able to catch the thief.

It was then the prince vowed before his father that he would himself go out that night and catch the thief. His father supplied him with one thousand mounted men, and with these he started towards the wood to trace the robber. Our hero Ratnam when he came to know that his father was in the wood, thought with himself that his mother's vow was accomplished. He now assumed the disguise of a betel-nut seller, and with a bag of nuts and a basketful of betel-leaves and a bundle of tobacco, set up a bâzâr in a wide plain in the wilderness with a glimmering light. The prince, when he saw the light, gave instructions to his soldiers to surround that spot in the form of a circle and himself slowly approached the place. Our hero, who was watching all that took place round him, slowly approached the prince, and falling down on his feet thus addressed him: "My lord, I am a very poor bâzârman selling betel-nut and tobacco for robbers that go by this way to rob. I get ten thousand per cent as my gain and hence have taken up this profession. Kindly excuse me." The prince was greatly pleased. He asked our hero Ratnam to assist him in catching the robbers. Said our hero, "My lord, you must order our men to be in ambush, and present themselves soon as we give a signal. You must now go into this tobacco bag. I will just shut the mouth of it, and open it in the pretence of taking tobacco out when the thieves come to me. You shall then catch hold of the robbers." The prince agreed to it, and undressing himself and removing all ornaments from off his body, he entered the bag. Ratnam tied the mouth of it and dressed himself in the clothes of the prince,—his father. He was so like him that when he put on the ornaments also, he resembled his father,—the prince himself. Ratnam now gave the whistle, and all the soldiers came out of the ambush. Pointing to the bag he said to them, "The thief is caught after all; take him up; he disclosed to me the places where the former booties were concealed by him. "Follow," said Ratnam to the soldiers of his father, who took him to be the very prince himself. He came to the spot where the coral legs of the cot, the ornaments, &c., of the prince, head-watch and the minister's son, were concealed. He ordered his soldiers to take possession of them and came to the palace.

The morning dawned. The news that the daring robber was caught spread throughout the town and all the gentry came to the palace. Our hero Ratnam, in whose face the old king his grandfather could not find any dissimilarity, thus addressed his grandfather; "There is the thief here and here are the booties that he plundered formerly in the palace, head-watch's house and from the minister's son." Then he opened the bag and let out the naked prince, whom he beat gently with the cord in his hand. The assembly was amazed. They found two princes, but one was naked. The naked and real prince now ran to a corner and concealed himself. His father, the old king, who now fully recognised his son in the running prince, ran after him, and after assisting him with the necessary clothes, asked him what the matter was. K*r*ish*n*a now explained everything of the treachery that was played upon him by the boy in the assembly, who called himself the prince. The old king was struck by the majesty of our hero's face, and asked him his history. "That would become plain if you send for your daughter-in-law imprisoned in the dark room of the house in the garden," said Ratnam. All these seemed an enigma to all in the assembly except K*r*ish*n*a. For to him the oath which the oilmonger's daughter Rukma*n*î took before him came to his mind. The daughter-in-law was sent for, by the old king. A concealed place behind a screen was given her. And from that place she related her whole story to the assembly from the time she first met the prince to that day, without omitting her adventures as the rope-dancer's daughter, &c. She now laid before the assembly the pearl-garland, diamond-garland and signet ring of the prince which she took from him when she met him in the hut as the rope-dancer's daughter. Ratnam now related all his adventures, and how he deceived the prince while asleep and while awake, as well as the head-watch and the minister's son, who now hung down their heads out of shame.

All in the assembly praised the skilfulness of Rukmaṇî and Ratnam and blessed them with long life. And the prince having no children by his first wife, gladly received in his palace with great pride Ratnam and Rukmaṇî. He excused the impertinence of his son who now, since his vow was over, humbled himself to the very dust before his father. The prince begged several excuses from his wife for all his ill-treatment to her, and from that day reigned most happily.

"And must not such a prince's son like Ratnam marry you. Oh! My gem of womankind!" Thus ended Buddhichâturya his twelfth story. The sun began to rise. The princess and the minister's son retired after their particular duties.

[MORAL.—The concluding moral in this story illustrates how vindictive persons, sacrificing their position, honour and occupation adhere to their oaths through all difficulties and successfully accomplish them. The queen, our heroine, joined the rope-dancers, performed in that menial capacity before her own husband, the prince, without his knowledge, and successfully accomplished her vows.]

CONCLUSION.

On the morning of the thirteenth day the minister's son was seated in the bathing apartment of the palace engaged in washing his teeth. Both the sisters—the princesses whom their husband, the minister's son Buddhichâturya, had been deceiving by relating stories for the past twelve nights—came up there to assist him in his bath. On their way the elder said to the younger, "Sister, do you see the real intention of our husband. He has been keeping us away for the last twelve days from the marriage-bed, and, to make us forget our amorous sports, has purposely been telling us stories. And moreover every time a story ends he concludes it by saying, "And should not a husband like the hero of the narrative marry you my gem of womankind?" Bearing in our mind that he had the marriage-band tied round our necks by female hands instead of doing it himself, we must infer, by his concluding statements at the end of every story, that he means not to marry us to himself. I think he has reserved us for some other prince. We have been silent till now, but let us take this opportunity of plainly asking him his intention."

Thus thinking within themselves the princesses approached Buddhichâturya—their husband, and revealed to him all their doubts. The minister's son with a sweet smile thus began:—" Dear ladies! I suppose you have had the dawn of intellect only to-day. And it was for this dawn of itself that I related to you so many stories. Good days are before all of us hereafter. Know then my history. I am the son of the minister of Mahêndrapurî. The prince of Mahêndrapurî is my king. After our school-life our amusements used to take place on the tank-bank of our town, where my prince was used to break the water-pots on the heads of the ladies who returned from the tank by shooting a dried mud-ball at the vessel. I, by immediately sending after it a wet mud-ball, was used to close the gap. Thus we amused ourselves during several years. On one occasion I left my king—the prince—on the tank-bund and went home for my breakfast. In the interval the daughter of the king's household priest, who had all along entertained a very great love for the prince, came to the tank, and seeing him all alone, wished him to gratify her desires. He refusing, she disfigured her body and in the state of a chaste woman who was roughly handled by a bad man, came and reported to her father that the prince had ill-treated her. The enraged father flew to the court and reported to the king his son's immoral conduct. The father, the most just king the world has ever produced, called the executioners, and without enquiring into the matter and finding out the truth, ordered them to cut off his son's head. One of the executioners came to me. I spoke kind words to them and bribing them rescued my prince. We then set out for some unknown country and reached the town of Indrapurî, in the temple of which my prince fell into a swoon before a picture in which were represented two ladies. They were the incarnations of beauty itself. All my efforts to bring the prince back to his senses proved vain. The doctors told me that unless the objects of the picture stood before him he would not revive. So I gave over the senseless prince to the charge of a respectable gentleman and started to find out the objects of the picture.

Know then that those objects were none other but yourselves. With great difficulty I traced out the painter, who told me that he never saw you in his life, but drew your figures from a hair of your head which was presented to him by an oil-rubber. I enquired who the oil-rubber was, and came to know that he was the head oil-rubber in your palace. I went to his house as his brother-in-law and was his guest for a few days. My object was to know first whether you were really the objects represented in the picture. For that I devised a scheme to have an oil-rubbing near that room adjacent to your window. The head oil-rubber, whose brother-in-law I was supposed to be, agreed to it. I placed before me a big dish of oil, in which the shape of anything above it, could very well be seen reflected. The head oil-rubber with all sorts of time-beatings began to rub the oil. You were then inside your room, and hearing a noise near the window, opened its doors and enquired the cause of it. Down in the oil I saw your forms reflected, and satisfied myself that you were the very objects represented in the picture.

Then it was that I began to ask whether your hands could be disposed of in marriage, if any suitable bridegroom would present himself. The reply to this was a great stroke to me. As I thought that all my troubles to secure you had proved vain, I went into the ocean to commit suicide. The great God Paramêsvara then presented himself before me and gave me hopes. He only asked me to be wandering in the streets of your town, which I did. He then appears to have come to your father as an ascetic. Your father invited him for a dinner, before partaking of which the pretended ascetic, on the plea that his host's daughters were, even after having attained their puberty,—unmarried,—disappeared.

The sudden loss of the ascetic infused great fear into the mind of your father. He cursed himself for all his former cruelty to the several bridegrooms who had presented themselves. The thought, that he had lost the company of an ascetic whom he took to be the great God himself, stung him to his heart. He at once wanted to give his daughters away in marriage to any suitable prince that he could procure for the occasion. His ministers were sent to search about the town for any travelling or sojourneying prince. As I was then wandering in the streets of this town, instructed to do so by the great God, the ministers took me to your father, where I agreed to marry you on condition that only Brâhma*n* ladies should tie the marriage-band round your necks. By acting in this way and by keeping you from off my bed for the last twelve days, I meant one of you to become my prince's wife. I must take both of you to my prince. She, whom he likes of you both, must become his wife; and the other must become mine."

Thus ended Buddhichâturya. The princesses listened to his adventures with great pleasure, and requested him to start that very moment towards the city of his prince. He asked them to take the permission of their parents: of course, the old king had no objection. A daughter cannot always remain in her father's house. So, there was a grand feast that day in the palace, and Buddhichâturya started off with the two princesses to proceed towards his country. His father-in-law gave him several horses and elephants as dowries for the princesses. A big army of infantry was also presented to the son-in-law.

With these and the princesses Buddhichâturya started to the city where the prince was lying entranced. On the way, he met the painter in his village, and rewarded him amply for all his troubles. Then journeying through mountains, forests, and over hills and rocks, Buddhichâturya reached Indrapura, the city where Madanakâma the prince, was living. He lodged all his followers, animals, and men in suitable quarters, and after bath and ablutions, entered the temple with the princesses to worship the God there. The prince Madanakâma was so much enslaved through love of the objects in the picture, that excepting his meal time, he always chose to remain in the circuit of the temple before the paintings.

Buddhichâturya, after his adoration of the God, went to the place where the prince was lying down, and made both the princesses stand before him. As a lion springing up after his couchant posture, Madanakâma rose up and touched the eldest of the princesses. The youngest stood behind Buddhichâturya. Thus, it was established that the first princess was to be the prince's wife. Buddhichâturya requested his prince to wait for the consummation of the marriage till they reached their own country and till their weddings were publicly celebrated. The prince readily consented.

They all left the temple and went to their quarters. The prince asked him how he succeeded in getting the princesses. Then Buddhichâturya related to the prince all his adventures, at which the latter was much pleased. Said Madanakâma, "You first protected me from the hands of the executioners, and again from a greater executioner—Love : I do not know how I shall repay you." The minister's son replied him that it was only his duty as a minister on both the occasions to have saved his master's life.

They all then started to their own native country—Mahêndrapurî. After a day's journey they reached a fine tope with a big banyan tree. Underneath that tree the prince pitched his tent. The minister's son was encamped near him at a short distance. In a third tent, surrounded by all the body-guards, lived the princesses. Evening came on. Exhausted by the troubles of the journey one and all the persons in the encampment were sound asleep. There was only one person in whom alone sleep found an enemy. That was Buddhichâturya, the minister's son. The night was half spent. At that time the hootings of two owls fell into his ears. He listened to them closely, for it must now be known to us that our hero Buddhichâturya was a great interpreter of bird's speech.

The owls happened to be a male and female, and after their amorous sports were over, fell into the following conversations. Said the male bird, "My dear love, the prince, encamped under our tree, is to die shortly by the falling upon him of a big branch of this tree which is shortly to break." "And if he escapes this calamity," rejoined the female bird. "He will die to-morrow in a river in which he is going to pitch his tent; the river will be dry when he pitches it, but in the mid-night a heavy flood shall rush down the river and carry him away," said the male bird. "And if he escapes this second calamity too" exclaimed the female bird. "Then he shall surely die by the hands of his wife when he reaches his town," said the male bird. "And if he escapes this third calamity too" exclaimed the female bird. "My dear love. This calamity must befall the prince without failure. He will never escape it. And if he does he will reign as a great king and king of kings for several hundreds of years," answered the male bird. It also spoke out to its love that he who, happening to know the secret, reveals it, shall have his head broken into a thousand pieces.

The three calamities and the curse on the person who would reveal them struck amazement in the mind of the minister's son. But he had no time to lose. He rose up, and going into the prince's tent removed him while he was asleep with his cot to another place far off from the tree. No sooner the cot was set in its new place than the branch of the tree broke, and in its horrible noise awoke all in the army as well as the prince. "What! I was sleeping under the very tent which that branch has smashed to pieces. How was it that I was removed to here," said the amazed prince. "I heard the noise of the breaking branch and removed your cot" was all the reply the minister's son gave for it. The prince was astonished at the carefulness of the minister's son. The sun began to rise and Madanakâma and his followers began their journey till they reached the banks of a river. All preferred to encamp on the embankment while the prince alone was obstinate in pitching his tent in the river bed. No one could persuade him. So, he was in the river bed, while all the others were in a safer place. The night came on. It was a fine moonlight night. The minister's son Buddhichâturya gave orders that none but the prince should sleep in the river bed. And as his followers regarded him with great respect, they could not refuse him. So all were sound asleep but the minister's son, as we very well know. The night was far advanced. Rustling of waters was heard at a distance. Buddhichâturya who, ever since he heard the owl, had banished sleep from his eyes, at once removed the prince with the cot to the bank. On waking up at the noise of the flood, the prince was amazed again with wonder at his escape, and thus addressed his minister: "What, I was sleeping in the river-bed which is all now deeply sunk in water. How is it that I am now here without any injury?" Buddhichâturya told him how watchful he was and how he removed him without his own knowledge to the bank. Again said the prince, "Language has no words to express my affection to you. From the very beginning of our life you have always been my saviour. There, in our town you saved me from the hands of the executioners. A second time you saved me from the sharp arrows of Cupid by procuring me, after a great deal of hardship, the object of my affection. Last night you saved me from the fall of the branch. To-night again you have saved me from the flood." By this time the sun rose, and all the retinue marched and reached before noon a village at ten *ghatikâs* distance from Mahêndrapurî. There the minister's son rented a house, and left in it all his retinue with the ladies, whom he asked to continue living there till their mothers-in-law would take them to their houses. Said Buddhichâturya to them: "Dear ladies! You must wait here till the twentieth day from this date, when my and the prince's mothers will come to you and take you to the palace for our weddings. Till then you must continue to live here. So saying, he sent away to Bhîmâpuram, whatever persons he brought only for assistance on the way. Then he, accompanied by the prince only, rode to Mahêndrapurî. All the persons in the palace were wonderstruck when they saw the prince, whom they had thought to have been executed for his offence towards his priest's daughter, returning. The king was informed of the safe arrival of his son after so long a time had elapsed. But the bad conduct or his supposed bad conduct was lurking in his father's mind; therefore he was not at all pleased to hear the news, and accused himself for having sent faithless executioners after his son. Except the king, every one in the palace welcomed the prince.

Madanakâma, when his palace was reached, asked the minister's son to go to his parents. Said he, "Enough of all your troubles till now. Be happy and easy for a day at least." The minister's son replied as follows: "My dear prince. One boon I would request you, and that is that I must be permitted, only this day more, to be with you. I must, without the knowledge of your wife, be in some part of your bed-room. If you would only grant me that much, all my desires are accomplished." The request, though seemingly indiscreet, must not be refused. For, it was his deliverer on several occasions who made the request; the prince therefore allowed him his boon.

The day was spent. The night came on. The prince finished his supper very early and retired to his bed-chamber; and Buddhichâturya slept, or rather pretended to sleep, below his cot. The fatigues of long marches and calamitous nights were so great that the prince overcome by exhaustion slept without waiting for his wife. The wife of the prince was a very bad woman. She had unlawful intimacy with a cripple who lived at a distance of two *ghatikâs* from the town in a ruined *mandapa*. That *mandapa* was connected with the bed room of the prince by a subterranean passage. The wife of the prince, after her supper, would lock herself up after, to all apparently, in her husband's bed room; but she would in the night visit the cripple outside the town by taking the course of the subterranean passage. Before dawn she would return to her chamber and come out as a chaste-woman, who was all the night pining away for her dead husband. To this wretched woman, who had thus surrendered away her honour to a cripple, the return of her lord was very painful. However she could not help coming to his chamber as usual with all formality that night; and when she did so, she found the prince sound asleep. She shook the bed, as it were, in anger. Still the prince did not get up. So accusing herself for having delayed so long, she hastened to a corner of that room and opened a closed stone which now appeared to Buddhichâturya, who from his place of concealment had seen all that took place, as a sort of lid to an opening beneath. In fact that was the subterranean way to the *mandapa*. She hastily descended and disappeared. The minister's son now began to suspect her, and wishing to know her destination, followed her behind quite unobserved. The prince's wife at last reached the *mandapa*, where her cripple was waiting impatiently for her. He accused her of her late arrival. She begged his pardon, and gave him all the sweet-meats, puddings, &c., she brought with her in a platter. He gobbled them all up in his hunger and spent the night with the prince's wife. In the course of the conversation that followed, the wicked wife of the prince said to her wicked cripple dandler that she would murder her husband the next day, and continue her visits to the *mandapa* in regular time. The cripple was startled. "Foolish lady. Do not do it. We must keep the tree if we wish to taste the fruit. If we cut down the tree where shall we go for fruits? If your husband continues to live we can continue to meet thus together, though our meetings are not lawful. But if you murder your lord, how can I afterwards touch you?" These words and several more the cripple spoke in advice to her, who seemingly agreed to all the justice of his arguments. The minister's son, who had concealed himself behind the *mandapa*, overheard all that took place, and noted down with a charcoal on the walls there what he heard them speak. Now that everything about the prince's wife was plain to him, he returned back before her to the room where his friend slept, by the subterranean route. Taking his position below the cot, he watched for the arrival of the prince's wife. He had not long to wait. For she came to the room a *ghatikâ* or two after him with a sharp knife secretly concealed in her hips, and again approached the bed of her husband. Pretending to shake the bed she secretly drew out her knife, and with it cut the throat of her lord. It was now that the minister's son accused himself of his carelessness, and coming out of his place of concealment held the hand of the murderess. She without the least fear bawled out that the minister's son had murdered her husband and is dishonouring her. This horrible news soon brought the minister and the king to the prince's bed-chamber. They enquired Buddhichâturya the cause of having murdered his friend. "My masters! What can I say now to you all when you put me that question. I had no leisure or opportunity to perpetrate this crime on my way and during my long company with the prince. I was waiting for this opportunity of finding my friend asleep in his bed chamber before I thought of murdering him." The plain way in which he spoke made every one believe that he had not done that crime. And it was more than plain that the prince's own wife killed him. Still the thought that the prince had long ago deserved death, that the executioners spared him most unjustly, and that after all God visited him with a most deserving death, made the king and the minister hush up the matter. The funeral rites of Madanakâma were all performed and his body was set on the funeral pile. The minister's son also attended the mourning. The thought that all his labours had been thrown away for nothing by the death of his friend was foremost in his mind. Like a mad man he lingered in the burning grounds long after every one had left that place. When there was none there except himself, he removed all the fuel which were just then beginning to catch fire, and shedding tears over the body of his friend, removed it to the ground. Then not to create any suspicion, he gathered all the bones of the dead bodies that were cremated on former days and re-arranged the pile. He then returned home with his friend's remains and safely locked them up in his box. The day was already far advanced. Everything he saw was distasteful to him. The prince's death alone occupied his thoughts. He went inside his bed room, and lying down on his cot was contemplating upon his adventures and how vain they had all turned out. He was not long contemplating, when the door flew open, and his wife entered with several nice dishes arranged in a gold platter. Buddhichâturya desiring to test his wife, pretended to sleep. She approached his bed, and finding him asleep, soon left the room. The crime in which Buddhichâturya saw the prince's wife involved, made him suspect his innocent wife also. So he followed close at her heels wherever she went. Outside the town, at a short distance, there was a Kâlî temple to which she went, and extolling the goddess with several prayers, thus addressed her : "My holy goddess. I promised to sacrifice to you my right hand, in case my husband returned all safe. Now that he has so come back, accept this hand of mine." Thus saying she took the sword in her left hand and lifted it up to cut the right arm by it. The holy Kâlî was highly pleased at the devotion of that woman and gave her reply to the following effect—"My daughter! I am highly pleased at your sincere love towards your husband, and great faith in me. Enough of your sacrificing your hand. It is the same as your having done it. In return, I confer on you the boon of your right arm reviving dead things—be it of any kind—animal or vegetable." So saying, the voice stopped. The minister's wife was exceedingly pleased and returned to her husband's room. On her way she spied a dried-up stalk of an old tree, and wishing to revive it applied her hands to its top. At once the tree grew up and began to put forth flowers. Buddhichâturya, when he saw all that his wife did and the tree that came to life, left off his dejections. He at once concluded that his friend, the dead prince, would come to life again. He ran in advance in great haste, and going into his bed-chamber, pretended to be sound asleep. His wife soon came there and slowly awoke him up. "My dearest lord! Long have you been in the seeking of adventures abroad. Glad that you have returned all safe. What have you brought me as presents?" Her husband at once gave her his keys, asking to open his big box and let in her right hand and take out what she found there. With great eagerness she went towards the box, opened it, and holding the lid by her left hand, let her right into it. And soon as her extraordinary hand fell on the remains of the prince, he came back to life and rose up with a great noise. The startled lady at once flew to her husband without knowing anything. He calmed her fears and said that the person in the box was none but the prince. By that time Madanakâma came out of the box and wished to know how he happened to be there after having safely gone to bed in his own room. The minister's son replied that he must wait eleven days more to hear the reasons for it, that he must till then never stir out of his room, and that himself and his wife would supply him with all that he wanted. Everything appeared quite an enigma to Madanakâma ; but he had no other course than to wait patiently till the promised day.

Here in the palace all the funeral ceremonies for the dead prince were regularly performed. The concluding day of the rites—(the thirteenth day among the Hindûs) came on. All kings and emperors from different parts of the world attended the funeral, which was performed in a large shed temporarily erected in the river-bed of that town. All the ladies of the palace too were present in closed sheds. The minister's son Buddhichâturya called his wife to his side and addressed her thus : " My dearest wife ! I now go to the funeral with my friend, the prince. You must also be there among the ladies. There, before the company, I shall reveal certain secrets, at the close of which my head shall break into one thousand pieces. Then, my coming back to life depends upon you only. You must boldly come forward and console the assembly, promising to bring me back to life and join with your hands the broken pieces of my head. I shall then revive and we will live happily in the world for a long time. Thus, Buddhichâturya instructed his wife and started to the river-bed with Madanakâma, the once dead prince, following him. When both of them reached the place of the ceremonies, all these rose up exclaiming : " There rides the prince who died thirteen days ago. There comes the prince, there comes the prince." The old king and the minister, the father of Buddhichâturya, came out and saw the prince. They were dumb with amazement for a time, till after all they came to the conclusion that the person who stood before them was none other but the prince himself. The whole assembly of kings and emperors was in utter amazement. " How came the dead prince back to life ?"

The father, after his confusion had abated a little, asked his son how he came back to life after having been murdered. And Madanakâma replied : " Dear father ! I know nothing about it. I was sleeping in my room and rose up from my slumber in a huge box in the room of my ever inseparable companion Buddhichâturya. He must know all about it, and you must ask him. The old king now turned to Buddhichâturya and requested him to quickly put an end to all this mystery. I am ready to relate every secret connected with these facts. But if I do my head shall split into a thousand pieces. Would you all like it.'' One and all in the assembly said that that was simply an excuse, as he who had the power of bringing the dead prince back to his life, must also have such power regarding himself. They all in one voice compelled him to relate every portion of his adventures, and Buddhichâturya without omitting a single item began from the beginning. Every point he related : the seemingly chaste daughter of the king's priest, the seemingly indecent behaviour of the prince, their escape to Indrapurî, Madanakâmâ's love to the objects of the picture on the temple walls at Indrapurî, his adventure to Bhîmâpuram, his desponding hopes about securing the hands of the Bhîmâpuram princesses, Paramêsvara's help in his cunning and apparent marriage of the princesses, his having kept them off for twelve nights by the narration of twelve stories, the ladies' doubt about the husband that married them in a queer way being their real husband, his clearing of their doubt, his coming back to Indrapurî to the prince Madanakâma with the ladies, the prince's choosing the eldest lady himself, his journey homeward with the ladies and the prince, the first day's halt, the owl's revelation of the three calamities, his successful saving of the prince from two of them, his inability to save him from the third one, the treachery of the prince's former wife, her criminal love towards the cripple in the *mandapa*, behind the back wall of which he noted down by charcoal what conversations took place between them a few *ghatikâs* before the prince's death, his lingering in the cremation ground and removal of the remains of his friend to the big box in his room, his wife's vow and the boon she had which brought the prince to life, and every minute point from beginning to end, Buddhichâturya related. The audience gaped their mouths and eagerly swallowing what he related. He closed his mouth, and his head split into a thousand pieces. "Buddhichâturya is gone. The great man in the world is gone for ever. We were fools in having forced him to relate the story," exclaimed all with tears in their eyes. Like the Goddess Pârvatî, the mother of the world—the wife of the deceased—the lady with the life-giving-right-hand, herself stood before the bewildered and weeping crowd. She asked them all to be quiet and went to the river to bathe. With her cloth wet and *kumkuma* in her forehead she stood before the shattered remains of her lord, and joined with her right hand all the blown-out pieces, when lo! like one waking from his sleep, our hero rose up. Great joy prevailed. "Our one man of the world is in life again. Victory to Buddhichâturya and his wife," exclaimed the whole assembly of kings. "She alone is the mother of the world said every one there."

"What remains to be done now," the assembly asked the old king. "I know nothing. Buddhichâturya is henceforth my lord and every thing, and he alone must say that." Our hero at once ordered the wife of the prince to be consigned to the lime kiln, which was immediately done. The cripple, for all his criminal intimacy with the prince's wife, as he spoke to the latter not to murder her husband, was sent for, and the wife of Buddhichâturya touched his defective leg, when lo he became a perfect man.

Then they all returned to the palace. Soon as the council hall was reached, Buddhichâturya asked his parents, the king and the queen, to go to the village in which the princesses of Bhîmâpuram were sojourning. They were immediately brought with all pomp due to their position. On that very day the wedding of the prince and of the minister's son with the elder and the younger Bhîmâpuram princesses respectively were celebrated. Even the God Pramêsvara with his consort Pârvatî attended the wedding; all the royal guests had great regards shown them. After the joys were all over they all took leave and went to their respective countries.

The old king gave the kingdom on that very day to his son and retired to enjoy the easiness of his old age. The old minister too resigned his seat to his intelligent son, our hero Buddhichâturya. Madanakâma with his new wife and Buddhichâturya with his old and new wives reigned over Mahêndrapurî with their old parents for a long time.

ERRATA.

P. viii	L. 3	from top	*for* Mîmâmâ	*read*	Mìmâmsâ
,, x	,, 2	do	,, சுணை	,,	சுண
,, xxxi	,, 2	from bottom	,, thinly	,,	thirty
,, xxxv	,, 13	do	,, nad	,,	and
,, 26	,, 20	do	,, instansly	,,	instantly
,, 30	,, 16	from top	,, her, when	,,	her. When
,, ,,	,, 18	do	,, pile, She	,,	pile, she
,, 44	,, 13	do	,, maturiry	,,	maturity
,, 63	,, 6	from bottom	,, he	,,	the

Books by the same Author.

FOLKLORE IN SOUTHERN INDIA.

Part I.—Containing the stories of the Three Deaf Men, Why Brahmans cannot eat in the dark, The Soothsayer's Son, Ranavirasing and Charity alone Conquers.

PRICE **One Rupee**, POSTAGE, &c., **1 Anna.**

Part II.—Containing the stories of Mr. Won't-Give and Mr. Won't-Leave, Mr. Mighty-of-the-mouth and Mr. Mighty-of-the-hand, Mother-in-law became an Ass, The Brahman Girl married a Tiger, The Story of Appayya or Fate reigns supreme, The Good Husband and Bad Wife and Bad Husband and Good Wife.

PRICE **8 Annas**, POSTAGE, **1 Anna.**

Apply to either of the four following :—

The Supt. Education Society Press,
Byculla, Bombay.

V. Kalyanaramayyar, Esq.,
Esplanade, Madras.

V. Sambamurtti Ayyar, Esq.,
Nungambakam, Madras.

C. Gopala Ayyar, Esq.,
Manager of The School-Master,
Madras.

Opinions of the Press.

UNDER the above title we have received from Mr. Naṭêsa Sâstrî a small collection of Indian Fables which forcibly call to mind the legendary tales with which bright memories of our early years are stored. The tales contained in this little book, however, differ considerably in one respect from those with which our youthful hours over the home fire-side were beguiled. Both alike amuse, and yet point a moral or proclaim a truth, but these fairy tales of an Eastern land, unlike our own, have blended with them peculiar mythological allusions which lend them piquancy. The East has ever been the home of legendary lore, but unfortunately ignorance of the language of this country on our part, and of ours on the part of the native, has for some time prevented the European from learning the style of fairy tale with which the Indian grand-dame beguiles the evening hour, seated among her dusky offspring, or the way-side improvisator rivets the attention of the passer-by with his stories of quaint imagery, and half historical, half fictitious, or half probable and half improbable tales. It is the love of the marvellous with which the Eastern mind is so deeply imbued, that has to a great extent clouded the early history of this land. To trace the story of the good old days when Pandya and Chola strove for mastery in Southern India is, owing to this, rendered well-nigh impossible. So intimately are copious myths blended with a little truth, that history has degenerated into fable, even in times so recent that in European city they seem but as yesterday. The little book before us goes far to show to the English reader what has hitherto been a closed book to many, the style of fiction which has thus impregnated the history of this part of the world. Historical allusions there are, but all blended, as we have said, with myth forming a quaint whole. In many instances the origin of proverbs and the reasons for certain Hindu customs are explained. Thus in one story we learn the legend on account of which the Brahman will not eat his food in the dark, while another explains the origin of the Tamil proverb, "Charity alone conquers." The English in which the tales are written is very good, and seldom does the author betray that the language in which he writes is any other than his own mother-tongue. We find in it few indeed of those Indian peculiarities of language or composition from which native productions are seldom free. It is throughout most readably written, and we should strongly recommend any one who takes an interest in the literature of the East to peruse its fairy tales.—*The Madras Times.*

It is due to the patient researches of a class of *savants* and investigators that the Folklore of so many countries constitute an agreeable part of the literature of the world. Men of the highest intellect have addressed themselves, with more or less credit, to the task of collecting those legendary tales, myths, and similar things founded on some incident or tradition about which there is no historic certainty, and which are coloured by the glow of an imagination that runs riot. Every nationality in India has its Folklore, but it is only a small part of it that has been explored and brought to light, and there yet remains a large field for the industry of those who will take the trouble to discover the sort of legends that are retailed and believed in by the great mass of the people, legends the recital of which in prose or verse amuse the untutored fancy in numberless households or on the way-side. The late Mr. Gover published a work giving an interesting account of the Folklore in the Madras Presidency, and especially that in vogue among the Tamil-speaking population. Had he not been cut off in the prime of life and from amidst his useful municipal labours, this work would have been greatly extended. We have received a brochure of eighty-three pages, entitled "Folklore in Southern India" by a learned Pandit (S. M. Na*tê*sa Sâstrî,) of the Madras Presidency, employed in the Government Archæological Survey. It is written in English in a pleasing manner, and is only the first part of the tales that make up the folklore in Southern India.—*The Madras Standard.*

[My thanks are due to *Mr. Streenivasiah, the Proprietor of the Madras Excelsior Press,* for the rapid and neat execution of this work.]